U0366096

弥合数字时代的
性别鸿沟

Bridging Gender Divide
in the Digital Age

赵晓蕾 沈开艳 主编

上海交通大学 出版社
SHANGHAI JIAO TONG UNIVERSITY PRESS

内容提要

在实现联合国可持续发展目标和可持续产业发展的进程中,性别平等和妇女赋权必不可少。数字时代的性别鸿沟问题是市场经济发展中产生的社会负效应,难以通过市场经济的自主运行自动弥合。基于此,本书在厘清数字经济时代的性别鸿沟的内涵、表现与成因的基础上,以上海为研究对象,系统梳理了数字时代背景下性别鸿沟的发展现状,深入剖析了以喜马拉雅、梦饷集团和美克生能源为代表的企业在弥合数字时代的性别鸿沟方面所作的突出贡献与创新举措,同时总结了数字经济发展中弥合性别鸿沟的国际经验与教训。最后,结合数字经济的最新发展趋势,展望了在未来数字经济时代中,性别鸿沟将呈现何种发展趋势。

本书内容含有中英文对照,适合高校、研究机构的研究者、政府公务人员以及对本话题感兴趣的读者阅读。

图书在版编目(CIP)数据

弥合数字时代的性别鸿沟 / 赵晓蕾,沈开艳主编
. —上海:上海交通大学出版社,2023.9
ISBN 978 - 7 - 313 - 28363 - 4

Ⅰ.①弥… Ⅱ.①赵… ②沈… Ⅲ.①性别差异一研究一中国 Ⅳ.①D669.1

中国国家版本馆 CIP 数据核字(2023)第 037683 号

弥合数字时代的性别鸿沟
MIHE SHUZI SHIDAI DE XINGBIE HONGGOU

主　　编:赵晓蕾　沈开艳	
出版发行:上海交通大学出版社	地　　址:上海市番禺路 951 号
邮政编码:200030	电　　话:021 - 64071208
印　　制:上海万卷印刷股份有限公司	经　　销:全国新华书店
开　　本:710 mm×1000 mm　1/16	印　　张:15.75
字　　数:256 千字	
版　　次:2023 年 9 月第 1 版	印　　次:2023 年 9 月第 1 次印刷
书　　号:ISBN 978 - 7 - 313 - 28363 - 4	
定　　价:128.00 元	

本书编委会

主　　编　赵晓蕾　沈开艳

编　　委　周　婷　文　雯　刘玉博　张伯超

　　　　　赵　锦　王　晖　李方卓

支持单位　上海社会科学院经济研究所

　　　　　上海财经大学

　　　　　上海国际金融与经济研究院

　　　　　联合国工业发展组织上海投资促进中心

Editorial Committee

　　妇女和女童代表着世界人口的一半,也代表着世界一半的发展潜力。产业中女性具有诸多独特的特质,包括强烈的职业道德、对细节的关注、协作能力和有效同时处理多项工作的能力。她们常常带来更加多样的观点,并为促进创新做出贡献。实现性别平等、赋能女性发展,是实现联合国可持续发展目标(SDG)和包容性可持续工业发展(ISID)的基本组成部分。在实现可持续发展目标9(建造具备抵御灾害能力的基础设施,促进具有包容性的可持续工业化,推动创新)的同时,工发组织还支持妇女学习技术技能,获得生产和资金资源,使她们能在社区的经济生活中有效竞争,为实现可持续发展目标5(实现性别平等,增强所有妇女和女童的权能)做出重大贡献。

　　联合国秘书长安东尼奥·古特雷斯(António Guterres)先生表示,实现性别平等、赋能妇女和女童,是我们这个时代未竟的事业,也是全世界面临的最大人权挑战。值得注意的是,数字经济作为未来产业的重要组成部分,可以为女性提供更多的就业选择和创业机会,包括电子商务、数字内容创作、直播、在线咨询等。与此同时,伴随着数字化和工业4.0的发展,数字时代的性别鸿沟呈现出新的特征。在数字技术的获取、数字技能的掌握、数字创新成果和数字技能提升方面,不平等现象日益显现。数字技术的性别偏见使得男性更容易利用数字技术和数字技能,这可能会阻碍女性从数字化中受益。此外,女性的数字身份和隐私保护严重不足,在高收入就业中面临着不平等局面。因此,需要着手准备制定新的战略和政策。提高女性参与度并弥合数字性别鸿沟有助于推动数字化的成功转型。女性在数据分析、设计和用户体验方面的技能有助于数字技术的应用,而女性在沟通和建立关系方面的能力将有助于更好地了解用户的需求。

　　政府可以通过顶层政策设计,提升女童和妇女的STEM教育,促进科技领域女性人才的发展,培养女性企业家,并在各个阶段给予支持以赋能妇女发展。

企业可以凭借自己独特包容的方式,帮助女性在职场中取得进步。在未来,缩小性别鸿沟将更加依赖于政府、企业和社会组织等的共同参与。

工业发展组织以"创新驱动进步"(progress by innovation)为指引,致力于通过加强对数字化的关注,更好地应对全球挑战,并利用最新理念和技术助力可持续发展目标的实现。工业发展组织把性别平等和增加女性权能作为一项核心任务,制定实施了一系列倡议和行动,以助力实现这一愿景——即女性能够在数字化时代平等地领导、参与包容和可持续的工业发展,并从中受益。例如,"制造业发展中的性别平等"(EQuIP 10)咨政工具为政府弥合性别差距,特别是制造业领域的性别差距提供了实用的政策指导。通过线上培训课程"女性企业家和经理人的数字商业创新",工业发展组织助力提高女性的数字技能水平,以支持女性领导企业的恢复与发展。此外,在每次项目开发中,工发组织都要求项目经理就新项目的主题提供深入的性别分析,并制定项目实施性别问题主流化战略。

2023 年国际妇女节的主题是"数字包容:创新和技术推动性别平等(DigitALL:Innovation and technology for gender equality)",与本书的内核完美呼应。《弥合数字时代的性别鸿沟》一书为缩小数字时代的性别鸿沟提供了极好的建议。除本书的高质量外,研究团队本身也正是这个课题的完美诠释。联合国工业发展组织投资与技术促进办公室(中国上海)团队荣获联合国工业发展组织性别平等动员奖(GEM)提名,这是对其在促进性别平等和增加女性权能方面所做努力的高度认可。

我认为,这份报告有三大亮点。首先,本书介绍了 UNIDO 聚焦性别平等的 EQUIP 10 咨政工具,为地方政府应对性别鸿沟问题提供了国际视野。EQuIP 10 作为国际化政策咨询工具,可以帮助政府了解女性参与制造业部门的程度和方式,并识别女性公平参与产业转型时的机会和挑战。其次,本书中来自在线平台、电子商务和能源等不同行业的三个生动案例,从初创企业到独角兽企业再到大型企业,都为数字时代的性别鸿沟问题带来了优秀的解决方案。它们的实践,为那些想要给可持续发展目标 5 做出贡献的企业树立起标杆。最后,"元宇宙趋势下弥合性别鸿沟的展望性分析"一章完美地呈现了元宇宙对性别鸿沟的短期和长期影响。在 AI 技术塑造未来的时代,这无疑带来了全新的视角,也给我们在全新领域弥合性别鸿沟带来了希望。

　　相信这本书会给社会不同领域的读者带来新的见解,并为在数字时代弥合性别鸿沟带来创新理念。正如书中所说,弥合数字时代的性别鸿沟需要企业、社会组织和社会其他群体的共同努力。让我们共同努力,迈向更加包容、可持续的未来!

Weixi Gong

龚维希　博士

联合国工业发展组织

全球投资和技术促进办公室和机构伙伴关系司司长

Women and girls represent half of the world's population and, therefore, also half of its potential. The unique characteristics of women in the industry include strong work ethic, attention to detail, collaborative skills and the ability to multitask effectively. They often bring more diverse perspectives and contribute to facilitating innovation. Gender equality and empowerment for women and girls are the fundamental part of achieving the UN Sustainable Development Goals (SDGs) and Inclusive and Sustainable Industrial Development (ISID). Parallel to UNIDO's work on SDG 9 (Build resilient infrastructure, promote inclusive and sustainable industrialization and foster innovation), UNIDO also contributes significantly to SDG 5 (Achieve gender equality and empower all women and girls) by supporting women in acquiring skills and gaining access to productive and financial resources that allow them to compete effectively in the economic life of their communities.

The UN Secretary-General, Mr. António Guterres has stated that achieving gender equality and empowering women and girls is the unfinished business of our time, and the greatest human rights challenge in our world. Especially, the digital economy, as a key component of future industries, can provide more employment options and entrepreneurial opportunities for women, including e-commerce, digital content creation, live broadcasting, online consultation, etc. However, at the same time, with the development of Digitalization and Industry 4.0, new characters of gender divide have emerged in digital age. Growing inequalities are becoming increasingly evident in the access to digital technologies, the master of digital skills, digital innovation achievements and digital skill improvement. The gender bias of digital technology makes it easier for men to adopt digital technology and digital skills, which may prevent women from benefiting from digitalization. Besides, women's digital identity and privacy lack protection, and face inequality in high income employment. Thus, new strategies and policies need to be ready. Increasing women's participation and bridging the digital gender divide will help drive the success of the digital transformation. Women's skills in data analysis, design and user experience can be conductive to the application of digital technologies, and women's abilities in communicating and relationship-building will contribute to better understand user's needs.

Government can empower women by top-level policy designing, improving the education of girls and women in STEM, facilitating the development of women talents in science and technology areas, cultivating female entrepreneurs and supporting them at all stages. Enterprises can help women advance their careers in their own unique and inclusive ways. In the future, bridging gender divide will rely more on the joint participation of government, enterprises, social organizations and other entities.

Guided by the motto: "Progress by innovation", UNIDO is committed to response better to the global challenges through enhanced focus on digitalization and support the achievement of SDGs utilizing the latest concepts and technologies. With gender equality and the empowerment of women lie at the heart of the mandate, UNIDO has developed and implemented a wide range of initiatives and actions to promote our vision that women can equally lead, participate in, and benefit from inclusive and sustainable industrial development in digital age. For instance, "Gender equality in manufacturing development" (EQuIP 10) policy toolkit provides practical policy guidance for government to bridge gender gap especially in manufacturing sector. Via online training course "Digital Business Innovations for Women Entrepreneurs and Managers", UNIDO supports the recovery and expansion of women-owned businesses by enhancing their digital skills. In addition, for every project development, UNIDO requires project managers to provide in-depth gender analysis regarding the topic of the new project and to develop gender mainstreaming strategies which will be applied in the course of the project implementation.

International Women's Day 2023 is themed as "DigitALL: Innovation and technology for gender equality". This perfectly echoes with the spirit of this book. The book *Bridging Gender Divide in the Digital Age* provides excellent suggestions to narrow gender divide in digital age. Besides its high quality, the research team can perfectly represent this topic. UNIDO ITPO Shanghai's team has been nominated in UNIDO gender equality mobilization award (GEM), which is high acknowledgement for its endeavors in promoting gender equality and women empowerment.

In my view, there are three major highlights of this report. First, it introduced UNIDO's EQUIP 10 focusing on gender equality and provides international outlook for local government to address the gender divide issue. EQuIP 10 serves as an international advisory tool that can help government understand the extent and way of women's participation in the manufacturing sector, and identify opportunities and challenges for women's fair participation in industrial transformation. Second, four vivid case studies from different industries such as online platform, e-commerce and energy, from startups to unicorns and to large corporations, all bring wonderful solutions to gender divide in digital age. Their practices will set examples to enterprises who wants to contribute to SDG5. Third, the novel chapter *Prospective analysis of bridging the gender divide under the trend of Metaverse* perfectly present short term and long term impacts of Metaverse on gender divide. This brings brand new perspective to the world in the age where AI technology is shaping the future, which also brings us hope to merge gender divide in a benad new field.

I believe this book will bring new insights to readers in different fields in society and brand innovative ideas on the topic bridging gender divide in digital age. Just as the book says, bridging gender divide in digital age will rely on the joint effort from enterprise, social organizations and other groups in society. Let's work together toward a more inclusive and sustainable future!

Weixi Gong

Weixi Gong, PhD

Chief

Division of Investment and Technology Promotion

Offices (ITPOs) and Institutional Partnerships

United Nations Industrial Development Organization

　　近年来,伴随着数字经济的迅猛发展,数字技术在广泛渗透与普及应用的过程中呈现出强烈的性别非对称性,数字时代的性别鸿沟问题引发了各方的关注。本书对数字时代性别鸿沟的内涵予以明确界定,并在此基础上梳理总结了当前数字时代性别鸿沟的主要表现,即:一是数字资源可达度存在性别差异,数字资源性别享有度严重不均;二是数字创新成果与数字技能提升存在显著的性别差异;三是女性数字身份与隐私保护严重不足;四是数字经济的发展加剧了企业雇佣层面的性别不平等。

　　在国际层面,数字时代的性别鸿沟已引起了包括联合国工业发展组织(UNIDO)在内的诸多国际组织的关注。UNIDO 提高产业政策质量(EQuIP)系列咨政工具第十项:制造业发展中的性别平等,为各国政府提供了国际化政策方案。这一咨政工具有助于政府了解女性参与制造业部门的程度和方式,并明确女性公平参与产业转型时的机会和挑战。通过帮助决策者明确选定的工业化轨迹变得更加性别平等的途径,从而从性别平等维度进行政策部署和资源配置,这一咨政工具能够使女性和男性有平等的机会对结构转型作出贡献并从中受益。

　　上海在数字经济基础上发展起来的互联网应用、人工智能、新基建等取得了长足的进步:数字经济规模、企业、人才、数据储备在全国领先,数字基础设施完备、政策配套完善,对中国数字经济的发展起到了引领作用。与此同时,上海数字经济的快速发展也为女性带来了众多机遇。具体而言,一是上海数字经济的快速发展衍生出更多适合女性的数字经济就业岗位和创业机会,拓宽了妇女的就业创业选择面,激活了妇女的就业潜能,例如数字贸易、电商、直播、在线医疗/教育等行业机会。阿里研究院的研究显示,数字经济为中国 5 700 万名女性创造了就业机会,无疑也为上海女性提供了广阔的就业空间。二是数字经济产生了各类新兴行业和职业,也提升了女性网络自雇创业、兼职创收的机会,帮助她们发挥特长和潜质,实现人生梦想与价值。以梦饷集团的爱库存平台为例,其店主群体绝大部分为女性,已有 1 000 万名消费者兼店主入驻,帮助超 200 万位店主成功实现创业和创收,成为 UNIDO 推荐的联合国优秀案例。

但与此同时,在数字经济时代背景下,弥合性别鸿沟也面临着诸多挑战:首先,数字时代女性的职业竞争压力进一步加大;其次,数字时代收入水平的性别差距更易拉大。

综上所述,数字经济对性别鸿沟的影响呈现出多面性、综合性的显著特征。一方面,数字技术的性别偏向性使得从总体来看更有利于男性利用数字技术和数字技能来提升其社会分工地位;另一方面,数字技术通过赋能模式和业态创新,为女性提供了增量就业岗位和机会,同时推动女性利用数字技术来平衡事业和家庭。

本书对弥合数字时代的性别鸿沟的国际经验进行了总结。① 女性平等参与和融入数字化世界,例如"eSkills4Girls"倡议、UNIDO 性别平等和女性赋权战略(2020—2023)(Strategy for Gender Equality and the Empowerment of Women 2020‒2023)等。② 弥合互联网获取和使用的性别鸿沟,例如基本数字篮子、微软宽带倡议;弥合数字节能教育性别鸿沟,例如非洲女性可编程倡议(African Girls Can Code)、"STEM for Girls"倡议等。③ 弥合数字技能岗位的性别鸿沟,如对女性的在职教育等。④ 全方位支持女性平衡家庭与事业,如家庭友好型工作场所认证等;鼓励女性成为数字行业的领导者和创新者,如 UNIDO 对女性企业家数字商业能力培训项目等。⑤ 发展平台经济,为女性就业创业赋能,例如 UNIDO 联合 IFAD 用数字平台赋能农产品价值链等。通过丰富的国际经验总结,发现数字时代对性别平等的呼声和响应更强,总体来看,一是确保所有成年女性和女孩能上网是弥合数字时代的性别鸿沟的基础,二是在女孩中普及数字素养教育是弥合性别数字鸿沟的长远之策,三是帮助女性就业创业者做好应对数字化转型的准备是减少性别数字鸿沟负面效应最直接的方法。

同时,本书通过生动的企业案例分析,展现了企业在弥合数字时代的性别鸿沟方面所做的努力。

(1)梦饷集团旗下的爱库存平台通过搭建网上基础设施平台、分销电商定位吸引女性参与创业,打造社群运营模式,发挥女性社交优势。妇女社群具有爱分享、活跃度高、善沟通的天然优势,能够比较精准地发现客户的潜在需求,从而抓住创业契机,开拓新的创业领域。

(2)喜马拉雅作为全球最大的音频内容平台企业,通过优质音频内容为女性提供知识、信息和精神慰藉,支持不同职业起点的女性找到热爱的事业,实现更大的社会价值,共享数字时代的红利;汇聚女性声音,搭建女性之间沟通、交流、互助的平台,向社会传递性别平等的理念,助力女性携手跨越性别鸿沟。

(3)美克生能源充分发挥科技女性在双碳赛道上的领航前行作用;消除女性的职场刻板印象,平衡职场生态;利用"奖学金""知识产权"等激励机制,帮助女性开发自身潜能,实现自我价值最大化;为女性员工提供安心、贴心的职场环境,让女性找到适合自己的职业发展道路,实现员工成长与公司发展相统一,在技术进步和数字化转型中发掘更多的"她力量"。

元宇宙被看作是下一代空间互联网的代表,未来数字经济的主要发展方向。元宇宙本质上是对现实世界的虚拟化、数字化过程,需要对内容生产、经济系统、用户体验以及实体世界内容等进行大量改造。短期来看,元宇宙技术完善阶段的性别偏向可能会加剧性别鸿沟,本书以元宇宙产业的计算层技术区块链技术中的加密货币技术为例进行了分析。长期来看,未来场景应用端有望塑造弥合性别鸿沟的主战场:一是众多元宇宙情境下的应用场景将不再具有性别偏向性;二是特定元宇宙应用将打破固有的性别门槛,推进应用层面的性别公平。

在弥合数字时代的性别鸿沟的过程中,政府和企业都是重要的参与力量:

首先,政府是弥合数字时代的性别鸿沟的顶层设计者。数字时代背景下,性别鸿沟的弥合属于市场负外部性问题,需要政府发挥"看得见的手"的作用,通过政策调节和行为规制,谋划弥合性别鸿沟的政策框架和有益举措,弥补数字技术普及应用在性别层面引发的市场失灵,确保不同性别群体能够尽可能共享数字红利,实现全面发展。

一是通过充分保障女性就业权利,尽可能减少数字经济快速发展过程中造成的女性摩擦性失业。例如,政府针对女性就业权益保障问题,出台较为详细的规划文件,从而促进妇女就业,提升妇女经济参与质量,并在就业权益方面明确性别平等指标。

二是助力科技女性人才的发展。事实上,上海市妇联、科委等部门已经出台了关于支持女性科技人才在上海建设具有全球影响力的科创中心中发挥更大作用的12项措施,希望借此可以增加高新技术企业中女性高级管理人员比例,缩小高级专业技术人才中男女比例差距,平衡各类人才项目入选者和科研项目承担者的女性比例,逐步提高获得发明专利授权者中的女性比例等。

三是培育和支持各阶段创业女性。《上海市妇女儿童发展"十四五"规划》将"创业活动率的男女性别比保持稳定"列入上海促进妇女创业就业、提升妇女经济参与质量的主要指标,与此同时,也提出了更为现实的操作性策略措施。

其次,弥合数字时代的性别鸿沟中的企业力量不容忽视。企业作为新模式、新业态的创造者和应用者,在推动数字经济创新发展及影响性别鸿沟方面发挥着重要作用。企业案例研究发现,以喜马拉雅和爱库存为代表的数字经济企业分别以自身独特的方式为女性发展和弥合性别鸿沟赋能。无论是数字经济企业,还是传统的制造与销售服务企业,都在弥合数字时代的性别鸿沟方面发挥着十分重要的作用。可以预见的是,弥合性别鸿沟,需要政企一齐发力,社会多元共治,才能达到理想的效果。

展望未来,我们提出以下几点想法:第一,数字时代的性别鸿沟将始终伴随着数字技术的更新迭代与普及应用;第二,当前应更关注数字技术创新供给对性别鸿沟的影响;第三,未来应更加重视多元数字化应用场景对性别鸿沟的影响;第四,企业在弥合性别鸿沟方面的影响力将持续增强。

In recent years, with the rapid development of digital economy, digital technology has shown strong gender asymmetry in the process of widespread penetration and popularization. The problem of gender divide in the digital age has caused concerns from different sectors. This book clearly defines the connotation of gender gap in digital age. And on this basis, it summarizes the main manifestations of gender gap in the current digital age: First, there are gender divide and gender inequality in the accessibility of digital resources and the digital resources accessed by different gender types is seriously imbalanced; Second, there is a significant gender difference in digital innovation achievements and digital skill improvement; Third, protection for women's digital identity and privacy is seriously inadequate; Fourth, the development of the digital economy has aggravated gender equality in terms of employment level.

At the international level, the gender divide in the digital age has attracted the attention of many international organizations, including United Nations Industrial Development Organization (UNIDO). Tool 10 of Enhancing the Quality of Industrial Policies (EQuIP) toolbox proposed by UNIDO calls out to promote gender equality in the development of manufacturing industry and provides international policy strategy for governments in different countries. Tool 10 will help the government understand the extent and way of women's participation in the manufacturing sector, and identify opportunities and challenges for women's fair participation in industrial transformation. This tool also enables women and men to have equal opportunities to contribute to and benefit from structural transformation by helping policy makers design industrialization path that is more gender equal, so as to carry out policy deployment and resource allocation from the perspective of gender equality.

On the basis of digital economy, Shanghai has made significant progress in the development of internet applications, artificial intelligence and new infrastructure: The city takes lead in terms of digital economy scale, enterprises, talents and data reserves. In addition, Shanghai has solid digital infrastructure and adequate policy support. Hence the city has played a leading role in the development of China's digital economy. Meanwhile, the development of Shanghai in digital age has brought more opportunities for women. Specifically, the rapid development of Shanghai's digital economy has generated more digital-economy jobs and entrepreneurial opportunities for women, which has offered women more options of employment and entrepreneurship, and activated women's employment potential, such as opportunities in digital trade, e-commerce, live broadcast, online medical/education and other industries. According to Alibaba Research Institute, the digital economy has created employment opportunities for 57 million women in China, and has undoubtedly provided a broad employment space for women in Shanghai. Also, the digital economy has generated various emerging industries and occupations, and has also improved the opportunities for women to start businesses online and earn part-time income, helping them to give play to their talents, reach their potential and realize their dreams and values in life. Take the Aikucun platform of Idol Group Co., Ltd as an example, the majority of its shop owners are women. More than 10 million consumers, working as store owners at the same time, have started their business on the platform and 2 million among them successfully achieved entrepreneurship and generated income. Idol Group's case has become and excellent practice recommended by UNIDO.

However, in the age of the digital economy, bridging the gender divide also faces many challenges. In digital age, women encounter even greater pressure of competition in the workplace and the gender income gap is more likely to widen.

To sum up, the impact of the digital economy on the gender divide is multifaceted and comprehensive. On the one hand, the gender bias of digital technology makes it easier for men to use digital technology and digital skills to improve their social division of labor status. On the other hand, digital technology provides women with incremental job opportunities through empowerment and business mode innovation, meanwhile promoting women to use digital technology to balance their careers and families.

This report summarizes the international experience in bridging the gender divide in the digital age, analyzing the following aspects: ① women's equal participation in and integration into the digital world, such as the "eSkills4Girls" initiative, UNIDO Gender Equality and Women's Empowerment Strategy (2020 – 2023), etc; ② bridging the gender divide in Internet access and usage, such as the basic digital basket, Microsoft Broadband Initiative, bridging the gender divide in digital energy-saving education, such as African Girls Can Code, "STEM for Girls" initiative, etc; ③ bridging the gender divide in digital-skill jobs, such as in-service education for women; ④ fully supporting women to balance family and career, such as family friendly workplace certification, and encouraging women to become leaders and innovators in the digital industry, such as UNIDO's digital business ability training program for women entrepreneurs; ⑤ developing platform economy to enable women's employment and entrepreneurship. For example, UNIDO and IFAD use digital platforms to enable agricultural product value chain. From the abundant international experience, it is found that the digital age has a stronger voice and response to gender equality. On the whole, first, ensuring that all women and girls have access to the Internet is the basis for bridging the gender divide in the digital age; second, popularizing digital literacy education among girls is a long-term strategy for bridging the gender digital gap; third, helping women entrepreneurs prepare for digital transformation is the most direct way to reduce the negative effects of the digital gender divide.

At the same time, the report also showcases the efforts made by enterprises in bridging the gender divide in the digital era. ① Aikucun platform of Idol Group Co., Ltd attracts women to participate in entrepreneurship by building an online infrastructure platform and e-commerce distribution platform. It aims to attract women to participate in entrepreneurship, and create a community operation model to utilize women's social advantages. Women's communities have the natural advantages of love sharing, highly active and good communication, which can accurately identify potential customer needs, so as to seize the entrepreneurial opportunities and open up new entrepreneurial fields. ② As the largest audio content platform enterprise in the world, Ximalaya Inc. provides women with knowledge, information and spiritual comfort through high-quality audio content. The platform supports women from different careers to find a career they love, realize greater social value, and share the dividends of the digital age; gathering women's voices and building a platform for communication, exchange and mutual assistance between women, Ximalaya delivers the concept of gender equality to the society, and helps women work together to bridge the gender divide. ③ Shanghai MS Energy gives full play to the leading role of women in science and technology positions on the carbon peaking and carbon neutrality track; the company eliminates the stereotype of female in workplace and balances the workplace ecology. By using incentive mechanisms such as "scholarship" and "intellectual property", MS Energy helps women release their potential and maximize their self-worth. It provides women employees with a comfortable and intimate workplace environment, so that women can find their own career development path, achieving the unity of employee growth and company development, and explore more "her power" in technological progress and digital transformation.

The Metaverse is regarded as the representative of the next generation space Internet and the development direction of the future digital economy. In essence, the Metaverse is a process of virtualizing and digitalizing the real world, which requires massive transformation of content production, economic system, user experience and physical world content. In the short term, the gender bias in the improvement stage of the Metaverse technology may intensify gender divide. Here, the report takes the crypto currency technology included in the computing layer block-chain technology of the Metaverse industry as an example for analysis. In the long run, the future scenario application end is expected to be the main battlefield to bridge the gender divide. First, many application scenarios in the Metaverse will no longer have gender bias. Second, specific Metaverse applications will break the inherent gender threshold and promote gender equity at the application level.

In the process of bridging the gender divide in the digital age, both the government and enterprises are important participants.

The government is the top designer to bridge the gender divide in the digital age. In the digital era, bridging the gender divide is a negative externality of the market, which requires the government to play the role of "visible hand". Through policy regulation and behavior regulation, the government should plan a policy framework and useful measures to bridge the gender divide, make up for the market failure caused by the popularization and application of digital technology at the gender level, and ensure that different gender types can equally share the digital dividend as much as possible to achieve comprehensive development.

First, by fully protecting women's employment rights, women's frictional unemployment caused by the rapid development of the digital economy could be reduced as much as possible. For example, the government should issue more detailed planning for the protection of women's employment rights and interests, so as to promote women's employment, improve the quality of women's economic participation, and clarify gender equality indicators in terms of employment rights and interests.

Second, government is to facilitate the development of women talents in science and technology areas. In fact, in this regard, the Shanghai Women's Federation, the Science and Technology Commission and other departments in Shanghai have issued 12 measures to support female scientific and technological talents to play a greater role in building a science and innovation center with global influence in Shanghai, hoping to increase the proportion of female senior managers in high-tech enterprises, narrow the gender divide in senior professional and technical talents, balance the proportion of women selected for various talent projects and scientific research projects and gradually increase the proportion of women among those who have obtained invention patents.

Third, cultivate female entrepreneurs and support them at all stages. The *14th Five Year Plan for the Development of Women and Children in Shanghai* includes "enable a stable gender ratio of men and women in entrepreneurial activities" as a main indicator of promoting women's entrepreneurship and employment and improving the quality of women's economic participation in Shanghai. The map also put forward more practical policies and measures for this end.

In order to bridge the gender divide in the digital era, the power of enterprises cannot be neglected. Enterprises, as creators and users of new business models and formats, play an important role in promoting the innovative development of digital economy and influencing the gender divide. The enterprise case study revealed that the digital economy enterprises represented by the Ximalaya Inc. and Aikucun empowered women to develop and bridge the gender divide in their own unique ways. Both digital economy enterprises and traditional manufacturing and sales service enterprises play an important role in bridging the gender divide in the digital era. It is foreseeable that it requires the government, enterprises and all sectors of society to make contribution to achieve desirable results.

Looking ahead, we propose the following ideas: first, in the digital age, the update iteration and popularization of digital technology will always be accompanied by gender divide; second, now more attention should be paid to the impact of digital technology innovation supply on gender gap; third, in the future, more attention should be paid to the impact of multi-scenario digital applications on gender divide; fourth, the influence of enterprises in bridging the gender divide will continue to increase.

目录

Contents

第 1 章
研究背景

中国已经迈入数字时代,大数据、物联网、人工智能、区块链等新一轮现代信息技术的迅猛发展成为推动社会经济发展的新动力。与此同时,在"数字工具的获取、数字技术的掌握以及数字世界的参与"等多个方面产生了新的不均衡,即"数字鸿沟"。5G 时代的数字红利,在不同性别的群体之间还没有实现均衡,数字时代的性别鸿沟依然存在。

1.1 数字时代的概念与特征

我国在 2021 年 3 月发布的《国民经济和社会发展第十四个五年规划和2035 年远景目标纲要》(以下简称《纲要》)中提出了"加快数字化发展,建设数字中国"的战略部署,要"迎接数字时代,激活数据要素潜能,以数字化转型整体驱动生产方式、生活方式和治理方式变革"。《纲要》明确宣示中国已经从后工业化、信息化时代迈进数字时代。

1.1.1 数字时代的缘起

从国际背景来看,联合国于 2019 年 6 月发布的《相互依存的数字时代》、世界贸易组织于 2020 年 11 月发布的《数字时代促进创新的政府决策》,均突出了鲜明的数字时代主题。

从科技和社会发展的角度来看,信息化是数字化的前期阶段,信息时代伴随着电子计算机和现代通信技术而生,其特征体现为各自分散建设的"信息孤岛"。而数字化本质上是更高级的信息化,表现为"万物互联、数据共享、平台赋能、信息主导、业务协同"。物联网、大数据、人工智能、区块链等数字化技术的迅猛发展和广泛应用,进一步加快了数字化迭代、转型的过程。

数字技术的应用催生了一个全新的数字时代,由信息领域向人类生活的各个领域全面推进。思科(Cisco)公司作为"数字法国""数字以色列"和"数字印度"的合作伙伴,对数字时代的内涵有着深入的见解,并对数字时代和信息时代做了时间上的区分,认为 20 世纪 90 年代到 2010 年为"信息时代",从 2010 年到 2030 年人们将逐步步入"数字时代"。

1.1.2 数字时代的内涵

数字时代影响着人们的社会生产、社会关系,特别是在社会伦理和精神文化等方面。[①]

在社会生产层面,数据成为重要的生产要素,数字经济蓬勃发展。数字时代,数字劳动作为一种复杂的知识劳动,以数据为生产资料,通过人们在网络空间耗费一定的劳动时间与劳动量来创造价值。[②] 新技术带来的倍增效益将是信息时代的 5~10 倍。数字时代给整个社会的生产、分配带来一次全新的洗礼,促成了全球层面经济和权力的重构。

在社会关系层面,社会关系走向复杂的"聚合离散",从"虚拟社会"向"镜像社会"转变。数字时代解构了传统的以血缘和地缘为纽带的社会关系,信息的极大流通能够让陌生人在网络空间快速聚集,形成一个虚拟的共同体。人们逐渐在多元意识的碰撞中寻找到属于自己的"部落群",现实社会中的关系越来越多地被嫁接在网络虚拟空间中。随着数字技术的进步,人们的活动轨迹可以被捕捉输入网络数据库中,"镜像世界"逐步取代"虚拟社会",和现实世界更加紧密地互动。

在社会伦理层面,社会伦理更加多元化、差异化,并以冲突和包容并存的形式在数字空间存在。更富个性化、多元和碎片化的社会形态催生出了不同的网络部落群体,这些不同的圈层在互联网上呈现出冲突又和谐的共同生活状态。腾讯发布的《2018 腾讯 00 后研究报告》显示,00 后崇尚"平等""包容"的价值观,更习惯和善于表达自己的情感和看法,也更容易接受他人的差异。

在精神文化层面,知识获取更为便利,知识更新迭代速度加快。在数字时

---

① 李华君.数字时代品牌传播概论[M].西安:西安交通大学出版社,2020:1-6.
② 吴欢,卢黎歌.数字劳动与大数据社会条件下马克思劳动价值论的继承与创新[J].学术论坛,2016,39(12):7-11.

代,网络数字文化得到了快速发展。人们能够通过网络迅速获取大量的知识和信息,促进了知识的飞速迭代与文化的国际沟通和交流。在文化思想层面,资源、环境、生态、人类未来、个体生存及自我、理想价值、性别意识等主题受到更多关注。

1.1.3　数字时代的特征

习近平总书记在给 2019 中国国际数字经济博览会的贺信中提到:"当今世界,科技革命和产业变革日新月异,数字经济蓬勃发展,深刻改变着人类生产生活方式,对各国经济社会发展、全球治理体系、人类文明进程影响深远。"①数字时代的特征体现在如下几个方面:

第一,数字经济为世界经济发展增添新动能。根据《全球数字经济白皮书(2022 年)》发布的数据,2021 年,全球 47 个主要国家数字经济增加值规模达到 38.1 万亿美元,同比名义增长 15.6%,占 GDP 比重为 45%。其中,发达国家数字经济规模更大,2021 年为 27.6 万亿美元,占 GDP 比重为 55.7%;发展中国家数字经济增长更快,2021 年增速达到 22.3%。中国数字经济规模达到 7.1 万亿美元,位居世界第二,占 GDP 比重为 39.8%②。数字经济的基础构成部分是数字产业化,主战场是产业数字化。数字产业化与产业数字化的深度交融改变了要素资源配置的结构与效率,对经济增长和社会生活方式产生了革命性的影响。

第二,数字生活让生活更加便利和智能。数字生活是以互联网和一系列数字技术应用为基础的一种生活方式,运用一系列科技手段让我们的生活更具品质。随着互联网技术应用的日益普及,互联网已经全面改变了全人类的生活方式。最新的科技手段依托统一虚拟网络的数字工具构建起一种便捷、舒适的高品质的数字生活模式。

第三,数字治理为推动国家治理体系现代化提供动力。数字治理把政府、市场、社会和个人以数据化方式动态关联起来,进一步形成各方多元互动、协同演化的数字时代共同体,促进数字社会健康、有序发展。数字治理的应用与发展,赋予国家"数字化国家能力",其中,信息汲取能力、数据治理能力、精准决

① 新华社.习近平向 2019 中国国际数字经济博览会致贺信[EB/OL].(2019 - 10 - 11)[2023 - 02 - 02].https://www.gov.cn/2019 - 10/11/content_5438401.htm.

② 陈维城,孙文轩.2021 年中国数字经济规模达 7.1 万亿美元[EB/OL].(2022 - 07 - 29)[2023 - 02 - 01].https://baijiahao.baidu.com/s?id=1739696825942008930&wfr=spider&for=pc.

策能力为国家经济工作赋能。

1.2 传统性别鸿沟的历史发展

现在的年轻人普遍拥有一定程度的数字意识和数字基础,但受传统文化性别不平等观念的影响,整个社会文化观念和规范的更新发展,并没有完全与 5G 时代快速的数字化转型相契合;相反,它以更加隐蔽的形式潜移默化地影响着男性和女性对数字技术的接受、使用以及在数字世界的参与程度。

1.2.1 传统性别鸿沟的历史起源

尽管人类社会发展进入了 21 世纪,男女之间性别不平等依然是人类社会不平等的一个重要表现,特别在广大发展中国家和地区表现得十分突出。在人类历史的发展进程中追究其根源,从采集狩猎向农业社会的转化是一个重要的节点。首先,农业社会的男性劳动力在犁耕的农业生产方式下相对于女性更具有比较优势,由此形成了男性在户外从事农业生产活动、女性在家庭内部进行生产活动的格局。其次,妇女将大量时间用于照顾孩子,而较少有机会从事其他农业生产活动,所以男性的权威在社会观念中得到加强。这种农业社会早期的社会分工决定了男性与女性在社会中的不同经济社会地位和角色,直至通过观念的深化,导致当前各国男女之间的性别不平等。

女性的社会地位并非一成不变,除了受到文化、宗教信仰等方面的影响,人们对男女平等观念的形成与演化也处在不断发展与完善的过程中。一方面,历史因素会对当前人们的行为以及观念造成持续的影响;另一方面,随着社会结构的变化和经济的发展,一些可以发挥女性劳动力作用的新兴行业和职业的出现,逐渐提高了妇女在经济社会中的地位和作用。

1.2.2 传统性别鸿沟的影响

在传统文化观念的浸染下,父母对子女未来发展的期待存在性别偏见。传统的社会文化规范,将数字领域包括学校和职场中与数字技术相关的专业和工作,大多视为"男性专属",父母对女孩选择数字相关专业的支持力度较小,认为她们更适合进入人文社会科学领域学习、工作,这最终导致女性在数字专业领域缺乏自信,在数字相关职业的参与度较低。根据国际学生评估项目

(PISA2015)的相关数据显示,15 岁女孩"设想自己在未来从事科学和工程领域工作"的可能性要低于男孩①。

传统的社会性别角色分工不太支持女性全身心地投入自身的职业发展。尤其是发展中国家的女性,因为长期留守家中或从事短期、不稳定的工作,进一步增加了其使用数字技术的难度,无形中阻碍了她们从事数字领域的工作。女性需要承担更多社会赋予她们的家庭责任,从而缺乏接受继续教育和培训的充足时间和精力,给她们进一步提升自身的数字技能、深度参与数字经济造成了隐性障碍,间接阻碍了她们在数字职业领域获得更高层次的职业发展。

传统性别观念中的刻板印象限制了女性在数字行业顶端领域的卓越发展。在数字领域的工作组织中,高级职位的男女比例严重失衡。例如,在移动行业,全球女性担任高级领导职位的可能性比男性低 20%。女性在数字专业领域所面临的严峻发展问题,在一定程度上也会进一步降低她们在数字专业领域的学习参与度和职业抱负。

1.3 全球致力于消除性别鸿沟的努力与实践

虽然新技术变革与传统文化限制对女性在数字时代的发展有一定的制约性,但全球的组织也在采取积极有效的措施去努力弥合性别鸿沟,促进女性自身发展,并扩大数字世界的包容性。

1.3.1 国家和国际组织层面出台相关政策、资金及文化保障

UNIDO 长期关注性别平等议题,把性别平等和增加女性权能作为一项核心任务,发布了多个关于性别平等和增强妇女权能的政策和战略报告,并在与德国发展合作组织(GDC)、德国国际学会(GIZ)联合开发的"提高产业政策质量(EQuIP)"系列咨政工具中,特别开发了"制造业发展中的性别平等"工具,为政府提供国际化政策咨询。

由联合国妇女署、国际电联、国际贸易中心和联合国大学联合发起的"数字时代构建性别平等的全球伙伴关系"行动方案,开发了一款"性别数字包容

---

① OECD. PISA 2015 Results(Volume I):Excellence and Equity in Education[EB/OL].(2016 - 12 - 06)[2023 - 02 - 01]. http://dx.doi.org/10.1787/9789264266490-en.

性地图",用于广泛收集和查阅全球各国为弥合数字性别鸿沟展开的实际行动,挖掘最好的实践案例并进行分享。"性别数字包容性地图"要求各国在弥合数字性别鸿沟的过程中形成"命运共同体",通过优秀案例的共享、学习与相互借鉴,缩小数字技术的接触、使用和深度参与方面的性别差距。

经济合作与发展组织(OECD)提出了一系列政策和行动方案,旨在引入性别分析,提供更多平等的教育和就业发展计划,关注低收入和发展相对落后地区的性别鸿沟问题。G20 成员在 2017 年德国举行的数字经济部长级会议上,制定了"数字化路线图:数字化未来政策",其中纳入了性别观点,并支持开发适合女性的数字金融服务项目,为女性深度参与数字世界提供更多的平台。

由德国发起的"女性数字技能培养"行动方案,旨在弥合低收入和发展中国家现有的数字时代性别鸿沟。其具体目标是增加女性参与数字世界的机会,包括教育和就业机会;通过收集和传播弥合数字性别鸿沟的知识、实践以及政策建议,促使不同的利益相关者共同帮助更多女性进入并深度参与数字经济。

1.3.2 高校和企业联合开展合作项目和学习平台

许多国家通过在学校与科技公司之间建立合作项目,为女性接触职场中真实的数字世界提供机会,并在参观和交流的过程中,逐渐培养她们对数字技术的兴趣。例如,微软与澳大利亚商业社区(ABCN)联合启动了"DigiGirlz"项目和职业生涯日(career days),旨在让高中生有机会接触高科技世界。其中,"DigiGirlz"项目通过举办各种数字研讨会,培养中学女生对数字技术的兴趣,并使她们能够充分了解数字技术领域的职业。这在一定程度上打破了学校与职场的界限,大大激发了个体对数字技术的兴趣。

在 5G 时代,技术的日新月异成为新常态,知识总量空前膨胀,只有终身学习才能防止数字时代的性别鸿沟进一步扩大。在这一背景下,联合国妇女署开发了一个创新学习平台——"虚拟技能学校",致力于为职业女性提供全面的支持服务和灵活的培训机制,通过构建终身学习体系,持续提升女性个体的数字技能水平,以帮助更多的女性获得继续教育和就业的机会。

1.4 性别平等的概念

传统性别鸿沟植根于性别不平等的传统文化观念,弥合性别鸿沟,最重要的首先是在观念上达成性别平等的共识。

1.4.1　性别平等的定义

UNIDO 将性别平等定义为"男女在权利、责任和机会上的平等",但这不意味着绝对的平等,而是确保在产业政策的设计和执行中,能够同等重视女性和男性的利益、需要和优先权。

1.4.2　性别平等的意义

性别平等及对女性给予经济赋权,是一个国家减少贫困、增加收入和减少社会不平等的一项关键战略。UNIDO 通过性别咨政工具(工具详情将在下节进行重点阐述)在多个国家和地区的实施已经证实了如下观点:

1)性别平等对地区经济和教育促进有显著的正向促进作用

(1)促进经济进步。由于男女对风险管理策略的不同,性别更平衡的企业生产率和效率更高,决策更全面,创新能力更卓越。女性拥有的特质,如更具环境友好意识,更加深入和持续的职业视角,更快、更灵活的业务接受度和更温和高效的沟通能力,等等,会在数字化和技术融合趋势下的工业发展进程中发挥更大的作用。增加女性在公司中的比例,包括在管理职位和董事会中的比例,可以显著提高业绩。

(2)利于教育促进,减少贫困。女性经济赋权对教育普及有直接影响,能够产生比政府鼓励女孩上学的大规模有条件现金转移项目更强烈的效果。女性更倾向于对社区和后代的投资,更加注重女孩和男孩的教育和健康,这比男性决策角度具有更大的溢出效应,可以再次促进持续的经济增长,有助于更持久的福祉。

2)性别平等在促进国家工业化转型方面发挥独特潜能

制造业中女性和男性的平等,即在各个部门和活动中公平分配女性工人,使女性得到跟男性一样的工资,并享有同等的工作环境,将有助于女性拥有维持未来经济竞争力所必需的技能和经验,积极推动工业技术变革,并提高农业和服务业的生产率。

(1)促进创新研发。加强女性参与制造业和研发这一观念可能会吸引更多的女性加入。私营部门 90% 以上的研发业务发生在制造业,确保女性公平参与该部门也意味着她们将接触或参与研发活动。

（2）加强教育投资。女性倾向于将更多的收入投资于教育，工业化转型时期，女性更注重提高子女的 STEM（科学、技术、工程、数字）素养，反哺性别平等。

（3）衍生就业机会。在解放生产力方面，制造业比其他行业更能促进性别平等。制造业和消费品的生产创新，如洗碗机和其他家用电器能减轻或替代女性承担的无报酬的家务和护理工作，让她们有更多的灵活性。创新和技术进步创造了对肌肉力量依赖较少的新职位，衍生出更多对女性友好的就业机会和领域。

1.5　UNIDO 性别平等咨政工具的内涵与实践成果

数字化、融合化的全球产业发展趋势要求产业政策必须综合考虑社会、环境和经济前景，有效的产业政策应以促进包容性和可持续工业发展过程为宗旨。UNIDO、德国发展合作组织（GDC）与德国国际学会（GIZ）联合开发了更有效的全球产业政策支持服务系列工具，即"提高产业政策质量（EQuIP）"系列咨政工具，旨在支持发展中国家和不发达国家的政策制定者制定和设计包容和可持续产业发展的循证战略，以增进当地的产业管理能力，并使其能够在战略设计、制定政策和国际产业参与发展方面拥有更大的发言权，从而提升国际伙伴关系。"制造业发展中的性别平等"（以下简称 EQuIP10）是系列咨政工具中重要的一项。

1.5.1　UNIDO 性别平等咨政工具的内涵

EQuIP10 作为一项国际化政策咨询工具，有助于政府了解目前女性参与制造业部门的程度和方式，并明确女性公平参与产业转型时的机会和挑战。通过对女性参与制造业和结构转型的情况和决定性因素进行分析，帮助决策者明确选定的工业化路径如何促进性别平等，从性别平等维度进行政策部署和资源配置，使女性和男性有平等的机会参与社会的结构转型。

（1）EQuIP10 希望解决的关键问题：提升妇女参与制造业的程度；制造业女性的工资、质量和就业类型与男性的区别及未来引导的方向；向制造业、技术密集型部门和更有效的生产过程进行结构转型时，引导妇女参与制造业的趋势和政策执行措施及执行保障；当地促进女性参与制造业的关键决定因素，制定针对性措施做好政策和资源的倾斜;衡量当地女性制造业的参与程度和参与质量,并做好持续监测评估和措施实施保障。

（2）EQuIP10 的分析路径: 决策者首先需要清楚地了解女性参与制造业及其分部门的现状和趋势,借此制定政策、战略和干预措施,释放女性的潜力,使她们公平地受益于该部门,同时为国家包容性和可持续的工业化、社会平等和整体经济增长做出贡献。

图 1－1 为工业化各阶段女性参与制造业的发展路径,分析人员和决策者可借此综合分析考察妇女在制造业的情况,从而确保决策者对本国制造业中性别平等的复杂问题有一个清晰的认识,以便在工业化转型中利用这些信息来制定性别公平的战略。

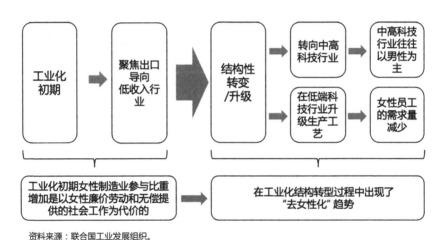

资料来源:联合国工业发展组织。

图 1－1　工业化各阶段女性参与制造业的发展路径

图 1－2 为衡量制造业中性别不平等的分析框架,分析人员可以通过这个分析框架逐一对应各项要素从而调整配置政策资源,以衡量制造业中的性别不平等。

框架第一部分通过评估劳动力市场男女平衡的基本指标和三个大经济部门（农业、工业和服务）的性别分布情况,帮助研究者了解制造业中性别不平等的背景。

框架第二部分描述了制造业中的性别平等背景情况,它为政策制定者提供了一个关于该国制造业中存在的性别不平等程度和类型的总体概念。框架兼顾了女性参与工业化进程数量和质量两个方面,因为简单地通过典型

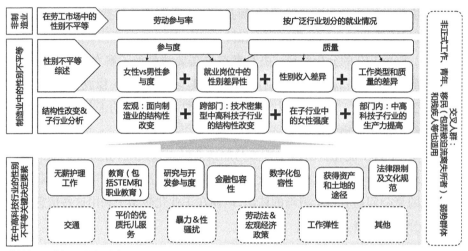

资料来源：联合国工业发展组织。

图 1-2　衡量制造业中的性别不平等分析框架

的血汗工厂工作来增加女性在制造业的就业,是不被认为性别平等或公平的。

　　框架的第三部分是关于结构变化和分部门分析的。结构转型是工业化的支柱,是该工具的核心。然而,由于制造业就业的去女性化,结构转型与制造业女性就业之间的关系并不总是正向的。为了衡量这种趋势,需要对结构转型中的女性参与问题从宏观到微观进行分析。

　　框架的最后一部分,对影响妇女参与制造业的一些关键决定因素进行了分析,这包括妇女比男子更多地从事无报酬照料工作的程度。这影响到她们从事有报酬的生产性就业的总倾向,是一个关键性的决定因素。

　　(3) EQuIP10 的指标体系。EQuIP10 工具推出后得到了广泛的应用和发展。它提出了一套完整的指标体系,在德国、越南等国家被采用。该套指标体系如表 1-1 所示:

表 1-1　EQuIP10 的指标体系梳理

一 级 指 标	二 级 指 标
背景情况	女性占总体劳动力的比例
	女性在农业、工业和服务业中的就业比例

一　级　指　标	二　级　指　标
制造业的性别平等概览	女性在制造业中的就业比例
	制造业中的性别差异度指数
	制造业中的性别薪酬差距
	女性在管理人员中的比例
	不同职级中的女性比例
	不同性别的最低薪酬差异
	不同性别的非正式雇佣比例
结构调整与制造业细分行业	基础制造业中性别平衡的结构性调整
	中高端科技领域中性别平衡的结构性调整
	制造业细分领域的女性就业密度
	生产力的变化与细分领域中的女性就业密度
关键决定因素	无偿护理工作中的男女比例
	不同教育水平的男女劳动力比例
	科学、技术、工程和数学毕业生中的女性比例
	职业培训学徒中的女性比例
	研发人员中的女性比例
	在金融机构中开设账户数量的男女比例
	从金融机构获得借款的男女比例
	融资创业的男女比例
	互联网使用中的男女差距
	使用移动现金账号的男女比例
	过去一年中使用电子支付的男女比例

一 级 指 标	二 级 指 标
关键决定因素	工作场所权利
	拥有土地和非土地性财产的法律权利
	在家庭之外拥有带薪工作的妇女权利情况

1.5.2 UNIDO 性别平等咨政工具的实践成果

（1）巴林 ITPO：巴林 ITPO 把帮助阿拉伯及世界女企业家克服文化和投资障碍作为主要工作方向。EQuIP10 咨政工具为巴林 ITPO 与政府沟通交流并执行工作提供了有力的工具。巴林 ITPO 通过其企业发展和投资促进（EDIP）计划，提供培训和指导，鼓励个体经营和企业创建，启动在线培训课程的开发，使女性能够抓住经济机会。

（2）俄罗斯：UNIDO 与俄罗斯联邦政府自 2018 年开始就促进女性赋权进行合作。以 EQuIP10 为实施工具，双方设立了促进妇女经济赋权和创业平台的合作项目，建立了强大的区域参与者网络，囊括政府、私营部门和相关民间社会组织。双方同时进行了全球推广宣传。UNIDO 邀请了来自世界各地杰出的女性经济赋权倡导者，在 2018 年第二届欧亚女性论坛，2017、2018 和 2019 年圣彼得堡国际经济论坛，以及 2019 年第二届 GMIS 上分享了她们的观点和政策建议，以促进全球知识共享。此外，还有 2019 年启动的在线培训课程，旨在提升女性企业家和管理人员在数字化方面的商业管理技能，目前正在试点。

第2章

数字时代的性别鸿沟：内涵、表现与成因

"性别鸿沟"在数字时代背景下具有全新的表现形式,其背后与数字时代相关的深层次原因同样值得深入探讨。本章将从数字时代性别鸿沟的内涵出发,聚焦其概念内涵的三大层次,重点分析数字时代性别鸿沟的全新表现形式,并分析其背后的深层次原因。经分析发现,数字时代为性别鸿沟的弥合带来了全新的挑战,赋予了性别鸿沟多维度的全新表现形式(也是数字时代性别鸿沟在细分领域进一步加剧的主要表现),其背后的深层次原因提醒我们必须通过多元主体共治的方式对其加以弥合治理。

2.1 数字时代的性别鸿沟的主要内涵

2.1.1 数字鸿沟的概念内涵与历史演变

数字时代的性别鸿沟可以理解为"数字鸿沟"(digital divide)在性别维度的现实表现,因此,要归纳总结数字时代性别鸿沟的内涵、表现与成因,需要先对"数字鸿沟"的概念内涵与历史演变特征趋势进行分析,从中挖掘数字时代背景下,"数字鸿沟"在动态演变发展过程中,其在性别层面的具体"鸿沟"的主要表现或影响。

近年来,伴随着数字技术的普及与扩散以及数字经济的迅猛发展,"数字鸿沟"现象引发了多方关注。根据既有研究,"数字鸿沟"已经成为拉大全球贫富差距的重要影响因素之一。"数字鸿沟"这一概念的最早提出可以追溯到20世纪90年代。1990年,美国著名未来学家托夫勒在其出版的《权力的转移》一书中,提出了信息富人、信息穷人、信息沟壑和数字鸿沟等概念,认为数字鸿沟

是信息和电子技术方面的鸿沟,信息和电子技术造成了发达国家与欠发达国家之间的分化。1999 年,美国国家远程通信和信息管理局(NTIA)在名为《在网络中落伍:定义数字鸿沟》的报告中定义:数字鸿沟指的是一个在那些拥有信息时代的工具的人以及那些未曾拥有者之间存在的鸿沟。这一阶段对"数字鸿沟"的讨论主要集中在数字设备、数字化基础设施的可及性差异所引发的国与国、人与人之间的发展差距问题,当前学界将其命名为"第一阶段数字鸿沟"。

进入 21 世纪以来,信息化基础设施的普及度快速提升,数字技术对经济社会各个领域的渗透融合愈发深远。在此背景下,"第一阶段数字鸿沟"问题的严重性开始逐渐消退,"数字鸿沟"问题开始出现全新的表现和变化趋势,即在数字化设备可及性差异缩小、数字化设备普及度大幅提升的背景条件下,由于数字技术与数字设备对经济、社会、生活的全方位渗透与影响,导致人们对数字技术的掌握以及数字设备的应用程度直接决定其收入水平和社会地位等;不同地区、不同群体在应用数字设备以及对数字技术的掌握方面出现显著差异,由此导致"第二阶段数字鸿沟",即不同群体数字技能掌握与应用性质差异问题。比如,移动支付技术可以提升支付效率与安全性,但由于生理缺陷或者对新技术、新事物的学习能力不足等原因,老年人以及部分残疾人在使用移动支付软件方面存在障碍或困难,由此引发不同社会群体之间在数字技术应用以及享受数字技术红利方面的显著"鸿沟"。

随着学界对"数字鸿沟"问题研究的不断深入,以及数字技术在生产端的快速渗透,经济数字化转型进程的持续加快使得学界对"数字鸿沟"的研究由第一阶段和第二阶段开始转向第三阶段,即考虑数字技术在不同经济社会领域的扩散导致不同社会群体在个体收入、教育程度、消费水平、社会地位等结果方面存在的显著差异究竟如何。如果认为前两个阶段"数字鸿沟"的内涵倾向于阐释不同社会群体在应用数字技术的可达性与熟练度方面所存在的差异及其影响效应,即更加侧重于需求侧的"数字鸿沟",那么"第三阶段数字鸿沟"则更加侧重于数字技术在经济生产与生活应用领域的自发扩散与渗透的经济社会效应,即更加侧重于数字技术在供给侧的普及渗透对不同社会群体所带来的差异化影响。

2.1.2 数字时代性别鸿沟概念的界定

"数字鸿沟"的内涵演变经历的上述三个阶段,实际上是与数字经济的历史发展轨迹相匹配的。

因此,在界定"数字时代的性别鸿沟"的概念与内涵时,可以将其理解为"数字鸿沟"在不同性别群体维度的表现。此外,"数字时代的性别鸿沟"亦可被理解为"数字性别鸿沟"是指:这一概念与 OECD 所提概念更趋一致①。2018 年,OECD 发布了《弥合数字性别鸿沟技术报告》,旨在通过识别、讨论和分析数字性别鸿沟根源的一系列驱动因素,指出"数字性别鸿沟"即"在国家、地区、部门和社会经济群体内部以及它们之间,信息通信技术的有效获取、数字技能水平等方面存在的性别差异"。其所提出的这一概念基本涵盖了"数字鸿沟"前两个阶段的内涵,但是对第三阶段内涵的诠释不够完整,因此,本书认为,数字时代的性别鸿沟的概念内涵也应当基于"数字鸿沟"的三个阶段来进行挖掘与概括。

本书中所提"数字时代的性别鸿沟"亦可理解为"数字性别鸿沟",其主要内涵包括三个层面:一是指数字化设施设备在不同性别群体中的可达性存在显著差异而造成的"鸿沟";二是指由于不同性别群体在数字技术的掌握以及数字设备的应用熟练度上存在显著差异而造成的"鸿沟";三是指数字技术在经济生产与社会生活等众多领域扩散、渗透与普及应用的过程中,导致不同性别群体在劳动就业、收入水平、教育程度和社会地位等方面形成的显著差异和"鸿沟"。

2.2　数字时代性别鸿沟的主要表现

结合上文所提"数字性别鸿沟"三个层面的概念内涵,本书认为数字时代的性别鸿沟具有以下几个方面的具体表现。

2.2.1　数字资源可达度存在性别差异,数字资源性别享有度严重不均

根据国际层面数据,全球范围内的数字性别鸿沟正呈日渐扩大趋势。国际电信联盟最新发布的研究报告——《事实与数据:数字化发展监测 2019》显示:截至 2019 年年底,全球范围内仅有 48% 的女性能够顺利使用互联网,而高达 92% 的国家和地区的女性上网比例要严重低于男性,这在一定程度上反映出当前数字化基础设施的可达性存在严重的性别差异。此外,在国家互联网服

---

① 2020 年 1 月 29 日,OECD 发布的《教育和技能在弥合数字性别鸿沟中的作用》(*The Role of Education and Skills in Bridging the Digital Gender Divide*)报告中就直接使用"数字性别鸿沟"这一概念。

务性别平等方面,根据国际电信联盟评估数据,仅有不到 1/4 的国家基本实现了互联网服务层面的性别平等,且在互联网使用的性别差异问题上,发展中国家的性别差距较发达国家更大,且两者之间的差距仍未出现显著收敛趋势,即互联网等数字化基础设施可达性的性别差异与所在国家或地区的经济发展水平呈显著负相关:经济发展水平越高,其数字化基础设施可达性在不同性别群体中的差距越小,反之则越大。

随着数字技术的普及和应用,"数字接入鸿沟"中的性别差异已逐渐消除,但在数字设备的使用形式或用途上,仍存在男女差异:男性日常上网更频繁,在互联网上开展更多的活动(如游戏等);女性则更多地使用互联网进行社交活动(如发信息、在朋友圈发照片等)。

2.2.2 数字创新成果与数字技能提升存在显著性别差异

2018 年 10 月,OECD 于 2018 年 10 月发布的《弥合性别数字鸿沟》报告披露:2010—2015 年,G20 成员中只有不到 9% 的发明专利来自女性;在信息通信技术(ICT)发明方面,这一比例降到了 7%;全女性发明者团队则更为罕见,专利授权比例仅占 4%。根据 OECD 相关数据统计:G20 国家 STEM 专业高校毕业生中,女性仅占 1/4,且这部分女性从事 STEM 专业对口工作的比例更低于男性;5G 时代的数字红利并没有在不同性别群体之间实现平衡,反而在一定程度上加剧了这一"数字性别鸿沟",其根源在于 STEM 教育中男女性别的不平等。报告警告称,按目前的增速,只有到 2080 年,创新领域才会实现某种程度的性别平等。

数字技能是指个人适应数字社会所必需的数字能力。性别刻板印象、社会性别角色分工等,潜移默化地影响着男性和女性对数字技术的接受、使用以及在数字世界的参与程度,进而造成了数字职业领域的性别隔离。学校教育中,与数字技术密切相关的 STEM 课程中,女性参与率低,整体毕业率低,退学或转专业的可能性高。女性学习 STEM 的兴趣不足,更加倾向于学习非 STEM 学科的其他科目。

2.2.3 女性数字身份与隐私保护严重不足

数字空间为女性提供了参与政治、社会生活,勇敢发声和展现自我的平台,也为老年女性、性少数女性、残障女性和流动女性提供了分享、交流和相互联结的安全空间。但网络空间中的数字身份安全仍极易受到威胁，特别是女性。比如，网约车司机根据用户信息选择作案对象，别有用心的人窃取和传播女性私密照片或视频、出于恶意威胁泄露真实身份或其他隐私等事件案例，都印证了数字身份安全的脆弱性。这使得女性不得不面对数字化或数字技术的暴力侵害，这种侵害的传播速度和影响范围非常广泛，而数字空间的匿名性又降低了这种暴力行为的成本和被处罚的风险。

2.2.4　数字经济发展加剧企业雇佣层面的性别不平等

根据《2019 中国职场性别差异报告》，在 2018 全年前 15 个高薪岗位中，除了排在第 14 位和第 15 位的战略咨询及证券分析师外，其余岗位女性占比普遍在 30%以下（见图 2-1）。目前技术领域热度最高的机器学习、深度学习、图像识别、架构师等人工智能和大数据相关岗位，女性占比不足 20%，甚至是个位数，而这些高薪酬岗位全部都是伴随着数字经济的发展和数字时代的到来所衍生出的新兴高技能岗位，女性在这类数字化高薪技术类职位中的低参与率使得薪酬差异日益明显。与此同时，近年来，随着数字经济的不断渗透和发展，各领域商业模式红利减弱，行业巨头转向技术驱动，高级技术岗位薪资持续飙升，进一步强化了相关领域内高收入男性的薪酬优势。

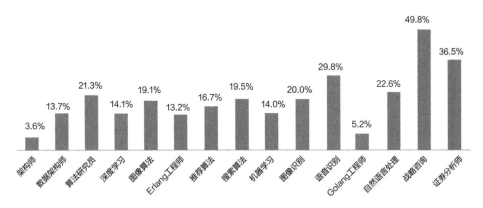

图 2-1　2018 全年前 15 个高薪职位女性占比

数据来源：BOSS 直聘研究院 & 职业科学实验室。

2.2.5　数字空间性别身份标签化，女性数字空间存在感偏低

数字空间是性别角色塑造的一个新场域，也是社会性别建构的重要部分，

然而很少有女性参与数字技术开发和决策,使得数字空间中的性别身份建构呈现出女性主体性不足、数字性别身份建构失真的特点。例如,由于人工智能领域女性工作者的缺位,开发者倾向于将性别刻板印象投射到机器人上,将探索外太空、救助人类、从事科研等工作的机器人设定为男性,而将从事沟通、服务工作的机器人设定为女性。在短视频流行的当下,也不难看到对女性形象污名化的现象,陈旧的性别刻板印象延伸将会加剧性别不平等。

2.3 数字时代性别鸿沟的主要原因

2.3.1 性别刻板印象和传统观念阻碍女性参与数字经济就业和创业

数字经济的发展改善了女性在参与劳动时的相对劣势,提高了女性在劳动力市场的特定价值,在数字经济发展中适合女性参与的社会劳动形式不断增加。但女性参与数字经济就业、创业仍然受到文化习俗等非正式制度的影响。传统性别角色观念对女性劳动参与具有显著的负作用,家庭责任分工及工作—家庭冲突机制使得女性承担更多的家庭责任而弱化了工作角色。即使在数字经济下,女性可以通过灵活就业或远程工作兼顾家庭角色,但女性仍然面临为就业、创业身份取得"合法性"的困境。特别是在农村地区、偏远地区,女性劳动者受到传统性别制度的影响更强,传统性别观念的壁垒依然存在,形成对女性参与数字经济就业、创业的阻碍。

2.3.2 女性的工作—家庭平衡压力较男性更大,阻碍其享受数字红利

数字经济发展中,线上工作、线下生活模式之间的界限变得更加模糊,新就业形态劳动者的权益保障有待完善。这样的界限模糊可能损害女性的工作与家庭之间的活动安排。现阶段,我国女性的劳动参与率明显低于男性。数字经济带来的工作责任将会给女性的就业带来更大的挑战。数字经济带来了更强的竞争、透明性和消费者的选择变化。数字经济中,女性通过数字平台创业、进行远程工作或参与新就业形态,可以改善家庭工作平衡,成为家庭的供养者。女性收入水平的提高也将为其家庭成员提供更好的生活环境,提高家庭成员的幸福度。但家庭生活要求女性高效利用个人工作时间,对女性的自我管理提出了更高的要求。女性在数字经济就业、创业过程中依然承担着家庭大量的无酬

劳动,需要合理处理家庭和谐和事业发展之间的矛盾。

2.3.3　数字技术性别偏向性更加有利于男性提升社会分工地位

数字技术在不断进步的过程中会在性别层面产生显著的偏向性,即数字技术进步对男性和女性劳动者的边际产出的提升效应具有显著差异和偏向性。从当前来看,尽管数字技术进步在推动经济数字化转型的过程中,为女性就业和发展提供了更多的机遇和平台,但是,将其与男性相比较,仍可发现当前数字技术进步更多偏向于男性劳动者。这主要表现为两个方面:一是在数字技术进步和普及应用的过程中,在数字技术研发设计以及数字技术与产业端融合的设计环节等高附加值工作岗位领域,更多由男性劳动者参与,女性受限于知识结构、社会传统观念以及职业标签等原因参与度偏低;二是在经济数字化转型过程中,工业互联网发展带动高端制造业数字化转型过程中所需的高技能劳动者仍然偏向于男性劳动者,女性在数字化转型过程中,更多参与消费互联网发展所衍生的低技能劳动领域,比如直播表演和带货等,由此引发男性劳动者和女性劳动者在数字化进程中就业领域的分化。在不考虑外部政策干预和引导的背景下,女性很可能更容易被低端(就业领域)锁定。

2.3.4　数字化渗透偏向于服务业,制造业数字化水平偏低,掣肘性别鸿沟弥合

中国的数字经济中,产业数字化所占比重已经超过数字经济整体规模的80%,是数字经济的重要组成部分。然而,当前中国产业数字化在不同产业间呈现显著差异,服务业的产业数字化水平明显高于制造业领域的产业数字化水平。根据 WIOD 数据库投入产出表测算结果(见表 2 - 2),中国制造业各细分行业的产业数字化水平大多不超过 20%,显著低于服务业各细分行业的数字化水平。根据中研网数据,服务业数字化水平是三大产业中最高的。2020 年,服务业数字经济比重为 40.7%,高于全部经济的 38.6%、工业的 21.0% 和农业的 8.9%①。由于制造业一直以来都是男性劳动者集聚就业的领域,女性劳动者受限于自身生理特征(体力、生育要求),在职业选择时会更加倾向于服务业领域,因此,制造业的数字化转型水平高低直接决定了女性在数字时代参与社会

---

① 数据来源:中研网,https://www.chinairn.com/hyzx/20220105/153131234.shtml.

图 2-2 中国制造业细分行业数字化水平示意图

数据来源：作者根据 WIOD 数据库投入产出表自行计算绘制所得。

分工领域能否进一步丰富和扩展。制造业数字化水平的提升会在一定程度上提升女性与制造业岗位的适配性,同时也会使得传统制造业蓝领职业岗位的社会印象发生变化。比如：数字化机械设备的使用使得制造业对员工体力和力量的要求不再居高不下,同时,原本从事体力劳动的制造业岗位也开始向数字化机械设备操作的技术领域靠拢,使得劳动者的劳动环境和社会评价更为体面,这都会消除女性对制造业岗位的偏见,改善其对制造业岗位的偏好,进而进一步扩展女性就业的可行行业领域。但是中国制造业行业数字化水平不高则会对上述机制产生严重掣肘。因此,必须加快推进制造业领域的数字化进程,为女性开辟更为广阔的行业空间。

2.3.5　网络空间治理规则不健全使得女性网络空间权益更易受侵害

网络空间治理规则的不完善,是造成网络空间中女性安全和权益受到侵害的重要原因。且由于女性的弱势地位,使得女性在网络空间中相较于男性更容易受到网络攻击和权益侵害等。2020 年《经济学人》的一项研究发现,"全球38%的女性直接经历过网络暴力"。根据这项研究,85%的人目睹过针对女性的网络暴力,且年轻女性更有可能经历网络暴力。

第 3 章
上海数字时代的性别鸿沟现状介绍

随着上海数字经济的蓬勃发展,一大批在线教育、在线医疗、在线文娱等数字经济相关企业也涌现出来,为女性的职业发展提供了大量机遇。与此同时,女性也面临着数字时代下新的职场压力与挑战。为此,中央和上海政府纷纷出台各类政策,保障女性就业权益,助力科技女性人才发展,支持女性积极创业。

3.1 上海数字时代的发展背景

在政府的大力支持和推动下,上海的数字经济迅猛发展,数字经济业态日益丰富,数字技术应用场景逐渐增多。一大批数字经济的头部企业(尤其是生活服务类企业)在上海生根发芽,展现出积极向好的发展态势。

3.1.1 上海数字经济相关政府政策的助推

近年来,随着数字经济在全球范围内的迅速兴起,各地政府纷纷鼓励和推动数字经济的快速发展。上海市政府也顺应此发展大势,高瞻远瞩、提前布局,2020 年以来出台了一系列推进和规范数字化转型和发展的政策文件,对城市数字产业化和产业数字化的重大意义、发展目标、总体要求、行动方案、保障措施等方面进行了具体部署,使上海数字经济的发展方向逐步明确,发展路径逐渐清晰,大大助推了数字经济发展的进程。

2020 年 12 月份出台的《关于全面推进上海城市数字化转型的意见》,明确了上海进入新发展阶段全面推进城市数字化转型的重大意义和目标,提出“到 2025 年,上海全面推进城市数字化转型将取得显著成效,国际数字之都建设形成基本框架,上海数字化基础设施国际一流,数字经济全国领先,建成世界级数字产业集

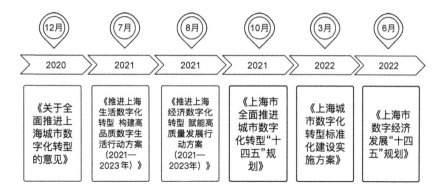

图 3-1　近年来上海市政府出台的数字经济相关政策文件

资料来源：作者整理。

群;到 2035 年,成为具有世界影响力的国际数字之都"的总体要求。同时提出"三个坚持"——"坚持整体性转变、坚持全方位赋能、坚持革命性重塑"的总体任务。

2021 年 7 月出台的《推进上海生活数字化转型 构建高品质数字生活行动方案(2021—2023 年)》,强调打造数字赋能生态,推进智惠基本民生,智享质量民生,智达底线民生,并提出加强数据赋能、人才培养、宣传推广、国际交流等保障举措;2021 年 8 月出台的《推进上海经济数字化转型 赋能高质量发展行动方案(2021—2023 年)》,从制造新模式、商务新业态、金融新科技、科创新生态、航运新枢纽、农业新体验、数据新要素、数字新基建等方面全面阐述了产业数字化的内涵和要求。

2021 年 10 月出台的《上海市全面推进城市数字化转型"十四五"规划》,强调通过完善城市基础设施、构建城市数据中枢体系、打造城市共性技术赋能平台等重点工作,推动上海经济、生活、治理等方面的数字化转型;2022 年 3 月出台的《上海城市数字化转型标准化建设实施方案》提出,要通过强化机制建设、技术协同、实施应用等保障措施,完善经济、生活、治理等方面的数字化转型标准;2022 年 6 月出台的《上海市数字经济发展"十四五"规划》,将拓展数字新产业、培育数据新要素、提升数字新基建、打造智能新终端、壮大数字新企业、建设数字新载体作为上海数字经济发展的重点任务,并从金融支持、人才培养、赛道机制等方面强调了保障措施。

进入 21 世纪以来,数字经济已成为推动国内外经济发展的主要力量,数字经济引领经济加速发展已成为各界共识。当前,数字经济发展的紧迫性凸显,新旧动能转化速度被迫加快,上海对数字经济的系统性认知和建设也不断加速,数字产业化与产业数字化不断孕育出新产业、新业态和新模式。2020 年以来,上海对推进城市全面数字化转型给予高度"定调",在信息化、数字化、智能化多年沉淀积累的基础上,促进数字动能迅速生长、深入融合,推动城市数字化时代加速发展。

3.1.2 上海数字经济的蓬勃发展

作为一个超大城市,上海人口规模大、流动性强,生活、生产需求均非常旺盛,给城市建设和发展、运行与治理等各方面带来了严峻挑战,对教育、医疗、养老等公共服务供给和保障水平升级提出了要求。作为国内大循环战略节点和国内国际双循环的战略链接,上海应充分发挥人才、技术、市场等方面的优势,更主动地服务于全国发展。因而,上海具有推进城市数字化转型的内在动力和外在压力。[①]

上海在以数字经济为基础发展起来的互联网应用、人工智能、新基建等方面取得了长足的进步,并在疫情期间成为"逆势飞扬"的新增长点,为疫后全国经济复苏提供了重要动能。[②]

数字经济在以上海为代表的综合型城市的 GDP 中占比较高。上海数字经济体量全国领先,具备丰富的数字人才、数字技术资源优势,数字基础设施完备,政策配套完善,数字经济带动作用明显,对我国数字经济发展起到了引领作用。上海的数字经济企业、人才、数据储备在全国处于第一梯队:商贸、港口、航运、物流、海关、商检、医疗、金融、通信等数据应用企业较多,网民普及率全国领先,网络购物用户等指标在全国位居前列,智慧社区、智慧医疗、智慧交通等数字领域也积累了海量数据;此外,上海还拥有基础雄厚的信息产业,数字经济业态丰富,数字技术应用场景多。[③]

《上海市数字经济发展"十四五"规划》提出了具体的发展目标:到 2025 年年底,上海数字经济发展水平稳居全国前列,增加值力争达到 3 万亿元,占全市生产总值比重大于 60%,产业集聚度和显示度明显提高,高潜力数字新兴企业加快成长,高水平数字消费能级不断跃升,若干高价值数字产业新赛道布局基本形成,国际数字之都形成基本框架体系。此目标的树立为上海下一阶段数

---

① 顾丽梅,李欢欢,张扬.城市数字化转型的挑战与优化路径研究——以上海市为例[J].西安交通大学学报(社会科学版).2022,42(03):41-50.
② 张伯超,韩清.疫情影响下上海在线新经济产业发展状况研究[M]//沈开艳.上海经济发展报告(2021):聚焦在线新经济和新基建[M].北京:社会科学文献出版社,2021:25-40.
③ 赵义怀.上海数字经济发展的现实基础、未来思路及举措建议[J].科学发展.2020,No.137(04):79-88.

字经济的进一步发展提供了强劲的动力和政策支持。

3.1.3　上海数字经济企业的涌现

在线新经济作为数字经济的重要内容,在疫情期间得到了爆发式增长,包括在线办公、无人工厂、在线金融、在线电商零售、在线教育、在线医疗、在线文娱等。伴随着疫情的持续,上海一批生活服务类数字经济的头部企业表现出惊人的发展潜力和契合时代需求的可持续竞争力,包括以喜马拉雅、梦饷集团等为代表的行业头部企业。

成立于 2012 年 8 月的喜马拉雅发展至今,其音频内容总时长超过 20 亿分钟,不重复收听超过 4 000 年。2021 年全场景平均月活跃用户已达 2.68 亿个,同比增长 24.4%,其中,移动端 App 平均月活跃用户高达 1.16 亿个,物联网、车联网及第三方月活跃用户达 1.51 亿个。移动端用户日均收听时长为 144 分钟,总收听内容时长为 17 441 亿分钟,在全行业收听时长中占比达 68%。喜马拉雅的付费用户及付费率均逐年递增,2021 年付费会员数量 1 440 万名,同比增长 52%,移动端用户付费率提高至 12.9%。在疫情最为严重的 2020 年 1—4 月间,喜马拉雅的企业营业收入同比增速达到 91.54%,其用户量和业务量激增;疫情期间推出在线课程以后,在线教育 App 的日活跃用户数量增加了 20%~100%。

创办于 2017 年 12 月的梦饷集团作为面向全球的去中心化新电商平台,致力于通过科技创新,助力数字经济发展,通过促消费、去产能、稳就业、助环保,在新电商领域为社会贡献力量。2020 年 11 月已获得 C 轮融资,目前该企业员工近 1 000 人,通过近 300 万名网络店主(其中 9 成为女性店主),将超过 10 000个品牌的高性价比商品销售至终端消费者,其月销售额突破 10 亿元,为店主增加收入近 50 亿元。在 2020 年 1—4 月间,梦饷集团的营业收入从 5 亿元增长到了 10 亿元,店主量增加了 60 万名,消费者数量新增 600 万名。[①]

3.2　上海数字时代发展下女性发展的机遇

在数字经济蓬勃发展的形势下,上海的制造业和服务业领域衍生出大量适

---

① 张伯超,韩清.疫情影响下上海在线新经济产业发展状况研究[M]//沈开艳.上海经济发展报告(2021):聚焦在线新经济和新基建[M].北京:社会科学文献出版社,2021:25-40.

合女性的职业机遇,助力更多女性实现弹性工作、兼顾家庭的愿望,同时还帮助女性提升自身素养,将终身学习内化为其生活方式。

3.2.1 数字时代为女性提供大量工作岗位

上海拥有全国城市第一的市场规模和全国城市第二的人口密度,拥有全国最完善的产业体系。近年来,上海数字经济蓬勃发展,产业发展与数字化融合度不断提升,从工业互联网、信息技术、人工智能到新零售、社区电商,从在线医疗和教育到在线金融、企业数字化服务等,上海已涌现出一大批数字经济头部企业,带动了上海经济多样性发展。

背靠上海强大的人才、技术、资本、信息等要素聚集优势,上海的企业立足中国、辐射全球,无论在数量增长还是能级提升方面都表现出显著优势。上海市商务委数据显示,截至 2021 年 11 月底,上海累计设立跨国公司地区总部数量 827 家,外资研发中心 504 家。在上海的跨国公司地区总部中,世界 500 强企业占比高达 15%,如沃尔玛、苹果、采埃孚、圣戈班、通用等。

上海已成为国内外数字经济头部企业布局的战略要地,既吸引了微软、亚马逊等全球科技巨头企业,也吸引了阿里巴巴、华为、腾讯、百度等国内龙头企业,更涌现出以喜马拉雅、爱库存、小红书、B 站等为代表的数字经济新兴企业,吸引了全国乃至全球范围内的大规模用户群体参与,打破了企业服务范畴在传统意义上的地域疆界,同时衍生出大量宝贵的工作机遇和就业岗位。

自新冠疫情暴发以来,企业的数字化转型意识更加强烈,随着 5G、人工智能、物联网、区块链等新一代数字信息技术的蓬勃发展与应用赋能的加速,上海企业的数字化应用和转型具备了坚实的技术支撑。越来越多的企业通过数字化方式构建自身的"风险防御体系",实现了日常运营的数字化、线上化、移动化。其中,制造业数字化转型发展的步伐明显加快,推动了由"上海制造"向"上海智造"的加速迈进。2022 年,上海规划通过分级分类推进智能工厂建设,加快布局数字经济新赛道,计划认定授牌 100 家左右"上海市智能工厂",争创 4~5 家"国家级标杆性智能工厂",向世界一流水平的"智造之城"迈进。

在此背景下,上海对数字技术人才的需求与日俱增。据直聘 BOSS 研究院数据,2020 年上海数字技术人才需求在技术人才需求中的占比达 14.3%,仅次于北京、深圳、杭州等地。上海数字经济的快速发展大大拓宽了女性的就业创业选择面,有利于激活女性的就业潜能,衍生出更多适合女性的数字经济就业岗位和创业机会,例如可大力展示和发挥女性自身优势的数字贸易、电商、直播、在线医疗、在线教育等行业机会。根据阿里研究院与中国就业形态研究中心课题组联合发布的《数字经济与中国妇女就业创业研究报告》,数字经济已为 5 700 万名女性创造了就业机会。

数字经济的发展和普及大大提升了女性就业和创业的能力,打破了传统就业模式的限制和禁锢,并由此产生了各类新兴行业和职业,提升了女性网络自雇创业、兼职创收的机会,也帮助她们发挥特长和潜质,实现人生梦想与价值。以梦饷集团的爱库存平台为例,其店主群体中绝大部分为女性,已有 1 000 万名消费者兼店主入驻,已帮助超过 200 万位店主成功实现创业和创收;另如喜马拉雅平台,其月活主播有 58.4 万名,其中女性占比高达 64.02%,她们中绝大多数是 80 后女性上班族,利用喜马拉雅平台进行创作、获取物质和精神的双重回报已成为她们新的生活方式,甚至改写了她们的生活和命运。

数字化还降低了一些行业的就业门槛,并衍生出一些新兴就业岗位。如随着分拣自动化系统的普及应用,终端分拣员等对体力要求更低的细分行业不断吸纳更多女性。数字经济和信息技术的发展还大大提高了女性求职的市场效率,甚至实现了工作搜寻的"零边际成本"和高度化"人职匹配"寻职方式,拓宽了女性的就业岗位获取渠道,有助于缩小就业岗位供求信息的不对称和由此产生的求职领域性别差异。

3.2.2　数字时代有利于女性平衡家庭与事业

随着经济的发展和社会的进步,上海女性在学历、职称等方面都有显著提升。从上海女性学历情况来看,2020 年上海约有 407 万名大专以上学历女性,包括 5.2 万名女博士、46.6 万名女硕士、211.3 万名本科女性和 144.1 万名大专女性。[①] 在数字时代,这部分具有较高学历和职称女性的就业岗位和机会得到大大拓展和提升。根据上海市第六次和第七次人口普查数据,上海 18~64 岁城乡女性就业率从 2010 年的 59.3%上升至 2020 年的 62.1%。其中,25~44 岁女性为就业主力,该年龄段女性就业率达 84%以上。

显然,25~44 岁就业主力军年龄段恰好与女性生育年龄段基本重合,这

---

① 国家统计局.中国人口普查年鉴—2020[M].北京:中国统计出版社,2022.

也给就业女性带来了家庭与事业平衡方面的较多困难。在生活模式上,由于社会性别观念、工时制度等因素,相较于日本等国家,我国的家庭分工模式具有"男女共同主内外"的特征,因此,女性在时间分配上具有"工作—家庭兼顾"特征。① 在上海这样的国际大都市,女性就业人员放弃工作、照料儿童的机会成本更大,更易陷入两难困境。

实际上,上海女性未就业的重要原因之一是"生育或照顾孩子",职场女性被迫造成工作中断。在幼年子女照料方面,母亲仍承担着主要责任。许多已育女性为照料幼儿牺牲了大量工作时间甚至职业机会。因此,上海女性对于实现工作弹性、兼顾家庭的愿望十分强烈。

随着数字经济的快速发展,女性打破传统就业模式下"工作—家庭"两难困境、加快走向二者平衡的契机不断涌现。尤其自新冠疫情暴发以来,在线新经济加速崛起,数字产业化和产业数字化的趋势越来越清晰,更多的企业开始尝试和推广远程办公。2020 年 1—4 月,上海在线远程办公 App 的平均新用户增长率达到580%。②

疫情还促进了在线新经济平台的发展和灵活就业形态的兴起。例如,上海喜马拉雅、爱库存等数字平台,吸纳了大量女性以灵活方式就业,替代了以前对就业的时间、地点束缚较多的全职形态的传统就业模式。这种灵活就业的职业范畴和领域也逐渐扩大,涵盖电商、文化、教育、医疗等各行各业,女性的就业模式更加友好,就业机会大大增加。实践证明,灵活就业模式能有效缓解女性就业压力,稳定就业市场,使女性突破空间限制、时间制约,获得更多的工作机会,实现居家办公、弹性办公,从而更好地兼顾家庭。

此外,数字经济还为女性减轻家庭负担、赋予平等发展机会贡献了不可估量的作用。通过互联网、物联网联动,家政服务业平台蓬勃发展,不断促进家务劳动由"家庭"走向"市场"。在科技赋能的支持下,女性逐步从繁重的家务劳动中解放出来,家庭生活质量得到显著提高。数字经济还优化了资源配置,使各类资源各得其所、充分配置,从而使社会经济的全要素生产率得到大幅提升,女性也随之从中受益。

---

① 焦健,王德,程英.上海与东京就业人员时间利用特征比较研究[J].未来城市设计与运营.2022,No.1(01):34-41.
② 张伯超,韩清.疫情影响下上海在线新经济产业发展状况研究[M]//沈开艳.上海经济发展报告(2021):聚焦在线新经济和新基建[M].北京:社会科学文献出版社,2021:25-40.

3.2.3　数字时代有助于提升女性综合素养

中央政府高度重视数字时代下居民数字素养不断提升的重要性与发展趋势。2022 年,网信办、教育部、工信部等多部门联合印发的《2022 年提升全民数字素养与技能工作要点》提出:要提升劳动者数字工作能力,促进全民终身数字学习;要搭建一批数字学习服务平台,从"数字原住民"入手,加快提升全民数字素养,营造"人人、时时、处处"可学的环境和氛围;要通过运用虚拟仿真、增强现实等新技术,使数字学习适应数字经济的需要。

上海政府亦十分重视城市数字经济蓬勃发展态势下教育的数字化转型,努力构建覆盖全市的终身教育数字化服务网络,不断完善教育数字治理,持续提升市民的数字素养,逐步实现教育资源精准供给,创造包容、普惠、友好的数字生活新图景,进一步形成与上海打造具有世界影响力的国际数字之都相匹配的终身教育数字化发展新格局。

2021 年上海出台《上海市教育数字化转型实施方案(2021—2023)》,提出到 2023 年将上海建设成为全国教育数字化转型标杆城市,形成一批高质量、可复制、可推广的教育数字化转型经验案例和示范场景。具体要求包括:积极探索教育数字化"新环境、新体系、新平台、新模式、新评价"建设,推进教育更高层次的优质均衡、个性多元;要探索发展基础/职业/高等教育基于人工智能的探究式、个性化学习,基于增强现实和虚拟现实等技术的沉浸式、体验式教学,基于 5G 的远端多点协作式教学,深化线上线下教育融合和创新;职业教育重点整合基于职业环境与工作过程的虚拟仿真实训资源和平台,开展数字化环境下的实训教学创新研究与实践,建设适应数字化教学需求的实训课程体系,支持国家职业教育虚拟仿真公共实训基地(上海)建设。

在数字经济环境下,女性的数字技术可及性大大提高,其受教育的条件障碍得到较大的突破,妇女和女童从数字转型中获益的机会和能力大大提高。女童在数字专业领域学科中更容易表现出色,如科学、技术、工程和数学(STEM)以及信息和通信技术(ICT)等,从而跨越这些领域的数字性别鸿沟,全面提升自身综合素养。

中央政府和上海政府对于利用数字经济提升居民综合素养提出了明确的目标和政策路径,为女性在数字时代中实现自我提升、保持终身学习、全方位提高文化素质与内在修养提供了十分有利的条件。教育的数字化转型改变了传统社会经济运行模式下教育服务供给和需求不可分离的局限性,突破了传统教育服务的"同步性""不可储存性"等低劳动生产率特征。信息技术的发展使教育服务可以以极低的成本实现远距离供给。[①] 对于女性而言,数字时代下的教育服务可为女性提供成本较低的各类教育服务,既可满足家务缠身的全职妈妈足不出户、宅家学习的需求,也可为工作忙碌的职场女性提供碎片化时间利用模式的分时教育。形形色色的在线学习平台、线上线下相结合的各类知识技能学习课程都为女性带来了丰富的教育机会。

当前,由大数据和人工智能技术(AI)驱动的新一轮技术变革,将人们从繁重的劳动中解放出来,使人们在科技的协助和支持下,变得更为智慧和强大。终身学习将成为人们生活方式的新常态,如通过雇主提供的培训项目,或通过个人渠道,持续学习新技能,改进思维方式,通过数字化手段实现技能提升和更新,适应未来职业发展的需要。数字时代的各类科技手段和工具将帮助女性在整个职业生涯中保持灵活性,根据市场需求的变化及时调整自身职业方向,培育个人素养。

值得一提的是,喜马拉雅股份有限公司作为近年来越来越家喻户晓的一家在线音频平台,为内容创作者和用户搭建了互联网连接交互的平台,其丰富的内容供给能够满足跨越各年龄段、不同身份和职业的用户对于内容的差异化需求,已成为众多女性用户日常生活中不可或缺的一部分。2021 年,其内容创作者数量超过 1 351 万名。喜马拉雅生产的音频总体数量为 3.4 亿个,有声书音频数量为 490 万个,涵盖 100 多种类型的广泛音频内容。喜马拉雅已建立整合全面的版权内容资源,确保了上游版权优势,持续生产优质的音频内容。截至2021 年 12 月 31 日,喜马拉雅与中信出版社等约 160 家头部出版社达成合作,与中国 140 多家头部网络文学平台建立了业务合作。

喜马拉雅拥有广泛的终端应用场景,很好地满足了女性利用碎片化时间进行学习、实现自我提升的要求,打破了学习在地域、时间、空间等方面的限制,契合了随时随地、化零为整的终身学习理念,为广大女性提供了宝贵的精神食粮。

3.3　上海数字时代背景下缩小性别鸿沟的挑战

数字时代背景下,女性在获取发展机遇的同时,也面临着各类压力与挑战,

---

① 江小涓,罗立彬.网络时代的服务全球化—新引擎、加速度和大国竞争力[J].中国社会科学.2019,278(02)：68 - 91,205 - 206.

包括更激烈的职业竞争,扩大的性别收入差距,较难获取创业赋能,等等。

3.3.1 数字时代女性的职业竞争压力进一步加大

自 2017 年"抢人大战"开启以来,各地对于人才的吸引集中在新基建、高精尖产业、金融贸易和现代服务业领域。上海对全国乃至全球人才产生了巨大的虹吸力,据直聘研究院发布的《2021 人才资本趋势报告》内容显示,北京、上海和深圳的人才吸引力位居前三位,上海城市内部职场竞争压力大大高于其他二、三线城市。然而,从上海常住人口的受教育水平来看,女性的整体职场竞争力并不乐观。根据《2021 年中国人口和就业统计年鉴》,上海城市地区女性人口中大专以上学历占比仅为 38.5%,不仅低于上海男性该占比(39%),而且低于北京城市地区女性该占比(48.8%)。

此外,近年来,随着上海从数字产业化走向产业数字化的发展趋势加快,数字技术正与几乎所有行业深度融合。面临应对疫情冲击和加快数字化转型的双重压力,企业对人才质量的要求也明显提高,工作岗位对职业技能的要求也发生了锐变。以硬技能为核心驱动的专业技术型岗位需求大幅增加,对人才的筛选和评估更侧重"技能驱动",复合技能人才较单一技能求职者更受青睐。

根据直聘研究院的数据,2020 年包括投资顾问、生物制药工程师、证券分析师、用户运营经理等在内的 13 种职业中,要求掌握数字化技能的岗位翻倍增长。诸多职位对女性数字技能的要求也不断提高,女性在人才济济的职场中得以脱颖而出的概率和难度无疑大大增加。

"梧桐果"的数据显示,在 2020 届高校学生中,女性占比为 52.04%,但工学和理学门类学生中女性仅分别占 36.11% 和 45.39%。显然,理工类学科女性的比例低将直接导致女性未来从事与数字技术领域相关职业的机会大为降低。数字经济时代下的岗位两极分化趋势将不利于女性获取更好的职业机会。

此外,在数字经济蓬勃发展的背景下,人工智能等前沿科技往往会迅速替代那些高重复、需要大量计算、技术含量较低的简单工作。上海女性在基础性岗位的占比明显高于男性,这部分是由女性的受教育程度所决定的(见表 3-1)。显然,人工智能对劳动岗位的替代对女性更为不利,缺乏职场竞争力的低学历女性也更易遭受被数字化科技手段所取代的风险。

表 3 - 1　上海城市地区分性别不同受教育水平人口数量及占比

性别	统计量	小　学	初　中	高　中	大专及以上
男性	数量（人）	898 956	2 720 336	2 099 209	3 875 357
	占　比（%）	9.06	27.41	21.15	39.05
女性	数量（人）	1 108 847	2 422 125	1 906 317	3 688 817
	占　比（%）	11.57	25.28	19.89	38.49

数据来源：《2021 年中国人口和就业统计年鉴》。

3.3.2　数字时代收入水平的性别差距更易拉大

在数字经济蓬勃发展的背景下,最直接受益的是以"新基建"为核心的软件、通信、互联网等行业。从图 3 - 2 可看到,2014—2020 年,在上海私营单位就业人员中,信息传输、软件和信息技术服务业与其他行业之间平均工资水平的差距进一步拉大,前者成为收入遥遥领先的行业,这与近年来上海数字经济的大力发展密切相关。

然而,《2021 年上海统计年鉴》显示,2020 年上海全行业和服务业企业中,信息传输、软件和信息技术服务业的从业人员占比仅分别为 5.9% 和 17.3%[①],其中,女性占比更低。同时,据《中国数字经济发展白皮书》,数字技术从业者的规模与收入存在明显的性别差距。报告显示,2020 年,数字技术类岗位中女性占比仅为 17.9%,性别比例严重失衡。互联网/IT 行业中,技术类岗位男性薪酬比女性高 16.5%。[②] 可见,产业数字化和数字产业化趋势的发展为男性提供了更多工资上涨的机遇,同时可能通过行业壁垒进一步拉大男女之间的收入差距。

受自身生理、专业等条件限制,众多女性从事着劳动密集型产业、生活服务业等中低端行业,如住宿和餐饮/批发和零售产业等。2020 年,在上海个体经营户从业人员总量中,女性占 52.6%,其中,在批发/零售行业和住宿/餐饮行业

①　上海市统计局.规模以上服务企业按职业类型分从业人员期末人数（2020）［EB/OL］.（2022 - 07 - 29）［2023 - 02 - 07］.http：//tjj.sh.gov.cn/tjnj/nj21.htm?d1=2021tjnj/C0217.htm.
②　李秀萍.全国妇联：完善数字经济领域妇女劳动权益保障［N］.农民日报,2022 - 03 - 10(4).

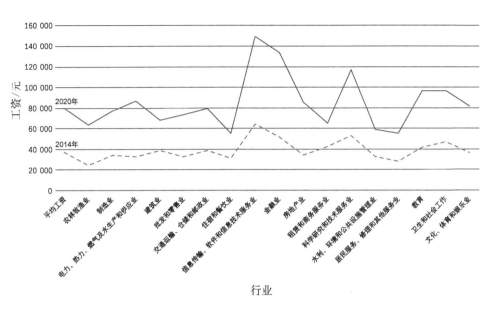

图 3-2　2014 年、2020 年上海按行业分城镇私营单位就业人员平均工资

数据来源：《中国统计年鉴》，http：//www.stats.gov.cn/tjsj/ndsj/.

中，女性分别占 55% 和 49%。① 然而，从图 3-2 可以看出，上海这些行业的平均工资处于各行业中较为低端的水平，近 5 年来的涨幅也不突出。

　　上海女性集中的许多行业（包括餐饮住宿、零售批发、休闲娱乐、家庭服务、教育托儿等）与数字经济结合度较低，更大程度地依赖于线下消费，因而受疫情冲击也更大。有数据表明，2015—2020 年，上海市女性行业岗位工资经历了波折起伏，其中，2017 年达到最高值，2018 年下降至 8 000 元左右，2019 年略有增长之后，2020 年再次下降至 8 071 元，仅为上海市平均工资的 61.34%。2017 年后，上海女性行业低收入岗位的占比逐年增大，尤其是 2020 年，较 2019 年增加了近 20 个百分点。其中，家庭服务、托儿所与学前教育等行业 2020 年的工资仅为 2019 年的 70%～80%。②③ 可见，女性大量就业于较难受益于数字

---

　　① 上海市统计局.上海市第四次经济普查主要数据公报（第一号）［EB/OL］.（2022-07-29）［2023-02-08］.http：//tjj.sh.gov.cn/tjgb/20200330/98f254db81fa405f95147551a548f9d4.html.

　　② 城室科技.疫情下女性就业情况变得更糟糕了吗？［EB/OL］.（2020-10-19）［2023-02-07］.https：//www.thepaper.cn/newsDetail_forward_9584732.

　　③ 其数据基于招聘网站的行业分类，与人口普查筛选所得的女性聚集行业（19 类）进行匹配，得到上海市 11 类女性聚集行业。依据招聘网站岗位的公司、发布日期、描述、工资等信息，对女性行业整体、11 类女性行业分别进行分析。

经济浪潮的行业,因而面临收入性别差距被进一步拉大的风险。在遭遇疫情等外生不利因素冲击、收入风险重重叠加、经济复原力不足的情况下,女性将更容易陷入经济困境。对于身处数字经济发展潮头的上海女性而言,其承受的风险和压力则更大。

3.3.3 数字经济对创业女性赋能不足

根据 2022 年 4 月上海海蕴女性创业就业指导服务中心主持的紫玉兰女性企业成长计划的《在沪创业女性问卷调研报告》,在沪创业女性所属公司的行业分布中,教育、培训、科研、院校等行业占比最高(为 28.30%);其次为广告、公关、媒体、艺术等行业(为 16.98%)。与数字经济联系较为紧密的行业占比较低,其中,IT、软硬件服务、电子商务、因特网运营类行业仅占 7.55%,制药、生物工程、医疗设备、器械类行业仅占 1.89%,银行、保险、证券、投资银行、风险基金类行业仅占 1.89%。

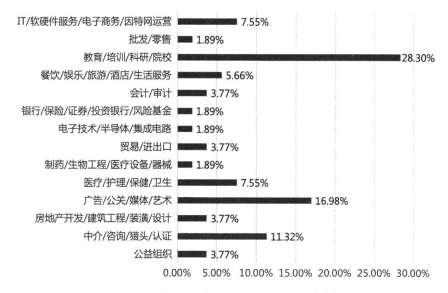

图 3 - 3 在沪创业女性所属公司所在行业分布情况

数据来源:2022 年 4 月紫玉兰女性企业成长计划《在沪创业女性问卷调研报告》。

由于部分创业女性对数字工具和技术的应用能力有限,特别是出于商业或经济目的来运用数字技术的主动性和综合能力不足,因而导致从数字经济中获利的性别差距也随之扩大。由于数字化程度不高,这些女性创业企业抵御疫情冲击的能力不强,疫情对企业的负面影响主要表现在获客量下降、资金不足和成本增加等方面。该问卷调研报告显示,在沪创业女性创办的公司数字化程度还停留在基础阶段,公司对于各环节的数字化转型升级需求较为迫切。其中,需求最大的依次为营销数字化、客户服务数字化、管理数字化等,此外,在供应链数字化、研发数字化、制造数字化等方面亦有一定需求(见图 3-4)。

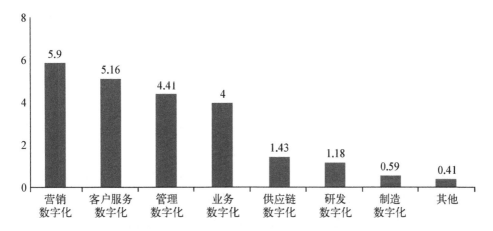

图 3-4　在沪创业女性创办公司的数字化需求

数据来源:2022 年 4 月紫玉兰女性企业成长计划《在沪创业女性问卷调研报告》。

3.4　各级政府为弥合数字时代的性别鸿沟作出的努力

随着我国社会经济的不断发展,女性对美好生活的需求与女性事业发展不平衡、不充分的问题仍然较为突出,如女性就业的社会环境和政策支持尚需持续优化,促进家庭生育的政策和社会支持体系仍需进一步完善。进一步解决女性发展面临的问题,促进性别平等和女性高质量全面发展,仍然任重而道远。

为此,中央和上海政府围绕缩小和弥合就业、创业等领域的性别鸿沟出台了许多政策文件,长期不懈努力,致力于帮助女性在快速发展的社会经济环境,尤其在不断变化的数字时代中应对挑战,得到更好的生存与发展机会,推动实现社会公平与性别发展平衡。

2021 年 7 月,上海发布《上海市妇女儿童发展"十四五"规划》,提出"到2025 年,上海妇女儿童发展水平保持'国内领先、国际先进',妇女发展水平保持中等发达国家水平"的总体目标。中央和上海政府陆续出台的政策,不断完善了女性在数字时代的就业创业环境,对于上海实现此目标提供了有利条件。

3.4.1 充分保障女性的就业权益

上海政府针对女性就业权益保障问题,出台了较为详细的规划文件。《上海市妇女儿童发展"十四五"规划》提出要促进妇女就业,提升妇女经济参与质量,并在就业权益方面明确了性别平等指标,包括劳动参与率的男女性别比保持稳定,城镇女性从业人员的比重保持在 40% 左右,男女收入比缩小,等等。为实现这些目标,上海提出了一系列策略措施,如保障女性就业制度安排,确保女性享有平等就业权利;规范企业用工行为,依法惩戒用人单位就业歧视行为,逐步消除行业、性别的职业隔离现象;支持女性生育后重返工作岗位,鼓励用人单位制定有利于职工平衡工作与家庭的措施。

为重点解决就业性别歧视问题,中央政府特别出台了相关文件,保障妇女平等就业权利,促进妇女平等就业,推动妇女更加广泛深入地参加社会和经济活动。2019 年 2 月,人力资源社会保障部、全国妇联等部门联合发布《关于进一步规范招聘行为促进妇女就业的通知》,明确禁止招聘环节中的就业性别歧视,包括在拟定招聘计划、发布招聘信息、招用人员的过程中,不得限定性别或性别优先,不得以性别为由限制妇女求职就业,拒绝录用妇女,不得询问妇女婚育情况,不得将妊娠测试作为入职体检项目,不得将限制生育作为录用条件,不得差别化地提高对妇女的录用标准。对性别歧视招聘行为,予以依法责令改正、罚款,或吊销人力资源服务许可证。同时采取联合约谈机制,纠正就业性别歧视行为,及时化解矛盾纠纷;利用司法救济机制为遭受就业性别歧视的妇女提供法律援助。

近年来,全国妇联高度关注数字经济时代背景下女性就业权益保障问题。在 2022 年 3 月全国政协十三届五次会议上,全国妇联提交了聚焦数字经济与妇女发展问题的界别提案,建言拓宽妇女在数字经济领域的就业渠道,提高妇女的数字化就业能力,完善数字经济领域妇女的劳动权益保障。鼓励网络零售、移动出行、互联网医疗、网络直播等行业企业,开发适合女性的新职业,并建立岗位职级体系,为女性高校毕业生就业打开新窗口;提高妇女数字化就业能力,加强妇女数字技能培训;完善参与数字化建设女性人才激励机制,促进高层次女性人才成长;推动数字经济从业人员参与社会保险,将新就业形态、灵活就业女性纳入生育保险,推动出台按比例申领生育津贴政策,等等。①

上海市妇联在推动女性就业权益保护方面也发挥了重要作用。例如,2021年上海两会期间,市妇联提交"修改完善《上海市促进就业若干规定》促进女性就业"的建议。《上海市促进就业若干规定》制定于 2005 年,至今没有修改。而《中华人民共和国促进就业法》于 2007 年颁布实施,2015 年修订过一次,其中设专章规定了"公平就业",但目前地方层面没有进一步的细化和具体化规定。市妇联指出,十几年来上海社会、经济发展发生了巨大变化,女性就业形势亦出现了许多新情况,迫切需要出台符合当前形势和要求的女性就业促进办法。当前女性就业后的隐性歧视面临取证、监管、查处等方面的难度;此外,促进女性就业的公共服务体系也有进一步完善的空间,如女性三期(孕期、产期、哺乳期)内的心理和情感需求,灵活就业女性的职业培训需求等,因而需要及时予以修订完善。②

2022 年,上海市妇联还着力推进就业创业巾帼行动,以提升就业服务水平,促进妇女更加充分和更高质量就业,做好"六稳""六保"工作。具体包括以下两方面内容。① 促进女大学生就业创业:实施女大学生职业飞翔"海鸥计划",推动高校建立完善"海鸥湾"工作机制,联合市女企业家协会开展"有志者等你来"2022 年应届毕业生就业行动,筹措百企万岗开展女大学生企业、社会组织专场招聘,为女大学生提供就业指导服务,多渠道助力女大学生就业。② 促进妇女稳就业提质量:加强女性在数字领域等方面的职业新技能培训,提高女性数字化能力,提升女性在数字新产业、新业态、新模式下的就业创业参与度;促进长三角女性就业创业区域联动,深化长三角女企业家的交流合作,创造更多的就业岗位。

综上所述,中央政府明确了女性在就业性别平等方面的诸多指标,包括劳动参与率、从业人员比重、收入水平等方面,并提出通过惩戒就业歧视、消除职业隔离、支持女性生育后重返职场等策略达成以上指标;中央相关部委从招聘环节入手,出台促进妇女就业的文件通知,规范招聘行为,为妇女提供法律援

---

① 李秀萍.全国妇联:完善数字经济领域妇女劳动权益保障[N/OL].农民日报,2022 - 03 - 10[2023 - 02 - 10].https://baijiahao.baidu.com/s?id = 1726707945558606779&wfr = spider&for = pc.

② 罗菁.维护促进公平就业,加强灵活就业群体保障! 上海今年将修订促进就业地方性法规[EB/OL].(2022 - 03 - 29)[2023 - 02 - 11].https://www.511ldb.com/shsldb/zc/content/017fd38ca47cc0010000df844d7e124a.htm.

助;全国妇联关注和聚焦数字经济与妇女发展的问题,努力拓宽女性的就业渠道,提高其就业能力;上海市妇联也长期致力于保障和改善女性就业权益,对落后于现实社会发展的文件规定提出及时修改的呼吁;还从校园到职场,全方位地培育女性的就业能力和参与度。可见,从中央到上海地方,各级政府为帮助女性应对数字经济时代下的就业挑战,一直给予关注并积极应对,通过出台各类政策法规,不断完善对女性群体的就业权益保障。

3.4.2 助力科技女性人才的发展

2021 年 11 月,上海市妇联、科委等 17 个部门联合印发《关于支持女性科技人才在上海市建设具有全球影响力的科技创新中心中发挥更大作用的若干措施》,提出 12 项针对女性科技人才的具体措施,包括更好发挥高层次女性科技人才在科技决策咨询中的作用,加大高层次女性科技人才培育支持力度,提升高层次女性科技人才的国际影响力和活跃度,推动落实高层次女性科技人才退休相关政策,深入开展"科技创新巾帼行动",支持女性科技人才投身浦东引领区建设,提升女性科技人才科研学术活力和社会贡献度,建立健全女性科技人才的评价激励机制,为女性科技人才创造生育友好型工作环境,加强女性后备科技人才培养,加强女性科技人才基础工作,等等。

2022 年公布的《上海市妇女儿童发展"十四五"规划》针对技术人才发展的性别平等,提出了诸多指标:高新技术企业中女性高级管理人员比例稳步增加,高级专业技术人才中男女比例的差距缩小,各类人才项目入选者和科研项目承担者的女性比例保持均衡,获得发明专利授权者中女性比例逐步提高,女性人力资本贡献率有所提高,促进女性科学素质达标率与公民科学素质达标率同步提高。与此同时,也提出了实现这些指标的策略措施:性别平等理念贯穿教育全过程,推动女性专业技术学习,保障女性平等获取职业技能的培训机会,提高女性网络素养,建构与女性生命历程各阶段相适应的科教文化服务体系,持续提升女性科学素养,全面提升女性的艺术文化素养,推进面向广大妇女的终身教育服务,等等。

2022 年,上海市妇联还大力推进科技创新巾帼行动,进一步激发上海女性科技人才的创新活力,更好地发挥女性科技人才在加快建设具有全球影响力的科技创新中心方面的重要作用。筹办浦江创新论坛女性科学家峰会,继续办好世界人工智能大会 AI 女性精英论坛,参与世界顶尖科学家"她"论坛;推进女性科技人才政策落实落地,加强政策研究,创造条件落实,千方百计为女性科技人才创造生育友好型工作环境;实施"女生爱科学"科技后备人才培养计划,探索研究女性科技创新人才早期培养模式,开展"女生爱科学"项目,引导激发女学生的科学思维和科学兴趣。

综上可见,上海市政府高度重视女性在科技发展中的重要作用,通过出台各种政策,助力知识和科技女性在数字时代更好地发挥自身才干、奉献社会。《中华人民共和国国民经济和社会发展第十四个五年规划和 2035 年远景目标纲要》还对科技领域女性的人才占比、贡献率、素质达标率等指标提出了明确目标,而且从培训机会、终身教育服务、科教文化服务等方面提出了策略措施。上海市妇联通过举办各类国际论坛、国内峰会,为女性科技人才提供展示风采的舞台;助推相关政策落地实施,为各年龄段女性提供成长和发展的有利环境。

3.4.3　培育和支持各阶段创业女性

《上海市妇女儿童发展"十四五"规划》将"创业活动率的男女性别比保持稳定"列入上海促进妇女创业就业、提升妇女经济参与质量的主要指标,并提出以下策略措施:加大女性创业扶持力度;弘扬女性创业精神、宣传女性创业典型,为女性创业提供资金支持、投融资渠道等方面的资讯与指导,完善促进女性创业的制度环境;引导女性融入长三角一体化发展,在开放的科技创新环境和新兴市场中贡献智慧;鼓励各类众创空间和孵化平台,为女性创业创新主体提供更多开放便捷的服务;探索建立女性创业激励机制,加大对女性在互联网、大数据等高新科技领域创业的扶持力度等。

2022 年上海市妇联推进"就业创业巾帼行动",具体内容包括实施女大学生职业飞翔"海鸥计划",继续开展上海市女大学生创新创业大赛,激发女大学生的创新创业热情,促进以创业带动就业;鼓励各区举办女性创业大赛,发掘和培育一批优秀女性创业项目和典型,针对"孵化项目""加速项目""重点培育项目"不同阶段的需求,以及女性创业的难点和痛点,提供精准服务等。

2016 年 2 月,上海第一家由妇联主管的女性创业就业指导服务中心——上海海蕴女性创业就业指导服务中心(以下简称"海蕴")成立。多年来,海蕴致力于为全职妈妈、职场女性及女性创业者提供系统性、创新性、实践性的创业就业知识技能指导咨询,帮助女性拥有独立事业并获得持续成长。目前,海蕴形成了"创懿家""紫玉兰"女性创业培训课程体系,私董会、项目路演、女性创业专访、专家面对面等核心产品和服务,其社群汇聚了数千位优秀女性创业者,正在为更多女性创业者提供持续的指导、培训、咨询和服务。

在上海市妇联的指导下,该中心于2018、2019年开展初创女性关爱与助力计划,通过定制化、问题导向的工作坊,帮助创业女性解决实际问题。开展女性创业"点亮"计划、女性创业大赛等项目;联合建设银行女性主题创业者港湾,成功对接普惠金融贷款,为企业缓解疫情期间的资金困难;持续开展面向小微企业女性创业者的赋能培训;通过上海市工商联、上市经信委的正式渠道,反馈女性小微企业受疫情影响的重点问题,并提出建设性议案。

上海已明确将"女性创业活动率"指标纳入"十四五"规划目标,并从资金、制度、环境等各方面提出策略措施。上海市妇联通过对创业女性进行指导咨询、持续赋能,为她们的创业事业排忧助力;还对在校女大学生开展培育项目,前瞻性地孕育女性企业家和创业者。可见,上海对处于创业各阶段的女性都努力提供大力支持,助力她们在创业道路上发光发热。

第 4 章
上海数字经济发展中弥合性别
鸿沟的案例解剖

本章将通过遴选上海具有代表性的生动企业案例,充分分析和展现企业在弥合数字时代的性别鸿沟方面所做的努力。其中,梦饷集团旗下的爱库存平台通过搭建网上基础设施平台、分销电商定位吸引女性参与创业,打造社群运营模式,发挥女性社交优势。妇女社群具有爱分享、活跃度高、善沟通的天然优势,能够比较精准地发现客户的潜在需求,从而抓住创业契机,开拓新的创业领域。喜马拉雅作为全球最大的音频内容平台企业,通过优质音频内容为女性提供知识、信息和精神慰藉。喜马拉雅支持不同职业起点的女性找到热爱的事业,实现更大的社会价值,共享数字时代的红利;汇聚女性声音,搭建女性之间沟通、交流、互助的平台,向社会传递性别平等的理念,助力女性携手跨越性别鸿沟。美克生在能源生态环境保护事业的双碳赛道上充分发挥女性的引领作用,为女性提供丰富的就业机会和清晰的职场路径,从而消除女性职场刻板印象,利用多种激励机制帮助女性实现自身价值最大化,营造良好的职场生态,在技术进步和数字化转型中挖掘更多的女性力量。

4.1 梦饷科技旗下爱库存平台案例

梦饷科技创立于 2017 年 12 月,成立 5 年来经历了特卖、店主和平台 3 个阶段。目前梦饷科技的定位为 B2R 分销电商,旗下拥有面向店主的爱库存 App、面向消费者的饷店小程序和面向机构的企业饷店 SaaS。从梦饷科技的发展过程来看,首先创立的爱库存平台,最开始的模式是"店主在社群中分享——顾客向店主下订单——店主接收订单后在平台下单"。店主在平台下单后,则可提取一定的服务费用作为推广收益,为兼职或全职店主带来收入。但这种运营模式的弊端在于客户不能直接触达购买页面,需要店主代其进行购买和售后等相关操作,影响了平台的运营效率。因此,梦饷科技开发了饷店平台,平台的店主可以分享饷店的小程序或 H5 界面到社群中,客户可以直接在饷店平台下单,操作更加便捷。升级后的饷店平台承载了此前爱库存通过百万店主,将 1 万多个品牌的产品向亿万消费端销售的定位。2021 年,梦饷科技战略升级为 B2R 分销电商(B 是指 Business,即商家;R 是指 Retailer,即零售商和 Reseller 分销商,又称店主),并且围绕 R 开发了播货机器人等赋能工具,进一步提升了 R 的工作效率。后文为叙述方便,当不特指爱库存或饷店平台时,将用"梦饷平台"进行统称。

梦饷科技绝大多数的店主和消费者为女性,店主将饷店工作作为自己的小事业或兼职。在充分发挥女性社群分享和沟通能力的优势,为更多女性提供就业机会,推动城市和农村女性创收,弱化女性在家庭中的刻板照顾者角色印象,提高女性的自我认同感,探索妇女权益保障组织新形式等多方面,梦饷科技正在推进数字经济发展背景下性别鸿沟的弥合。

4.1.1 平台助力女性发挥优势,开拓女性创业市场

1) 分销电商定位吸引女性参与创业

梦饷科技创立了 B2R 分销电商模式(见图 4 - 1),B(供应商)在商业模式生态圈中是上游品牌方,目前梦饷科技已经与来自世界各地超过 10 000 个国际国内品牌商都建立了合作关系,其中包括耐克、阿迪达斯、雅诗兰黛、李宁、多芬、UGG、沙驰、Swiss 等;R(分销商/零售商)是生态圈中的下游分销商/零售商。通过基于 SaaS 店铺管理软件和工具以及商品和服务一体化的供应链管理解决方案,将采购仓储、物流、售后客服、IT 系统等要素整合为标准化服务,连接供应商(B)、分销商/零售商(R)与消费者(C)。

R(分销商/零售商)按照规模可以分为小 R、中 R 和大 R。小 R 是指规模小的分销商,以个体为主;中 R 是指中等规模的分销商/零售商,以中小型机构为主,能够接触和服务中等规模数量的消费者,中 R 有的是分销商,有的是零售商;大 R 是指大型机构,能够接触和服务大规模数量的消费者,大 R 大部分是零售商,直接面向消费者提供零售服务。

目前梦饷科技约 300 万名 R 中主要是小 R,小 R 中 95.5%为女性店主。

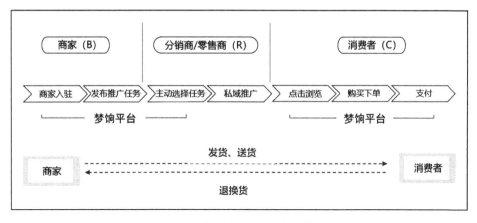

图 4-1　梦饷科技 B2R 商业模式

　　从梦饷科技的发展过程来看,发展初期的爱库存平台专注于服装品牌的库存特卖,积累了一批女性客户的驻足和女性店主的入驻。原因在于女性在品牌质量和价格优势方面兼具敏感度,平台中的商品比全网平均便宜 20%左右,因此吸引了大量女性到平台消费。由于灵活就业的便利性,根据统计,48.2%的店主加入梦饷是通过朋友推荐的,41.5%是从购买者成为店主的。相较于面对面的求职应聘,成为梦饷平台店主所带来的隔离感会大大弱化,消费者会更容易完成向店主职务的转化。

　　在初期积累了大量的女性消费者和店主后,叠加女性社交优势,为后续持续吸引女性消费者和店主带来了持久的动力。目前,梦饷科技女性消费者兼店主人数占比为 95.5%,截至 2021 年,已有 1 000 多万名消费者入驻,已赋能约300 万位店主实现创业创收。作为新经济平台,梦饷科技充分利用线上新经济模式,疫情期间提供了 22 万多个就业机会,成为以线上新经济模式促进就业和创业的典型,也成为推动妇女创业与就业的重要平台。

　　2) 8S 赋能为女性提供创业便利

　　社群经济是移动互联网时代、数字经济时代的原生产物,它改变了中心化传统电商时代"人—货—场"的关系和商业模式。卖方有一手货源,中间流转过程缩短,成本降低,因此能够吸引妇女成员参与社会经济活动。

　　具体来看,梦饷为店主提供了 8S 赋能:SaaS(software as a service,软件和技术服务)、supply chain(供应链)、skill(技能培训)、service(客户服务)、share value(价值传播)、social relationship (社交关系)、social value(社会地位)、

standard(行业标准)。

其中,SaaS 是指为店主提供所需要的开店、客户管理、订单管理等软件、App 和小程序等。供应链是指通过招商、品控、仓储、物流等环节,为店主提供完整的供应链服务,店主不必进行商品进货、备货、发货,就能拥有上万家品牌的商品。技能培训是指提供店主所需的各类技能培训,包括社群运营技巧、商品和品牌知识、管理培训、心理培训、育成成长、家庭关系维护等。客户服务是指提供所有客户的售后服务,为店主解决客户的售后问题之忧。价值传播是指提供店主品牌文化知识、商品知识等内容,同时店主传递共同价值观,成就他人。社交关系是指灵活就业模式使得店主能够有更多的时间回到社会,回归社交关系,这份事业保障能够让她们有充足的信心使亲子关系、夫妻关系和婆媳关系更亲密,使邻里关系更和睦。社会地位是指灵活就业模式使得店主获得经济收益从而地位提升,并且店主实现了自我成长和自我价值,取得了社会地位。行业标准是指建立了 S2R2C 新电商行业标准,规范和促进行业发展,让店主在一个合规、有序的行业环境中健康发展。

3)社群运营模式发挥女性社交优势

"社群"是指具有共同目标或者共同兴趣,能够即时互动、高效协作且一致行动的群体。社群经济的核心是通过社群将网民的力量聚集起来,形成具有经济效用的生产力,它强调社群的集体力量和该集体力量的生产性及其经济方面的效用①。社群经济是一种"去中心化"的电商运营新模式,是一种链接人、信息、服务、内容和商品的载体。

女性在数字经济发展过程中迎来了新一轮发展机遇。农耕经济的时代和后来的纯工业时代,人类靠体力生存,商业也要靠体力去发展。而在如今的数字经济时代,女性的社交属性、情感沟通优势,以及社交和沟通能力背后带来的力量,对商业的推动大大超越从前。

社群经济为女性走进社会创业提供了更多可能。一方面,社群成员拥有共同的信仰和价值观,更愿意向同一目标努力。女性社群具有爱分享、活跃度高、善沟通的天然优势,能够比较精准地发现客户的潜在需求,从而抓住创业契机,开拓新的创业领域。社群电商发展的关键在于分享交流,目前梦饷店主每天平均转发次数为 95 次,爱豆助手为 490 次。同时,社群为女性创业提供了相互学

---

① 彭兰.如何在网络社群中培育"社群经济"[J].江淮论坛,2020(03):123-129+144.

习、交流的平台,社群成员通过互动、交流、协作以及相互感染产生对社群的依赖以及信任,从而提高女性创业率。

4.1.2　平台助力女性自我成长,提升女性业务能力

1）创业服务——"百宝箱"数字服务

梦饷平台是一家面向全球的分销电商平台。该平台整合供应链、SaaS 店铺软件、运营、数据、培训合规等一站式服务,全面赋能店主创收创业。各类电商平台的出现为数字经济提供了新基础设施,赋能女性灵活就业,助力数字经济发展。在数据赋能方面,梦饷科技推出了"百宝箱"商家自运营工具,通过平台大数据和人工智能技术实现精准的人货匹配,勾勒"顾客画像",有效地为女性创业者减少运营成本,提升运营投产比,加速线上线下的一体化融合。女性创业者通过该平台赋能服务获得创业"捷径",缩短了因寻求创业资源、了解新电商创业信息的机会识别时间,以较低的成本实现创业营收,从而为社会创造价值。

2）业务培训——"爱豆学堂"课程服务

为助力新创业者快速成为业务主干、创业生力军,帮助其提升自身综合素质与能力,了解未来的职业发展与成长路径,增强社会身份认同感和归属感,梦饷科技为女性创业者创设了在线电视学堂——爱豆学堂(梦饷平台的店主在公司内被称为爱豆,英文单词 idol"偶像"的谐音)。目前,爱豆学堂已经形成了较为系统的课程体系,从新手小白的互联网知识了解、App 详细操作等基础培训到专业选品、营销方法的职业技能培训,从树立健康、积极心态的课程到情绪管理课程,从规范职场行为、职场礼仪培训到政策、法律知识学习,爱豆学堂为处于每个阶段的店主提供了契合自己需求的课程。在梦饷科技创业的女性表示,在创业的过程中拥有学习能力非常重要。通过"爱豆课堂"学习店主培训内容,分层运营客户,分类产品类型,发挥个人沟通能力和社群运营能力是成功的关键。

4.1.3　平台助力女性经济独立,推动女性创业创收

1）城市女性自主兼职缓解经济压力

调研[①]结果显示,梦饷科技受访女性中大约七成为兼职店主。在"为何选

---

① 调研为上海市浦东新区妇联委托复旦大学家庭发展研究中心沈奕斐教授团队在梦饷平台对店主的调研。

择成为平台专业的从业者"的回答中,"可以增加收入"是首要因素(83.4%)。受访女性在平台取得的收入通常用于家庭日常花销以及自己零花,这部分收入使得受访女性购物更加愉快,缓解了家庭经济压力,同时也提升了生活品质。

为了让更多的女性实现经济独立,对于最受关注的收入层面,梦饷科技在内部设置了温饱线和幸福线两个目标值:一、二线城市的店主月入5 000元即达到温饱线,月入10 000元达到幸福线;二、三线城市的店主这两个数字则分别为2 000元和5 000元。目前有54%的分销商已经把梦饷平台当作个人的小事业,不仅解决了自身的就业问题,大部分人的月收入更是达到了3 000~10 000元。

2)农村市场有效下沉增加女性收入

梦饷科技已拥有约300万名店主,其中95.5%为女性店主,店主中53%的女性店主来自一、二线城市,有47.09%的人来自三、四线的中小城市、县镇和农村。梦饷平台遍布全国各地,最东最北至黑龙江、南至海南、西至新疆都有梦饷平台女性店主的身影。截至2022年,梦饷平台创造了近50亿元收入,特别是农村店主增加收入10亿元。

在数字经济发展过程中,我国各地区由于资源禀赋和技术差异,国内三线以下城市、县镇与农村地区的市场范围大但分散,在提供数字化服务时,服务成本更高,平台经济更难以开展。梦饷科技为助力乡村振兴,2022年在农产品上与陇南西和县合作,促进西和县女性经济独立,让西和县女性拥有更多的机会参与社会活动。2021年举办了"乡村振兴好货节",与新疆喀什地区莎车县阿热勒乡桑霍伊拉(15)村、云南省怒江傈僳族自治州泸水市六库镇六库村建立了企村结对帮扶关系。"乡村振兴好货节"的商品以新疆莎车、云南大理、云南怒江三地的农特产品为主。除了在平台端上线产品,梦饷科技直播团队还前往云南等地,开启直播带货模式。梦饷科技通过"一加一减"和"一上一下"提供长期、可持续的梦饷方案。其中,"一加"和"一上",是指让每个村增加一名店主,同时促进乡村农产品上行,精准匹配农户与消费者的需求,给店主增加收入;"一减"和"一下",是消费成本减一点,同时让工业品下行,让消费者以更少的金钱,获得性价比更高的商品。梦饷科技产品围绕品牌特价销售,物价优惠,能够有效推动销售市场下沉,为三、四线城市和农村女性带来就业机会。

4.1.4 平台助力女性居家就业,平衡两性分工矛盾

1)现实层面——弱化女性角色刻板印象

首先,平衡家庭与事业依然是女性职业发展的重要障碍和焦虑来源,在家庭生活和参与经济活动的矛盾中,母职角色依然使女性处于两难困境。数字经济能够提供更多满足家庭照料和工作平衡的新模式,减少女性因职业发展无法全身心投入家庭照料,或者因家庭而退出劳动力市场的情况(管健,2019)。梦饷平台的调研显示,96%的平台妇女已婚,其中97.7%的已婚妇女有子女。然而,超过五成的女性反映其配偶不能与其共同承担家庭照料责任,这就使得女性在照顾家庭和外出就业两方面存在矛盾。63.9%的受访女性认为在梦饷平台创业可以自由安排时间,54.2%的女性认为能够兼顾家庭。数字技术的发展使得企业办公场所也越来越不受地理位置的限制,居家办公逐渐成为一种新趋势。这种变革可以节省通勤时间,让女性能够同时执行多个工作和生活任务,还能充分利用碎片化时间,实现工作和生活角色的快速灵活转换。灵活、自由的工作方式越来越得到女性的认可,成为女性就业的重要选择因素。弹性的时间能够解决女性工作需求和平衡目前家庭角色的分工。尽管受访女性不能改变现有承担更多照料者角色的分工,但弹性的工作时间可以在平衡现有家庭角色分工的前提下,为女性提供更多的工作机会,实现个人价值,提升其家庭经济地位。

其次,数字经济的发展也能帮助女性减轻家庭负担。网购、外卖以及网上支付各种账单等互联网使用行为能够减少家务劳动的时间,使女性有更多的精力投入工作,提高女性的劳动参与率。

2)精神层面——提升女性自我价值认同

从提升家庭幸福感方面来看,店主这份工作对受访女性的家庭生活的影响偏向积极。在夫妻关系方面,52.6%的受访女性表示店主工作对夫妻关系有积极影响;在亲子关系方面,31.8%的受访女性表示店主工作对亲子关系有积极影响;在自我认同感方面,76.6%的受访女性表示店主工作对自我认同感有积极影响;在家庭地位方面,46.0%的受访女性表示店主工作对家庭地位有积极影响。

从提升女性自我价值的认同方面来看,做好店主需要多重能力,例如人际沟通能力、顾客需求能力、商务推广能力和视频/图片拍摄和处理能力。在推进

这样一份创业工作的同时,会让女性提升对自我价值的认同感。对于梦饷科技受访女性店主而言,68.9%的女性认为店主这样一份工作最突出的意义在于充实生活,开辟新的事业路线,提升自我价值感,以及学习新知识的机会。在这样一份充盈的获得感中,86.7%的女性会持续从事店主的工作。

4.1.5 探索妇联组织新内涵,满足女性在数字经济时代的多元需求

上海市妇联紧扣构建新发展格局,推动高质量发展,积极跨前服务,团结动员妇女在参与发展新技术、新产品、新业态、新模式中建功立业。上海市妇联依托新经济电商平台——梦饷科技,建立了全国首家平台型妇联。结合梦饷平台的特征,可将其定位为平台型妇联。

平台型妇联具有以下组织特征:① 在参与主体上,平台型妇联是面向互联网平台妇女参与者和企业妇女员工的妇联组织;② 在组织形态上,平台型妇联是线上妇联工作网络和线下妇联组织网络相结合的复合型组织体系;③ 在领导成员上,平台型妇联的执委会成员应该由平台支持企业的妇女领导、妇女员工以及平台妇女参与者代表等多元组成;④ 在机构设置上,平台型妇联应该构建妇女工作和业务工作相互支持的融合型妇联组织机构;⑤ 在队伍建设上,平台型妇联队伍建设应该构建专职、兼职和挂职相结合的干部队伍。

2020 年 11 月爱库存妇联组织正式成立,是面向平台妇女参与者和企业妇女员工的、以推动平台健康发展与妇女全面发展为诉求的新型妇联组织。具体工作内容包括:① 开展网络宣传教育,探索线上线下互动的精神文明路径;② 发挥社群经济优势,促进妇女灵活就业,拓宽女企业家销售路径;③ 构建复合维权体系,做好面向店主的普法工作与权益保护;④ 建立相应的研究机制,探索数字新经济条件下妇联的工作规律。

调研结果显示,在爱库存妇联实际提供的服务中,成长服务和家庭教育服务需求最高,妇女维权服务次之。在梦饷科技创业的女性店主中,整体性别平等意识较高,认为两性应该共同承担家务,并认同两性在能力上各有所长。相对来说,比较不认同“丈夫的发展比妻子的发展更重要”和“男人应以社会为主,女人应以家庭为主”这样的观点。由此可以看出,梦饷科技平台的店主女性的性别平等意识较好,对于性别平等有一定认知。在性别平等意识较好的背景下,梦饷科技平台的店主中更多的受访女性希望妇联能够围绕就业信息、公益活动、业务培训、育儿知识等开展妇女和儿童相关权益保障活动。超过九成

女性愿意参与爱库存妇联的建设工作,这些女性更加关注女性个人成长和工作就业方面的活动。

4.1.6　主要结论

1) 梦饷科技降低灵活就业门槛,为女性提供数字技术赋能

梦饷科技是一家分销电商,为注册的店主们提供线上数字店铺和全品类的供应链服务,同时还提供销售技巧、选品技能、社群管理等线上培训,以及平台客服服务。这些数字技术对店主低门槛开放,只要店主具备基本识字和智能手机操作能力,且愿意投入一定的精力和时间,就能充分运用梦饷科技提供的数字技术和服务,并获得可观的收入。这无疑有利于女性店主加强自身的数字技术。

2) 梦饷科技打破时间和空间的限制,让女性平衡工作与家庭

很多女性组建家庭后,便开始了家庭与职场并行的紧张生活,尤其当女性有了子女后,时间、精力、心力的有限往往给女性带来了挑战。许多女性在承担本职工作压力的情况下还负担着大量的家庭无酬劳动。部分女性为了更好地照顾家庭,甚至选择退出职场,这些群体中不乏受教育程度较高的女性。

对于照顾家庭的女性而言,传统职场对时间和空间的限制使其对重返职场多了诸多顾虑。梦饷科技提供的线上灵活就业模式恰恰能为女性提供平衡家庭与事业的工作方式。梦饷科技的很多女性店主在照顾家庭的同时,可以不限时间和地点地从事自己的数字分销工作,并且从中获得经济收入,助力家庭消费。在此过程中,女性借助数字经济手段缩小了自身与男性之间的收入差距,甚至通过数字平台实现了一定程度的收入阶层跨越。

3) 梦饷科技制定行业规范,为女性店主权益保驾护航

梦饷科技作为分销电商领先企业,对数字分销者的行为规范、纳税标准做了严格设定,这为从事数字分销的女性提供了安全的职业发展环境,有利于女性店主在数字分销领域的长期耕耘。在梦饷科技,当店主月收入超过500元后必须办理个体工商户或企业资质,并根据国家规定进行纳税。这让很多全职妈妈店主也能为社会经济发展做出贡献,体现"巾帼不让须眉"的力量。

4) 梦饷科技打造平台型妇联,满足女性在数字时代的多元需求

梦饷科技因服务约300万名女性店主,为了更好地满足女性店主成长的需求,梦饷科技成立了全国首家平台型妇联——爱库存妇联。爱库存妇联主要在

组织体系搭建、网络宣传教育、促进妇女就业、平衡家庭事业、妇女权益保护、探索研究机制这六大方面发力,帮助女性在数字时代的就业、创业、权益、思想教育等方面实现突破,助力女性店主成长为更好的自己,在数字时代下焕发特有的光芒。

4.2 喜马拉雅案例

成立于 2012 年的喜马拉雅是数字时代下生长起来的在线音频平台,其音频服务涵盖了从胎儿期到 100 岁不同年龄阶段的用户群体,累积了包含 101 个品类的 3.4 亿条音频内容。2022 年前三季度,喜马拉雅全场景平均月活跃用户已达 2.82 亿名。喜马拉雅用知识、信息、娱乐等丰富的内容陪伴并帮助用户的终身成长,让人与人之间增加理解和包容,推动社会向多元性和包容性发展。

喜马拉雅作为一种伴随媒体,具有为女性经济赋能和心理赋能的独特优势。女性声音是喜马拉雅上的主旋律,女性在喜马拉雅通过技能学习、声音创业,实现了自我成长;通过表达自己、找到知己,实现了思想的交流碰撞。喜马拉雅已经成为弥合数字时代性别鸿沟的重要力量。

4.2.1 为女性提供知识、信息和精神慰藉

数以千万的女性在这里保持收听习惯,获取信息和新知。在喜马拉雅,女性用户占 47.6%,以一、二线城市的 80 后女性为主,她们喜爱收听有声书娱乐,也关注育儿知识、个人成长等。喜马拉雅为女性群体进行音频内容选题策划,创建喜播教育平台,为女性进行学习赋能,打造“超级情感节”“喜妈 FreeDay”等女性专题活动,构筑女性专属社群,为各行各业、不同年龄阶段的女性,提供在数字时代生存和发展的基本要素。

为女性提供陪伴、精神慰藉和精神食粮。喜马拉雅的女性用户覆盖普通白领、流水线女工、快餐店店员、家庭主妇等不同职业、不同年龄阶段和不同地域,喜马拉雅用音频陪伴她们,为她们提供精神慰藉,她们也在喜马拉雅找到了可以支持她们的内容和力量。

数字时代也是一个容易产生焦虑的时代,长期承受工作压力和家庭照护负担的女性,心理焦虑更为严重,女性用户对于解决生活困惑的精神食粮的需求不断提升。喜马拉雅大数据显示,恋爱脱单、婚姻家庭、个人成长是女性用户需

求较高的热门品类。经过近 10 年的积累,喜马拉雅平台已汇集了数百万张情感专辑,满足女性用户的情感需求。2020 年 10 月,喜马拉雅联合平台主播和社会各界人士,举办首届"超级情感节",发起女性话题讨论,分享女性成长经验,助力女性个人成长。

4.2.2　发挥女性优势,为女性提供数字时代的新职业机会

发挥女性在个人成长、亲子儿童、情感、有声直播等内容创作领域的优势。喜马拉雅让更多女性通过内容创作和声音传达,实现自我价值。2021 年喜马拉雅内容创作者达到 1 351 万人,其中大部分为女性,远多于男性主播。

为女性创作者赋能。每个月有数十万女性创作者活跃在喜马拉雅,喜马拉雅利用云剪辑和 AI 文稿为女性创作者进行工具赋能;利用 A+有声出版和"春声计划"为女性创作者进行资源赋能;借助喜播教育平台对女性进行学习赋能;创建女性事业部为女性主播专属运营赋能。

跨界联合为女性创作者的内容产品拓展产业链。在喜马拉雅月活跃女主播中,年轻上班族占比近 50%,在喜马拉雅上创作是她们的业余爱好或副业。喜马拉雅上女性创作者的创作内容覆盖了亲子儿童、情感生活、个人成长等多个领域,组成多元化生态,尤其在亲子儿童、情感、有声直播等内容创作领域,女性创作者的规模及热度常年高于男性 20%～30%。为了将女性创作者的优势和内容影响力进一步放大,2021 年 10 月,喜马拉雅与中国妇女出版社达成战略合作。双方主要聚焦家庭教育、女性社科等品类的版权合作,致力于为女性打造优质丰富的精神食粮,实现内容增值。

4.2.3　为女性提供新职业教育,打造"产教融合"体系

喜马拉雅旗下在线教育培训及人才服务品牌——喜播教育,以"再小的生命也能吐露芬芳"为品牌使命,探索多元化的职业人才教育体系,为用户提供终身职业教育与职业生涯规划服务,已累计帮助超过 251 万名女性朋友接触播音等新职业。她们从用户中来,渴望自己发声,将要和正在成为声音行业的新兴力量。

以喜马拉雅生态圈为核心培养女性新职业人才,使女性能够适应新职业,找到新的就业机会。喜播教育采取线上与线下相结合的教学模式,让学员在喜播教学与服务平台上,拓宽兴趣爱好,提升职业素养,学习职业技能;以市场需

求为导向,以能力培养为核心,通过喜马拉雅官方"有声演播训练营""有声书主播攀登计划"等培训项目,对女性学员进行新职业教育和新商业教育,完成从"学业"到"就业"的闭环。

喜播教育已培养了超过 396 万名学员,月活跃学员中女性占比达到 63%以上,远高于男性;女性学员及签约学员相比男性高出 26%。喜播教育超过 251万名女性学员中,妈妈身份的女性学员达到 27%以上,31~40 岁的女性占比近34%,二线城市的女性学员占比近 43%,她们期望能够学习新职业,找到新机会。

通过灵活用工服务,为女性提供兼职机会,加大副业收入。在喜马拉雅严格的签约条件下,喜播教育培养的签约学员中女性占 63%,她们通过培训实现了梦想,突破了自我,收获了物质和精神的双重财富。

2022 年 6 月 29 日,上海市女企业家协会联合喜播教育将线下招聘会放到线上,开展了"有志者,等你来"直播招聘专场。此次线上招聘会吸引了来自互联网、医疗、制造业、零售等行业 100 多个企业的参与,共收到 6 000 多份简历。在直播期间,主播、女企业家在线进行岗位招聘,与粉丝互动,解决女大学生和女性的二次就业问题。这种创新式的直播招聘方式,打通了女性求职就业的线上渠道,让社会更加关注和重视女性就业,也让更多的女性求职者与企业建立连接,充分体现了喜马拉雅为女性赋能的企业社会责任。

4.2.4 搭建女性之间沟通、交流、互助的平台,掀起女性声浪

不断融合碰撞的女性思想,创造女性互助(girls help girls)的场域氛围。喜马拉雅平台上的女性主播中,不但有学者、明星、媒体人,还有平凡普通的女性,她们在自己的生活和事业中奋力拼搏,同时用声音分享知识,表达观点,激励女性用户;喜马拉雅平台上的无数女性用户,不但获取了优质的内容与创作,也获得了陪伴、慰藉和成长的力量。女性用户将自己身边的故事反馈给创作者,也反哺了创作者。这种创作者也是用户、用户也可以成为创作者的氛围,形成了女性之间的双向激励。

喜马拉雅在公司内部成立"女性事业部",联合女性主播、创作者及用户,依据女性在工作、生活及心灵成长上的痛点,持续创作并发出女性向的内容和声音,把"帮助女性做更好的自己"作为喜马拉雅持续的事业。

通过公益活动为女性发声,为推动形成性别平等、包容多元的社会氛围持

续努力。喜马拉雅成立以来,很多优秀的女性主播成长起来,给用户树立榜样;征集和传播女性用户故事,通过喜马拉雅一次次的女性向活动,将女性故事、声音及观点传播出去,感染更多人;通过整合女性在生活、事业上的痛点及诉求,联合女性主播、创作者和各界女性,为女性发声,如"超级情感节""她酒馆""喜妈 FreeDay"等品牌活动已成为行业标杆,累计千万用户参与,覆盖上亿人次曝光。

在每年的国际妇女节,喜马拉雅以主题活动的形式为推动性别平等发声,塑造女性榜样,助力女性成长。2020 年 3 月 8 日,喜马拉雅发布"致敬女声力量"公益海报,让全社会看到女性的贡献和力量,致敬疫情之下平凡伟大的女性,塑造女性榜样;2021 年 3 月 8 日,喜马拉雅推出"伴你同行·女性成长计划"特别活动,以优质内容和精神食粮,陪伴和激励女性成长;2022 年 3 月 8 日,喜马拉雅发起"听见她声音"为主题的三八节特别活动,为普通女性展现自我提供发声渠道,传达"每个女性都值得被看见、每个女性的声音都值得被听见"的积极态度。同一时期,喜马拉雅发布女性态度视频与态度宣言。聚焦社会热门女性议题,呼吁社会关注女性的成长与发展,看见女性的价值,鼓励女性打破性别偏见,活出自我;开展女性话题直播与讨论,为女性提供发声渠道。2022 年 3 月 8 日—3 月 13 日,喜马拉雅直播间上线多场女性力量主题的语音直播与讨论;喜马拉雅用户可以就女性话题发表自己的观点,并上传音频内容至喜马拉雅圈子,提高社会对于女性问题的关注度。喜马拉雅还联合品牌扩大性别平等声量。喜马拉雅联合巴黎欧莱雅发起"我说我值得"活动,鼓励每位女性肯定自我,展现自信的人生;喜马拉雅联合苏宁百货以"女性的力量值得被看见"为主题征集音频作品,记录各行各业女性对家庭和社会的贡献,用有声的方式传递性别平等的理念。

4.2.5 帮助女性共享数字时代的红利

助力不同职业起点的女性找到热爱的事业,女性主播的商业价值得以发掘。数量众多的草根女性在喜马拉雅成长起来,找到了自己热爱的事业,在用声音陪伴并帮助他人的同时,也实现了自己的价值。

上海女孩马寅青是一位女性视障主播。马寅青借助自己喜欢和擅长的有声书演播,在喜马拉雅做主播,同时自主创业,创办了一家有声书演播公司。马寅青的公司员工中有 3/4 是视障人士。马寅青打破了世俗偏见,以乐观阳光的心态、坚韧不拔的努力,在声音的世界里闯出了自己的天地,并且帮助和激励了很多视障伙伴。2021 年 9 月,马寅青登上 2021 福布斯中国 30 Under 30 榜单,是 2021 年唯一的声音创业入选者。

有声主播"早安酱"从播音小白跨越成为娱乐主播,又在一个契机下进入有声书演播领域,目前在喜马拉雅已有近百万名粉丝,有声作品播放量超过 6.1亿次。2017 年,早安酱告别单打独斗,组建团队,成立了自己的音频内容工作室,年营收达数百万元,登上喜马拉雅 2020 年度最具商业价值主播榜。

众多女性学者、明星、媒体人联手喜马拉雅,发出女性的声音,讲述女性的故事。喜马拉雅上的众多女性主播,如社会学家李银河、情感专家苏芩等,是各自领域中优秀的女性,她们在喜马拉雅通过音频鼓舞和激励他人,给听众以启迪,彰显当代女性的力量,同时她们自身也受到更广泛的关注和肯定,事业迎来了第二增长曲线。

帮助女性实现社会价值,得到社会的认可。女性创作者在喜马拉雅已创作了多个累计播放量超过 1 亿次的单个内容专辑,涵盖儿童、情感、音乐、娱乐等多个方面,陪伴、帮助了无数听众成长,也影响了数以亿计的听众。

帮助女性实现自我认可,心理上更加充实自信。喜马拉雅的女性用户在使用喜马拉雅的时光里,普遍感到"获得力量""变得充实""独立""自信""成为更好的自己"。喜马拉雅的女性学员在学习和培训的过程中,新职业意识逐渐觉醒,她们不断战胜自己,向理想中的自己一步步靠近,通过喜马拉雅平台实现了更大的人生价值。

4.2.6 主要结论

数字时代下生长起来的在线音频平台喜马拉雅,为女性提供了丰富的知识产品,帮助女性跨越数字时代下的知识和信息鸿沟,这些精神食粮也有助于女性缓解生存焦虑,建立积极健康的生活方式。喜马拉雅旗下的喜播教育平台为女性提供了新的职业教育机会,使女性能够掌握数字时代的新职业技能,找到适合自己的新职业,弥合了数字时代的性别职业鸿沟。喜马拉雅为女性主播和女性创作者赋能,助力女性发挥在内容创作领域的优势,支持不同职业起点的女性找到热爱的事业,实现更大的社会价值,共享数字时代的红利。喜马拉雅汇聚女性声音,搭建女性之间沟通、交流、互助的平台,向社会传递性别平等的理念,助力女性携手跨越性别鸿沟。

4.3　美克生能源科技女性赋能数字化转型案例

放眼全球,科技女性一直是生态环境保护事业的开拓者、创新者和参与者。在中国生态文明建设的实践中,女性正以特有的细腻、细心与细致,展现出非凡的创新力与领导力,推动能源转型,助力电力结构变革,推动中国经济社会高质量绿色发展。

伴随着中国双碳目标的实施,能源变革成为主战场,电力升级成为主力军,无论是能源、储能还是电力,都需要缜密、科学、系统的落地方案。创立于 2018 年的美克生能源,是一家专注于"血液级"电池安全预诊断技术,并向客户提供绿色能源资产综合解决方案的国家高新技术企业。公司立足于中国"双碳"目标,是数字能源及储能安全领域的"双独角兽"企业。

4.3.1　双碳赛道任重道远,科技女性领航前行

美克生能源的董事长魏琼女士,不仅是一位重视科技的女企业家,更是一位新能源领域的资深实干家,充分发挥了科技女性的引领作用。在创办美克生能源之前,她曾参与编制"十三五"电力规划、上海市政府信息等重大行业报告,负责电力科研、基建、技改等重大项目多达 16 余项,筹建运营 10 余个地区标志性重点新能源项目,在促进国家绿色能源改革、传统电力改革方面,起到了引领性的推动作用。在创办美克生能源后,魏琼女士集结全球优秀人才,在科技创新领域、商业金融领域、团队塑造领域,带领美克生能源完成了多项重大发展和突破。

1）发挥科技女性优势,实现多项行业引领性技术突破

美克生能源为女性员工创造公平的平台和环境,发挥科技女性的优势,激发每个人的内在目标与公司目标共成长,每一个男性和女性都能实现自驱动、自增值、自进化。美克生能源拥有超过 30% 的女员工,在算法工程、项目管理、市场营销等重要岗位的管理者及一线员工中均有女性的身影。

通过充分发挥科技女性的力量和优势,美克生能源科研团队独立研发了电池安全预诊断系统(PSS),可以提前 15 天发现电池隐患并提示采取防范措施,实现了"预防做在消防前",独家解决了电池安全这一储能行业的痛点刚需问题,保障了储能资产的安全稳定运行。PSS 目前已成功应用于中国多个示范性

储能电站中,如中国首个出海的最大储能电站英国门迪电站、电网侧全国首个最大规模梯次利用储能电站南京江北电站、安徽最大规模储能项目淮北皖能储能电站一期。该产品填补了国内储能领域的市场空白。2021 年,PSS 系统作为重要研发课题的应用板块,荣获了国家电网科学技术进步奖一等奖,这是国家电力行业在科学技术方面含金量最高的奖项之一。此外,它还荣获了中国发明协会发明创业奖二等奖、中国电工技术学会科学技术奖二等奖。

2)发挥科技女性链接商业金融资源的影响力,助力科技自立自强

女性善于沟通的天然优势,强大的资源整合能力,为美克生能源的发展搭建了坚实的竞争壁垒,在推动和践行绿色低碳发展方面作出了积极探索,成为举足轻重的"她力量"。

为保障美克生研发发展,为企业创新注入资本动能,在魏琼女士的带领下,美克生能源充分发挥科技女性链接商业金融资源的影响力,自 2021 年 3 月至今,已获得从天使轮至 C 轮共 5 轮风险投资,投资者包括红杉资本、源码资本、君联资本、香港新世界集团、纪源资本等多家顶级投资机构,融资总额已达数亿元,并获得多家著名的投资公司支持,打造百亿级专项绿能基金,全面助力绿色低碳,服务科技强国战略。

4.3.2　消除女性职场刻板印象,在数字化转型中提升女性员工获得感

数字化转型使得体力劳动强度大、重复性高和危险性大的工种正在逐渐被设备所取代,具备创造性的工种逐步成为企业主流。美克生能源作为一家高新技术企业,凝聚女性力量,平衡职场生态,为所有男性和女性提供更具创造性、获得感的工作,让男性与女性都能够充分发挥价值,构建出各司其职、自驱自主、共同进步的生态系统。

科技创新是一个基于智力的竞争领域,越来越多的女性立足高科技行业,凭借较强的抗压能力、缜密的全局思考能力、优秀的研发突破能力,表现出科技女性的不可替代性。美克生能源在人才的招聘上,不对性别设限,注重团队的男女平衡,为女性提供丰富的就业机会;在人才的培育上,提供平等的资源与机制,激发团队共同成长;在人才的使用上,以成果为导向,为女性提供大量的表现机会和展示舞台。目前,在美克生能源的团队中,女性中高层管理者占比达到 30%。

4.3.3　建立学习激励和知识产权保护机制,助力女性实现自我价值最大化

1)实施"奖学金"制度,构建学习型组织,助力女性成长

为了更好地助力男性女性共同成长,美克生能源设立员工奖学金制度,基于不同等级的专业技能学习给予一次性奖金与每月补贴,并将学习成果作为调薪、晋升、评优的重要依据,以鼓励员工在繁忙而充实的工作之余,积极充电学习,提升自己的知识储备和工作能力。

"奖学金"制度的实施,有效地推动了美克生能源构建学习型团队文化,塑造了积极向上的组织氛围,让女性员工在不用担心资金压力的情况下,扫除了职场学习成长的后顾之忧,将更多精力用于自身的技能提升,拓宽女性人才职业发展通道。在"奖学金"制度的激励下,美克生能源女性员工通过开展技能学习,并将学习成果积极转化,实现了更高效的产出,更突破性的创新,以及自我和公司的共同成长。

2)实施"知识产权"激励政策,鼓励女性参与科技创新

推动知识产权的保护,提升女性的知识产权保护意识。为提升公司科研创新能力和知识产权管理水平,美克生能源于 2022 年 7 月正式发布《知识产权申请奖励办法》,鼓励全体员工参与专利、软件著作权等知识产权的撰写、申请和管理工作。该项制度的实施,有效地鼓励了更多女性参与科技创新,保障了女性的科研成果,对女性的职场晋升与未来发展具有非常重要的长期价值,对美克生能源的科研工作起到了显著的激励作用。截至目前,公司已经累计完成300 余项知识产权和发明专利,其中,有相当一部分成果由女性参与完成。

4.3.4　搭建安心、贴心的职场环境,为女性员工提供全方位的工作保障

美克生能源始终坚持和完善女性员工权益保障机制,以"安心、贴心、舒心"为宗旨,为女性员工提供优良的工作环境和工作保障。

1)注重高科技人才引进,帮助女性人才落户

美克生能源在人才引进过程中,打破性别偏见,使男性和女性享有同等机会和公平待遇,大量归国女性高才生、高等院校毕业的女性人才加入美克生能源。美克生能源持续关注上海落户政策,积极加强与政府的沟通,为女性员工争取更多的落户名额,帮助更多女性员工成功落户上海,排除女性在上海发展的后顾之忧。2021 年,美克生能源向松江区政府相关部门积极申请,运用上海

市人才引进策略中的"高新技术产业化重点领域人才"适用原则,成功帮助首批人才完成上海落户,帮助女性员工解决因户口影响子女上学的问题,更好地实现家庭与工作的平衡。

2) 为女性提供平等的晋升通道和灵活的调岗机制,满足女性的职业发展需求

美克生能源的女性人才占比越来越高,女性员工发挥出优秀的业务才能和领导才能;平等的晋升机制,让女性员工通过清晰的路径参与高级岗位竞聘,为女性职业发展打开无限空间。

员工基于对自身认知的变化,以及平衡工作与生活的需要,通常会希望在保持工作稳定的情况下,调整岗位工作内容。美克生能源为员工提供灵活的调岗机制,让女性在职场探索中既能够找准自我定位,又能够保证价值实现。

3) 为女性提供充分的就业保障,更好地实现家庭与事业的平衡

美克生能源规定女性员工享有丰富的假期,包括法定节假日、年假、婚假、产假、育儿假、病假、事假等,以及定期的免费体检、节假日关怀、生日关怀等,为女性提供全方位的生活呵护。在女性生育的前、中、后期,美克生能源密切关注女性员工的身心健康状态,为女性员工提供有竞争力的薪酬,保障其职场发展,并为生育后女性员工的返岗做好调适准备工作,帮助女性员工更快地返回职场。

4.3.5　主要结论

美克生能源充分发挥科技女性在双碳赛道上的领航前行作用,实现行业引领性技术突破、技术创新与金融资源链接,助力企业站在能源科技领域最前沿;在人才招聘、培养和晋升环节,美克生能源凝聚女性力量,为女性提供丰富的就业机会和清晰的职场晋升路径,消除女性职场刻板印象,平衡职场生态;利用"奖学金""知识产权"等激励机制,帮助女性开发自身潜能,提升研发本领,实现技能提升,实现自我价值最大化;美克生能源通过为女性员工提供安心、贴心的职场环境,让女性能够基于自身的优势潜力,选择适合自己的职业发展通道,实现员工成长与公司发展相统一,公司发展与市场需求相统一,在技术进步和数字化转型中发掘更多的"她力量"。

第 5 章

数字经济发展中弥合性别鸿沟的
国际经验或教训借鉴

怎样弥合数字经济时代的性别鸿沟是全人类面临的共同问题,需要世界各国、社会各界携手探索。不拘泥于一城、一国认识,放眼全球角度,可以借他山之石,更有效地在数字时代促进性别平等、赋能女性。本章将研究国际社会对数字时代性别平等的认识,分析世界范围内国际组织与企业弥合各方面性别鸿沟的案例,总结弥合数字时代性别鸿沟的国际经验。

5.1 国际社会对数字时代性别平等的认识

数字化时代机遇与挑战并存。数字技术的发展和应用使人类的生产和生活更加便利,也带来了广泛的数字红利。尽管数字化创造了新的生产和生活空间,但是数字要素在人群中的分布是不均等的,人们对数字工具的掌握程度也有高低之别,部分群体没有充分享有数字红利,与数字化相关的不平等已经出现。在数字时代,性别不平等仍然是实现包容和可持续发展的一个重大挑战。

5.1.1 走向女性数字包容

实现性别平等是推进数字时代的包容和持续性发展的应有之义。女性不能被数字时代遗漏,女性应该在数字时代获得充分的经济社会参与,充分融入数字技术的学习、开发和应用等各个环节。性别平等是推进数字时代包容和可持续发展的重要驱动力,只有使女性平等地参与和融入数字化的世界,才能发挥女性对数字化转型和技术创新应有的贡献。

走向女性的数字包容是推动包容和可持续发展的重要方面。近年来,国际社会充分意识到性别平等对于数字时代实现包容和可持续发展的重要意义,加快弥合数字性别鸿沟的全球步伐。2016 年 9 月,主要由国际电信联盟(ITU)、联合国妇女署(UN Women)、全球移动通信系统协会(GSMA)、国际贸易中心(ITC)、联合国大学(UN University)联合发起的"数字时代性别平等全球合作伙伴'EQUALS'",致力于推动技术领域的性别平等,为女性争取与男性同样的互联网连接、技能发展和职业机会。2017 年,德国担任 G20 轮值主席国期间,G20 成员国携手联合国教科文组织(UNESCO)、联合国妇女署、国际电信联盟、OECD 发起 G20"eSkills4Girls"倡议,向着"女性和女孩的数字包容"迈出了重要的一步,其目标是在全球范围内增加女性和女孩在数字世界的参与,提升相关的教育和就业机会。2020 年 9 月,联合国开发计划署(UNDP)和联合国妇女署发起 COVID‑19 全球性别响应追踪,分析各国为女性提供的经济和社会保障措施,确保以性别平等的方式应对 COVID‑19 的冲击。

作为推动女性经济赋权的重要平台,UNIDO 关注数字化发展中的女性群体。UNIDO 充分意识到在实现包容与可持续性工业发展中推动性别平等和向女性赋权的重要性,致力于解决工业领域中的性别不平等以及推动包容性增长。UNIDO 性别平等和女性赋权战略(2020—2023)(*Strategy for Gender Equality and the Empowerment of Women 2020‑2023*)明确提出"性别平等和向女性赋权是 UNIDO 实现包容与可持续工业发展任务,实现可持续发展目标(SDGs)的根本"。

UNIDO 倡导以人为中心的方法,用数字化推进包容与可持续的工业发展,让所有人从工业化和数字化中受益。2021 年 6 月,在芬兰政府的资金支持下,UNIDO 发起了新的"性别分析和项目性别主流化 UNIDO 指南",该指南以 UNIDO 的国家项目(country programmes,CPs)和国家伙伴项目(programmes for country partnership,PCPs)等重要项目为例,说明工业发展项目可以以性别平等为目标进行设计,最终实现工业发展与性别平等的互相促进。

5.1.2 构建弥合数字性别鸿沟的系统性体系

弥合数字性别鸿沟需要国际组织、各国政府、企业和非营利组织做出系统性的努力。国际组织推动国际社会达成性别平等的共识,是促成政府、企业、非营利组织合作的桥梁与纽带。从全球来看,发达国家处于数字技术发展和数字化转型的前沿,发展中国家的数字化推进相对滞后。国际组织将发达国家推进数字化的有效措施引入欠发达地区,使全球优秀企业帮助欠发达地区完善互联网基础设施,在推进数字教育和数字技能培训的全球普及方面发挥了重要作用。

各国政府负责制定性别平等行动计划,协调不同部门的努力。不同国家处于数字化发展的不同阶段,在推动数字时代性别平等中面临的主要任务不同,实施战略也存在一定的差异,如欠发达国家更注重互联网基础设施的建设和移动互联网设备的普及,发达国家更关注女性数字技能人才队伍的壮大,发挥女性对科技创新的作用。

企业站在数字化转型的一线,推动性别平等有利于企业的长远发展,也体现了企业的社会责任。ICT 领域的企业,应在数字技术发展的导向上、数字技术标准的制定上,保持性别敏感,树立性别中性意识,及时发现和解决技术发展中的性别歧视;非 ICT 领域的企业,应在用工和人才培养方面主动融入性别视角,为女性员工量身定制职业生涯规划,通过支持技能升级(upskill)和培养新技能(reskill),帮助女性员工做好应对数字化转型的准备,推进职业领域的性别平等和包容多元。

相比于政府和企业,非营利组织集合了社会中不同领域的女性,可以更好地回应数字化时代女性的需求。非营利组织联合国际组织、政府、企业,共同推动向女性赋权,使女性得到更全面的权益保障,获得更多的发展机会,如 Girls Who Code、Code First Girls 等非营利组织,通过与各方合作开展面向女性的数字技能培训,构建女性社群,在推动数字时代的女性赋权、缩小性别数字技能差距、改变技术领域的性别不平等方面,做出了重要贡献。

5.2　弥合互联网获取和使用的性别鸿沟

5.2.1　平等连接互联网是弥合数字性别鸿沟的第一步

互联网是数字时代重要的基础设施,每个人都应该平等地获取和使用互联网。在全球范围内,因为社会偏见,女性比男性更少有机会接触互联网设备和充分地使用互联网;部分女性因生活在偏远的、数字基础设施不发达的地区,无法被互联网所覆盖;部分女性因家庭贫困负担不起上网的费用。种种原因将女性排除在数字世界之外,无法与互联网连接,导致她们在知识、信息,以及教育、医疗和金融服务的获取上均受到限制,这对她们的个人发展以及整个社会的包容和可持续发展都造成了不利影响。因此,拆除阻止女性获取和使用互联网的种种障碍,缩小性别之间在互联网资源获取和使用上的不平等,是弥合数字性别鸿沟、迈向数字平等的关键一步。

5.2.2 国际经验与案例

数字技术的平等获取是通向性别平等,向所有女性和女孩赋权的第一步。当今世界,智能手机是最便捷、也是最普遍的上网工具,高传输速度的宽带给使用者带来了更好的上网体验。政府与私营部门合作,以免费或更低的价格为女性提供智能手机和高速宽带,是缩小互联网获取和使用上的性别差距最有效的方式。

1) 国际组织案例:基本数字篮

在发展中国家,互联网基础设施不完备,互联网覆盖率低,移动宽带使用价格高,以及社会对于女性接触数字技术的固有偏见等原因,导致互联网连接上的性别不平等。2021 年,联合国妇女署、国际劳工组织(ILO)和拉丁美洲和加勒比经济委员会(ECLAC)提出"基本数字篮"这一概念,即为没有实现互联网连接的女性,提供包含手机、笔记本电脑、平板电脑、互联网连接在内的"基本数字篮",以弥合数字性别鸿沟。"基本数字篮"概念的提出,表明国际组织和政府充分意识到互联网连接对女性赋权的重要性,提出一揽子解决方案来全面跨越互联网连接的性别鸿沟。

2) 企业案例:微软宽带倡议

女性能否充分地连接互联网是数字性别鸿沟的直接表现。近年来,全球重要的互联网技术企业支持欠发达国家和地区加快互联网基础设施建设,降低上网成本,在推动互联网覆盖上发挥了重要作用,体现了企业在推动弥合数字鸿沟和数字性别鸿沟上的社会责任。微软宽带倡议(Microsoft Airband Initiative)致力于将互联网带给全球更多的女性,使女性平等地获取和使用数字技术服务,弥合数字性别鸿沟。

5.3 弥合数字技能教育的性别鸿沟

向女孩普及数字素养教育关乎数字化的未来。青少年时期是开发女性数字潜能的最佳时期,今天在数字技术领域学习的女孩是未来从事技术行业女性人才的储备池。过去,由于社会偏见,家庭和社会对女孩的教育投入,尤其是对 STEM 领域的教育投入是不充分的,导致今天毕业于 STEM 专业的成年女性仅占少数。未来想要有更多的女性进入 STEM 领域,发挥女性在 STEM 领域的潜能,首先应当改变今天的教育模式,将数字素养教育的性别均等化放在缩小数字性别鸿沟的重要位置。

5.3.1　向女孩普及数字教育的重要性

数字时代的女性赋权首先是教育赋权。因社会期望和固有规范的限制,女孩进入 STEM 或 ICT 相关的学习和职业领域的比例明显低于男性。实际上,女孩对 STEM 领域的学习和探索兴趣不亚于男孩,女孩的学习能力也不弱于男孩,只要打破社会对女孩学习技术的偏见认知,给女孩提供与男孩同等的学习资源和学习平台,女孩在科学领域的表现将更加优异。鼓励和支持女孩接受数字素养教育,为她们未来的职业生涯提供了导航,既有助于打破数字性别鸿沟,构建女性数字人才库,也是为了创造未来更加包容、可持续发展的世界。

5.3.2　国际经验与案例

打破数字教育领域的性别鸿沟是各国努力的方向。过去,地方性的学校能够为女孩提供的教育资源是有限的,实训基地也是有限的;在数字时代,线上教育平台的出现,包括导师、教学资料在内的教育资源实现了全球共享,哪怕是贫困落后地区的女孩也有机会通过线上教育平台,获得 STEM 领域最优质的课程资源,与优秀教师互动,与其他地区的青少年共同学习,这是数字技术发展带来的弥合性别鸿沟的重要机会。用数字技术工具克服数字性别鸿沟,不但将有力地改变女性的未来,也能够潜移默化地改变社会对女性接受技术教育、从事技术领域工作的固有偏见。

1) 国际组织案例:非洲女孩可编程倡议

非洲是数字化基础设施基础最为薄弱、居民数字素养水平相对落后的地区。联合国妇女署联合非洲联盟委员会(AUC)和国际电信联盟实施了非洲女性可编程倡议(African Girls Can Code Initiative,AGCCI),对非洲女孩的编程和数字技能进行培训。2018—2021 年,非洲女孩可编程项目完成了第一阶段,向超过 600 名女孩传授了数字知识和技能,赋予她们追求 ICT 领域教育和创新的机会。

2022年,联合国妇女署、非洲联盟委员会、国际电信联盟、联合国教科文组织、联合国非洲经济委员会(UNECA)、联合国儿童基金会(UNICEF)发挥各自专长,在坦桑尼亚发起了非洲女孩可编程倡议的第二阶段,致力于在4年时间里向2 000名17~25岁的非洲女性和女孩传授数字知识和技能,为她们将来步入信息与通信技术部门提供机会。

2) 企业案例: IBM——STEM for Girls

IBM印度公司发起的"STEM for Girls"倡议,致力于提升面向女孩的STEM教育,从计算机编程、数字技能学习、职业指导、社会技能学习等方面,为女孩的未来职业铺路。在面向女孩进行STEM教育的同时,也对教育者和家长进行培训,从而更深入地改变社会对女孩接受技术教育的看法和认识。

5.4 弥合数字技能岗位的性别鸿沟

女性既可以是数字技术的使用者,也可以成为数字技术发展的推动者。当前对于女性劳动者数字技能开发和利用的不到位,阻碍了女性创新潜能的发挥,也造成了性别职业分割和性别工资差距。

数字技能岗位的性别鸿沟需要企业携手职场女性一同跨越。职场中的性别平等和性别包容决定了女性员工的职业发展。如果企业能从性别平等的角度出发,给予女性平等的职业发展机会,重视对女性员工的技能投资,支持女性员工生育后顺利回归职场,实际上是达到了一种"双赢",不但能对女性员工的职业发展起到引导和支撑作用,也会对企业的长远发展和文化塑造产生积极影响。

5.4.1 数字时代的女性就业与包容性职场

传统经济条件下,女性的职场困境主要表现为进入劳动力市场的机会不均等,工作环境对女性不友好,职场女性的工作与家庭责任难以平衡,女性的职业生涯发展阻力重重。在数字时代,自动化技术的应用节约了人力,同时要求劳动者具有编程和操控数字设备的能力,女性在这方面不占优势;在纺织、服装、食品加工等女性就业更加集中的劳动密集型产业,"机器换人"的风险更高。女性在面对原有职场困境的同时,还要面对数字技能缺口,职场生存和发展的难度更大。

新冠疫情的发生使女性身处的就业环境更加脆弱。一方面,疫情推动数字化转型加速,在流水线上执行常规任务的女性置身于更高的失业风险之中;另一方面,由于疫情封控,家庭中的育儿和家务负担加重,进一步挤压了女性的劳动时间投入,一部分女性被迫离开职场。后疫情时代,建立一个包容、可持续、有韧性的数字化时代更具迫切性。

5.4.2　建立终身学习与技能提升体系

传统经济时代,女性集中在非 STEM 领域就业。数字化时代,以自动化和人工智能为代表的技术进步将显著地改变企业和未来的工作,工人的数字技能对于企业的劳动生产率和竞争力将产生重要影响。跟不上数字技能要求的女性,将面临被自动化替代和被劳动力市场淘汰的风险。因此,帮助女性进行能力构建和技能发展是数字时代向女性赋权的重要方面。

1) 国际组织案例: 国际劳工组织对 STEM 领域女性技术人员的技能开发项目

通过数字技能培训,帮助女性获得平等的就业机会,实现就业质量提升是向女性赋权的重要内容。2017—2021 年,国际劳工组织与摩根大通基金会(J.P. Morgan Chase Foundation)合作,在印度尼西亚、泰国、菲律宾实施为期 4 年的 STEM 领域女性劳动技能的开发项目。该项目通过提升女性对于 STEM 领域相关技术技能、软技能的获取和利用,对女性进行数字赋权。

该项目根据女性的能力特征和职业发展需求,设计并提供有针对性的技能开发计划、就业能力培训计划和课程: 对于接受职业教育的女性毕业生,提供就业前的技术技能和就业技能培训,帮助她们进入 STEM 相关领域就业;对于在 STEM 领域初级岗位工作的就业不充分的女性,进行技能升级,帮助她们实现 STEM 领域更高质量的就业,拓展职业前景;对于在 STEM 领域工作、具有中等技能水平的女性,提供高水平的技术技能和管理技能培训,使其晋升到更高的职位。

2) 企业案例: LinkedIn Learning 线上学习平台

数字技术发展日新月异,女性要保持不断学习的状态,随时做好技能更新的准备。企业积极投资终身学习领域,主动支持女性进行技能升级和学习新技能,将有助于女性获取适应数字经济的新技能。近年来,在数字技术的推动下,教育培训从线下搬到线上,LinkedIn Learning 等学习平台广受欢迎。该平台提供了大量的专业技能学习和培训课程,可供学习者自学;该平台还与企业部门合作,帮助职场人士进行技能提升。线上学习平台的广泛应用,打破了学习和培训的时间和空间限制,有助于学习者自主选择学习内容,灵活安排学习进度,降低了学习者的学习成本和企业的培训成本,可以在一定程度上帮助女性弥合数字知识和技能缺口。

5.4.3 全方位支持女性平衡家庭与事业

传统观念认为女性应当承担主要的育儿和家庭照顾责任,导致女性在事业上的时间和精力投入不及男性。帮助女性实现家庭与事业的平衡发展,对女性职业潜能的开发,对企业和社会发展是有益的。家庭友好型政策(family-friendly policies)和灵活工作安排(flexible working arrangements)是推动性别平等的重要方面,将家庭友好型政策与灵活工作安排落地需要政府和企业的共同努力。

1)国际组织案例:家庭友好型工作场所认证

联合国儿童基金会澳大利亚委员会(UNICEF Australia)连同其他合作伙伴,共同开发了一套家庭友好型工作场所认证标准,为构建家庭友好型工作场所提供指引,既保护了妇女和儿童的权益,也推动了职场的性别平等。获得家庭友好型工作场所认证的企业,为女性平衡职业与家庭责任创造了条件,构建了包容多元的职场文化,既有利于企业吸引和留住女性人才,也有利于提高社会生育率。

2)企业案例:谷歌重返职场计划

女性在职业生涯中,可能因为育儿、家庭照顾,在某个时期离开工作岗位。在处理好家庭事务后,她们希望再次回归职场。在数字时代,技术的更新迭代和岗位角色的快速流动,使这部分女性重返职场时会面临一些困难。女性需要企业或组织提供一定的支持,指导她们在原有基础上学习新的技能,引导她们重新适应新的岗位角色并获得工作机会。

帮助女性维持家庭照护与劳动就业之间的和谐关系,是企业性别包容性和社会责任感的直接体现,也有利于企业吸引和留住女性人才,充分发挥女性人才的创造力,进一步提升企业的竞争力、凝聚力,为企业赢得社会赞誉。以谷歌为例,谷歌为希望重返职场的女性提供为期 6 个月的带薪培训项目"Google

Next Innings Program"。该项目专门提供给休假 6 个月以上且有至少 3 年工作经验的女性,为女性重返岗位提供过渡和缓冲。该项目配备富有经验的专业人员进行指导,接受培训者能够获得与专家沟通的机会。由于该培训项目是带薪培训,所以能够更好地激励女性参与培训,消除了女性对培训机会成本的担忧。由于有最富有经验的专业人士进行指导,女性培训者可以以最有效的方式学习新技能,重返技术前沿。在培训期结束后,企业也为接受培训的女性提供了重新进入全职工作的机会。该项目为女性重新融入职场提供了全路径的支持,激励更多的女性投身技术行业,也为技术行业留住更多的女性人才。

5.4.4 鼓励女性成为数字行业的领导者和创新者

女性领导者是女性群体中的榜样,多元、平等、包容的职场是培养女性领导者的土壤。但是从全球范围来看,女性领导者的比例仍明显低于男性,尤其是在技术领域,女性的职业发展道路比男性面临更多的障碍,不利于发挥女性人才对创新和可持续发展的价值和贡献,必须打破职业发展上的性别鸿沟。

在鼓励支持女性成为领导者方面,企业必须有明确的态度和行动计划,在实际行动中确保女性员工获得平等的职业发展机会和进入领导岗位的机会,这些做法将推动女性人才和女性榜样的形成,在更大程度上发挥女性在技术创新和管理领域的优势,也有助于促进社会逐步消除对女性领导者和企业家的偏见,形成更加多元、平等、包容的社会。

1)国际组织案例:UNIDO 对女性企业家数字商业能力培训项目

UNIDO 在实现数字性别平等中突出女性作为企业家的重要角色,加强对女性企业家在能力构建方面的支持。UNIDO 开发了女性企业家和经理人的数字商业创新(digital business innovations for women entrepreneurs and managers)线上培训课程,该课程主要包含数字技术基础、数字营销、数字项目管理、电子商务等内容,致力于帮助女性捕捉数字技术发展带来的收益。

2)企业案例:惠普 Catalyst@ HP 项目

技术领域的性别不平衡以及技术领域职业发展路径的性别不平等是存在的,但是改变这一状况,建立多元、平等、包容的职业发展环境,将驱动创新性思考和解决方案的提出,是企业在数字时代取得竞争优势的关键。

惠普是技术行业的领先企业,拥抱多元性和包容性是惠普发展的重要原则。2021 年,惠普提出,到 2030 年,领导岗位上的女性比例将从目前的 30% 左右提高到 50%。在实践中，惠普在打造多元性、包容性职场，构建有利于女性的职业发展环境方面，做了许多有意义的探索。为加快包括女性群体在内的在技术和领导岗位缺乏代表性的群体在组织内部的职业发展，惠普发起了Catalyst@ HP 项目。该项目在设计上要求参与者与高管结对，由高管负责对参与者的职业发展进行督导。通过培训、实践、分享相结合的学习模式，既帮助女性等项目参与者掌握了职业发展的核心技能，也助力其顺利晋升或进入新岗位。

5.5　发展平台经济为女性就业创业赋能

5.5.1　平台经济为女性打开就业创业新空间

平台经济对女性的经济赋权主要体现在两个方面：一是电商平台的出现，使女性商户获得了更大的市场发展空间，可以更加高效地与客户连接，获取更多的商业资源，既有利于充分发掘女性的商业潜能，也促进了女性的经济独立；二是"零工经济"为女性创造了灵活就业选择，支持女性在工作和照顾家庭中维持平衡，提升了女性的就业参与和经济能力，对于女性所在家庭的福利提升也有好处。

通过发展平台经济向女性进行经济赋权，仍面临一些困难和阻力。社会上仍然存在对女性创业者的固有偏见，女性面临的创业挑战仍然很多，女性灵活就业者也受到有意或无意的歧视。从事零工经济的女性在劳动力用工平台上得不到健全和完善的劳动保障，更长的工作时间和更低的薪酬使女性劳动者的权益受损，这些都是未来需要改进和完善的方面。

5.5.2　国际经验与案例

1）国际组织案例：UNIDO 联合 IFAD 用数字平台赋能农产品价值链

2021 年 6 月，UNIDO 和国际农业发展基金（IFAD）发起了一个以女性和青年为中心，通过数字平台提升水果价值链的项目，该项目主要在越南同塔省和槟椥省实施。该项目通过与当地农民合作开发智能农业模式，将小农户与水果批发和加工处理企业相连接，打通柚子、芒果等越南特色农产品价值链，通过数字平台向女性和青年赋能。

2）企业案例：Facebook“SheMeansBusiness”项目

平台经济为女性创造新的商业发展空间，数字企业利用平台资源优势支持女性从事线上商业经营是数字时代为女性经济赋能的一种重要方式。Facebook 发起的“SheMeansBusiness”项目，致力于帮助女性企业家从事平台商业经营，既可以触达更多的消费者，也避免了经营实体店所需要投入的高成本。该项目通过对女性企业家进行平台商业经营培训，教授女性企业家如何创设商业经营主页，如何进行数字营销，以及如何与消费者沟通交流，帮助女性提高平台商业运营技能，使女性经营的商业企业融入数字经济。通过进阶式的金融知识和财务管理方法指导，帮助女性企业家掌握科学的经营和管理方法，增强商业经营韧性，该项目已覆盖亚太、欧洲、拉美、非洲等地区的女性。

5.6　弥合数字时代性别鸿沟的国际经验总结

5.6.1　数字时代对性别平等的呼声和响应更强

全球各国都在为数字化转型做积极的准备，但是数字化转型没有天然地消除性别不平等，女性在数字化时代仍处于劣势。如果能够意识到性别之间在数字经济参与、数字教育、数字技能上的差距对经济社会发展的不利影响，采取系统且有针对性的措施对女性和女孩进行数字赋能，将性别数字鸿沟加以弥合，受益的不仅是女性、女性所在的家庭，也将推动数字化转型，为人类带来更大的发展空间和机遇。

对女性进行数字赋权是实现女性数字包容的核心。无论是数字基础设施的覆盖，数字要素的配置，还是数字红利的分配，都应当从性别平等的角度进行考虑和规划，确保数字化转型带来的机会是平等的，数字化转型的红利是共享的。

5.6.2　弥合数字时代性别鸿沟的主要经验

对女性的数字包容是数字包容框架中的一个重要组成部分。政府、企业、社会组织将弥合性别数字鸿沟提到重要的发展议程，是迎接数字化时代的一种积极态度，有助于人类向包容性、可持续性的数字化时代转型。

在推进性别平等的方法上，应当注重因地制宜，推动国际组织、政府部门、私营部门和社会机构的通力合作,加快向性别平等目标迈进的步伐;在推进性别平等的具体内容上,围绕为女性提供数字设备、向女孩普及数字素养教育、支持女性在创业就业中跟上数字化转型的步伐等方面,进行系统化的推进:

第一,确保所有成年女性和女孩能上网是弥合数字时代性别鸿沟的基础。提高互联网的可及性和可负担性,让所有的成年女性和女孩都拥有可触达的上网设备和经济上可负担的宽带互联网。只有连接互联网,成年女性和女孩才能进入数字世界,获取更多、更广泛的信息,获得更好的教育,实现更高的收入,这是实现性别数字平等的第一步。

第二,在女孩中普及数字素养教育是弥合性别数字鸿沟的长远之策。数字素养教育是一项长期投资,女性在青少年时期培养起来的对 STEM 领域知识的兴趣和获得的数字素养,为未来的数字化发展构筑了丰沛的人才池。

让女孩享有与男孩平等的数字教育机会,需要学校、家庭、社会的共同努力。在校内的课程安排上,要主动改变带有性别偏见的课程设置。在课程内容设置和讲授方式上要避免性别歧视,推动性别主流化;在校外的素养拓展上,给予女孩更多参与实践的机会,鼓励女孩追求感兴趣的数字技术内容。家长、老师、社会作为教育事业的推动者和主导者,对女孩接受数字教育具有重要影响。通过讲座和培训等各种方式,让家长、老师、社会从意识上逐步扭转对于女孩接受数字教育的偏见。相关各方携手为女孩打造有利的教育环境,将更好地支持和帮助女孩获得充分的数字素养教育。

第三,帮助女性就业创业者做好应对数字化转型的准备是减少性别数字鸿沟负面效应最直接的途径。性别数字鸿沟对经济社会造成的负面影响主要表现为女性劳动力的流失,女性创新人才的浪费。女性劳动者在数字领域的职业表现和职业发展前景不及男性劳动者,既与女性承担的家庭照顾责任有关,也与社会对女性职业发展的固有偏见,以及企业为女性提供的职业发展机会较少有关,这也意味着弥合性别之间在数字领域职业表现和职业发展前景的差距,需要从帮助女性平衡家庭与工作关系,为女性提供广阔的职业发展机会,以及创造适于女性创业就业的社会环境等方面着手。

首先,在帮助女性平衡事业与家庭关系上,政府和企业可以分别从公共政策和企业人力资源管理方面做出一定的安排。政府积极发展公共育儿事业,向家庭提供灵活多样的育儿选择,为家庭提供育儿补贴,减轻女性的育儿和家庭照护负担;从社会层面倡导和推动男性承担育儿和家庭照护责任,减轻女性发展事业的后顾之忧。企业在帮助女性平衡事业与家庭关系上,可以更贴近女性员工的职业特点,在内部建立多元、包容的企业文化,推动弹性工作制,允许远程办公等灵活的工作安排;为每位女性员工量身定制职业发展规划,给予女性必要的鼓励和支持,这将最大程度地减少女性员工的流失,吸引和留住女性人才,增强企业发展的韧性。

其次,企业在为女性提供平等包容的职业发展环境上起着重要作用,让女性享有与男性平等的劳动力市场参与权利和职业发展机会。打造一个平等包容的职场环境,既体现在企业内部的制度设计上,也体现在企业的软环境方面。企业应为女性提供平等的职业进入机会、在职技能培训机会和晋升机会,不因女性怀孕和生育,在招聘和晋升环节歧视女性;为女性提供与男性平等的在职技能学习和培训机会,为生育后的女性员工重返岗位提供必要的能力培训;建立家庭友好型的工作模式,如弹性工作制、远程办公等,为女性尤其是职场母亲,提供更加友好的办公环境;设定合理的企业领导岗位性别比例;在企业内部塑造性别平等、包容多元的企业文化,定期对企业的性别平等措施和结果进行评估和审计,做到及时纠偏。

最后,提供适于女性就业创业的商业环境。数字时代为女性带来了新的就业创业机会。政府和企业应为女性提供适应数字化时代的新职业教育和新商业教育,使女性通过开放式学习平台、经济上可负担的技能培训,学习新技能和完成技能升级,唤醒女性的新职业意识,主动获取新职业机会;为女性创业者和女性企业家提供平等的创业和发展机会,对女性企业家进行数字经营能力和企业管理能力培训,帮助建立女性企业家社群,使女性在就业创业领域有更大的空间,发挥更大的潜能和优势。

第6章
元宇宙趋势下弥合性别鸿沟的展望性分析

元宇宙(metaverse)被视为下一代空间互联网的代表,未来数字经济的主要发展方向。当前现实世界在向元宇宙领域进军的过程中会对性别鸿沟产生何种影响,本章将对其进行初步分析。

6.1 "元宇宙"的概念及发展导向

6.1.1 "元宇宙"的概念

元宇宙是利用科技手段进行链接与创造的、与现实世界映射与交互的虚拟世界,具备新型社会体系的数字生活空间。与现实世界平行,反作用于现实世界,多种高技术综合,是未来元宇宙的三大特征。元宇宙本质上是对现实世界的虚拟化、数字化过程,需要对内容生产、经济系统、用户体验以及实体世界内容等进行大量改造。但元宇宙的发展是循序渐进的,是在共享的基础设施、标准及协议的支撑下,由众多工具、平台不断融合、进化而最终成形。它基于扩展现实技术提供沉浸式体验,基于数字孪生技术生成现实世界的镜像,基于区块链技术搭建经济体系,将虚拟世界与现实世界在经济系统、社交系统、身份系统上密切融合,并且允许每个用户进行内容生产和编辑[①]。根据左鹏飞(2022)的观点,元宇宙将从以下方面影响人类生活和经济社会发展:一是从技术创新和

---

① 胡喆,温竞华.什么是元宇宙? 为何要关注它? ——解码元宇宙[EB/OL].(2021 – 11 – 19)[2023 – 02 – 10].https://baijiahao.baidu.com/s?id=1716854014749625905&wfr=spider&for=pc.

协作方式上,进一步提高社会生产效率;二是催生出一系列新技术、新业态、新模式,促进传统产业变革;三是推动文创产业跨界衍生,极大地刺激信息消费;四是重构工作生活方式,大量工作和生活将在虚拟世界发生;五是推动智慧城市建设,创新社会治理模式①。

6.1.2　元宇宙主要的发展导向

目前针对元宇宙的探讨一直甚嚣尘上,但是,不可否认的是,当前的技术水平还远未达到充分实现社会生活元宇宙化的发展阶段,这也导致未来元宇宙背景下的社会经济发展主要应用场景以及新模式、新业态的完整蓝图无法在当下被完全预测。因此,当前主要国家政府和生态主导型企业大多将元宇宙化作为发展导向,在当下及未来可预见的一段时间内,大力支持和发展基于元宇宙化的支撑性技术和关联性产业。即在政府界和产业界,其发展元宇宙的当下发力点仍然主要在技术端和产业端。考虑到本书聚焦于数字时代背景下的性别鸿沟问题,因此,本节将重点围绕当下各国政府和企业重点发力的产业端和技术端展开分析,探讨其对性别鸿沟的潜在影响,对未来元宇宙发展至成熟阶段后的社会、生活、经济等多维领域的应用场景及其对性别鸿沟的影响,本书将以较为谨慎的态度进行初步分析。

作为“地平线上的新技术”,“元宇宙”的准确定义目前仍处于“分歧与共识并存”的阶段,但业界普遍认可,“元宇宙”代表着空间互联网,是下一代互联网的重要发展方向,也是对互联网时代数字产业的全面升级,或将在部分领域引发颠覆性创新。就推动产业发展而言,“元宇宙”的最大价值在于“由虚促实”,通过数字技术构建更大规模、更沉浸式的虚拟数字世界,反哺“产业元宇宙”发展,即利用扩展现实、数字仿真、数字原生等技术手段赋能现实,以降低成本,提升效率。元宇宙的加快发展将加快推进城市数字化转型,推动实现经济高质量发展,鼓励“由虚促实”的产业发展导向,将赋能各类实体经济,以虚拟仿真、跨空间融合、数字沙盘推演等解决各类现实问题,降低社会生产、运行、治理与决策成本。

从元宇宙所涉及的产业链条与核心技术要素来看,其大致可以分为链接层、交互层、计算层、工具层和生态层。具体而言,链接层,主要涵盖支撑“元宇

---

① 胡乐乐.“元宇宙”解析［EB/OL］.（2022-04-06）［2023-02-01］.https：//baijiahao.baidu.com/s?id=1729338881562621670&wfr=spider&for=pc.

宙"运转的新一代数字基础设施,包括算力芯片、存储芯片、传输芯片、电源芯片和通信芯片等是新一代智能终端硬件的核心,与 5/6G、IoT 等网络传输软硬件共同构成支撑元宇宙运行的基础设施。据行业测算,"元宇宙"发展将带动 5~10 倍的带宽流量增长,是未来 5G+ 应用的主要方向。交互层,主要涵盖为用户提供沉浸式体验的新一代智能交互设备,包括 VR/AR/MR 技术、全息影像技术、脑机接口及传感技术。随着新型显示技术突破和设备小型化方案成型,目前 VR/AR 技术已临近成熟,即将进入大规模商用的临界点;脑机接口/全息显示等技术仍处于预研阶段。计算层,主要涵盖为"元宇宙"应用提供强大支撑的新一代计算平台,包括云计算、边缘计算、人工智能、区块链等。据行业判断,"元宇宙"发展面临着巨大的算力缺口,将推动"云+边"的新型分布式计算架构成为主流。工具层,主要涵盖为构建"元宇宙"提供关键"桥梁"技术的新一代数字工具,包括内容生产工具、底层图形视觉引擎、数字孪生和虚实交互工具等。生态层,主要包括"元宇宙"落地带动形成的新一代数字生态和应用,包括办公、社交、文娱、医疗、智能制造、仿真模拟等场景应用。

6.2 元宇宙对性别鸿沟的短期与长期影响

如上所述,当下各国政府和生态主导型企业大多从技术侧和产业侧布局和发力元宇宙新赛道。截至目前,除电子竞技领域外,基于元宇宙导向落地的较为成熟的应用场景仍然屈指可数。由此可见,当下元宇宙仍处于技术完善阶段,其未来的场景应用仍然具有高度的不确定性。本节将从短期和长期视角分析元宇宙发展对性别鸿沟可能带来的影响。短期视角重点从当下各国政府和企业着手发力的技术和产业维度展开分析,长期视角则重点从应用场景视角展开分析。

6.2.1 短期影响:技术完善阶段的性别偏向或将加剧性别鸿沟

在全球竞争空前激烈、数字经济"换道超车"的态势下,"元宇宙"作为面向未来的重要方向,前景巨大,具备颠覆现有数字产业的可能。但是,就当前而言,元宇宙的相关技术和应用场景方面与其完全体的元宇宙成熟发展状态仍有较大差距。未来一段时间内,全球各国都将在元宇宙的相关技术侧持续发力,布局其元宇宙产业相关技术发展战略。从全球范围看,美国作为"元宇宙"概念的发源地,早在 2015 年就在 META、微软、谷歌等企业的带动下开始布局,已在欧洲集聚了主要的头部企业和关键核心技术,处于引领地位;日本侧重于内容端的生产;韩国则倾向于政府侧应用推动。由此可见,在未来可预见的一段时间内,元宇宙的发展重点将侧重于技术端的攻关和研发,因此,元宇宙短期内对性别鸿沟的影响将从技术侧开展分析。

元宇宙技术侧或将引发更加激烈的性别偏见。在各国各地政府纷纷发力布局元宇宙产业及其相关技术的过程中,由于元宇宙相关技术均属于前沿信息技术范畴,同步伴有区块链等具备金融属性的技术领域,因此,在未来可预见的一段时间内,受制于信息技术和金融领域固有的性别偏见,元宇宙将具有从技术侧加深性别鸿沟的风险。在此以元宇宙产业的计算层技术区块链技术中的加密货币技术为例进行分析。

加密货币技术与性别鸿沟。长期以来,人们一直期望加密货币在许多领域中充当平等的力量,包括在性别偏见方面。加密货币领域的技术创新旨在确保一种开放的、点对点的互动形式,原则上不依赖于参与者的身份。显然,我们应该期待这能成为反对身份歧视的平等力量。然而,现实却截然不同。根据几乎所有可用的指标,加密货币在很大程度上是由男性主导的。主要原因为:

金融和技术领域根深蒂固的性别偏见。女性在金融领域依然处于弱势地位——而且越是高级别的职位,差距越大。在金融公司担任领导职务的女性人数占比仅为 21.9%,按照预测的速度,到 2030 年只能达到 31%。因此,这是一个漫长的等待,进展甚微。

在科技领域工作的女性人数也低得不成比例,在领导和高级职位方面,差距变得更大。虽然女性占科技行业劳动力的 28.8%,但她们只担任了 5% 的领导职务。即使按照一贯的增长速度,科技行业也需要 12 年的时间才能达到男女平等的比例。

这些不平等现象有着根深蒂固的根源。例如,长期存在的文化偏见,导致很多女性放弃学习 STEM(科学、技术、工程和数学)科目,这从根本上持续限制了立志于扎根科技行业的女性人数。在英国,女性只占高等教育中 STEM 学生的 35%——在工程和技术科目中,这一比例下降到 19%。而且,问题不仅仅是能够获得进入该行业所需资质的女性较少,女性离开科技行业的比例也比男性高得多,部分原因是她们在工作场所必须忍受性别歧视。

近年来,已经出现了许多重大举措来纠正这种严重的不平衡。尽管如此,仍有许多工作要做。因此,我们当然有理由认为,加密货币技术的创新可能是解决方案的一部分。加密货币的发展与对开放和匿名的数字交互的追求是密不可分的——这种追求既是技术层面的,也是道德层面的。其目的是避免中心化的控制和中心化机构基于身份验证的把关,这些机构有权决定谁可以或不可以参与。通过隐藏用户的身份,基于区块链的交易在理论上应该会提供一个公平的竞争环境,每个人都可以自由参与。

尽管有这样的希望,但迄今为止,加密货币似乎继承了科技和金融行业的许多性别偏见,而不是消除它们。这种加密货币的可能性与现实之间的矛盾也许在 NFT 领域体现得最明显。NFT 市场可以让新兴艺术家以以往不可能的方式展示他们的作品,有望为历史上以男性为主的艺术世界增加多样性。然而,人工智能公司 Limna 最近透露,NFT 艺术家中只有 29% 是女性,这和传统艺术市场的性别差距如出一辙。

区块链服务平台 LongHash 在 2018 年的一项研究表明,只有 14.5% 的区块链初创公司有女性团队成员,只有 7% 的高管职位由女性担任。同时,从加密货币行业诞生起,所谓的"加密货币兄弟文化"就在业内盛行,这也一直阻碍着女性的参与。2018 年北美区块链会议就是这一问题的例证,尽管它涵盖了 80 多位演讲者总计 10 个小时的演讲,但其中只有 3 位是女性。尽管根据其创始意图,加密货币行业完全有能力避免这些歧视性的陷阱,但男性依然保持着统治地位。

6.2.2 长期影响:未来场景应用端有望塑造弥合性别鸿沟的主战场

在未来,元宇宙相关技术的不断进步和完善,将进一步夯实元宇宙相关产业的发展以及多元应用场景的快速普及落地。各地政府必将加快推进数字技术、应用场景和商业模式融合创新,拓展"元宇宙"在商业、教育、娱乐和文旅等领域的深度应用,促进生活消费品质升级,开启沉浸式体验、跨空间融合的数字世界新入口。元宇宙发展至上述阶段后,得益于多元应用场景的普及应用,通过元宇宙技术加持后的各个场景将成为弥合性别鸿沟的主战场。

一是众多元宇宙情境下的应用场景将不再具有性别偏向性。比如在商业领域,元宇宙技术将加快促进商业流通领域创新,满足新场景、新体验、新消费需求,实现线上线下融合共生。届时,各地政府和企业将鼓励和主动在各类场馆、停车场所等打造虚拟全场景导览应用,提升室内导航、商业导购、泊车寻车体验。同时,各类商业综合体将实现转型发展,进一步创新元上购物体验。融合沉浸式、数字人等技术,优化直播带货、虚拟店面等线上购物体验。各大商业体将通过叠加虚拟地标、虚拟促销、互动游戏、全息广告等,拓宽商业运营新思路,创造虚实融合的消费新体验。

　　二是特定元宇宙应用将打破固有的性别门槛,推进应用层面的性别公平。比如:在制造领域,元宇宙将深入推进制造业数字化转型,加快虚实融合技术与生产制造场景的融合,赋能工业智造。① 推广生产协作工具。元宇宙技术的成熟应用将支持集成扩展现实、多维仿真(CAD/CAE/CFD)、机器人等技术的虚拟生产协作平台在工业制造领域应用,实现产品仿真设计、测试验证和优化的可视化实时协作。未来众多数字孪生工厂将不断涌现,数字孪生工程将建设高精度、高还原、可交互的虚拟映射空间,对工业制造全环节进行建模仿真、沙盘推演,破除数据孤岛,实现各环节协同和生产流程再造。② 发展 AR+智能制造。推动 AR、三维可视化技术在运维巡检、远程维修、资产管理等方面的应用,提升生产、运维效率。上述这些全新应用将打破过去制造业中浓厚的男性从业色彩,越来越依仗体力优势的男性制造业岗位将有望被女性从业者所部分替代,制造业领域的性别门槛将因为元宇宙技术的加速普及应用而弥合男女因生理结构不同所造成的鸿沟和差异。

第 7 章
研究结论与未来趋势

7.1 主要结论

数字时代的到来,对整个社会的生产关系、社会关系、精神文化和社会伦理将产生重大影响。数字时代背景下,数字技术的广泛应用与普及推动了数字经济的快速发展壮大,数字技术的性别偏向性和渗透领域的非对称性,使得数字时代的性别鸿沟呈现出全新的演变趋势。在数字时代背景下,性别鸿沟的最新表现主要有如下几个方面:一是数字资源可达度存在性别差异,数字资源性别享有度严重不均;二是数字创新成果与数字技能提升存在显著的性别差异;三是女性数字身份与隐私保护严重不足;四是数字经济发展加剧了企业雇佣层面的性别不平等;五是数字空间性别身份标签化,女性数字空间存在感偏低。

数字经济对性别鸿沟的影响也呈现出多面性、综合性的显著特征。一方面,数字技术的性别偏向性使得从总体来看更有利于男性利用数字技术和数字技能来提升其社会分工地位;另一方面,数字技术也通过赋能模式和业态创新,为女性提供了增量就业岗位和机会,同时推动女性利用数字技术来平衡自身事业和家庭。综上所述,数字时代的到来,对性别鸿沟的弥合既是挑战又是机遇。

7.1.1 政府是弥合数字时代性别鸿沟的顶层设计者

数字时代背景下,性别鸿沟的弥合问题属于市场负外部性问题,因此需要政府发挥"看得见的手"的作用,通过政策调节和行为规制等方式,弥补数字技术普及应用在性别层面引发的市场失灵,确保不同性别群体能够尽可能共享数字红利,实现全面发展。国内外政府重点从提升妇女参与不同产业分工的程度,提升女性就业工资和就业环境质量,强化政策引导女性就业和保障女性权利等方面展开,具体分析内容如下。

1) 我国政府: 积极谋划弥合性别鸿沟的政策框架和有益举措

我国政府主要从如下方面弥合数字时代的性别鸿沟: 一是通过充分保障女性就业权利,尽可能减少数字经济快速发展过程中造成的女性摩擦性失业。例如: 上海政府针对女性就业权益保障问题,出台了较为详细的规划文件。《上海市妇女儿童发展"十四五"规划》提出要促进妇女就业,提升妇女经济参与质量,并在就业权益方面明确了性别平等指标。为重点解决就业性别歧视问题,中央政府特别出台相关文件,保障妇女平等就业权利,促进妇女平等就业,推动妇女更加广泛深入地参加社会和经济活动。二是助力科技女性人才的发展。例如: 2021 年 11 月,上海市妇联、科委等 17 个部门联合印发《关于支持女性科技人才在上海市建设具有全球影响力的科技创新中心中发挥更大作用的若干措施》,提出 12 项针对女性科技人才的具体措施。2022 年公布的《上海市妇女儿童发展"十四五"规划》针对技术人才发展的性别平等,提出了诸多指标: 高新技术企业中女性高级管理人员比例稳步增加,高级专业技术人才中男女比例的差距缩小,各类人才项目入选者和科研项目承担者的女性比例保持均衡,获得发明专利授权者中女性比例逐步提高,等等。2022 年,上海市妇联还大力推进科技创新巾帼行动,进一步激发上海女性科技人才的创新活力,更好地发挥女性科技人才在加快建设具有全球影响力的科技创新中心中的重要作用。三是培育和支持各阶段创业女性。比如: 上海市政府推出的《上海市妇女儿童发展"十四五"规划》将"创业活动率的男女性别比保持稳定"列入上海促进妇女创业就业、提升妇女经济参与质量的主要指标。2022 年,上海市妇联推进"就业创业巾帼行动",具体内容包括实施女大学生职业飞翔"海鸥计划",继续开展上海市女大学生创新创业大赛,激发女大学生的创新创业热情,促进以创业带动就业。

2) 国际组织与其他国家政府: 强化互联网平等使用,注重数字技能教育平衡

国际组织和其他国家政府重点从推进互联网的平等互联和在性别间的普及应用推进和弥合性别鸿沟,此外,国际组织还十分重视在数字时代背景下提升女性群体的数字技能,注重数字技能教育在性别间的平衡发展。在互联网平等使用方面,最典型的案例是在 2021 年,联合国妇女署、国际劳工组织和拉丁美洲和加勒比经济委员会提出"基本数字篮"这一概念,即为没有实现互联网连接的女性,提供包含手机、笔记本电脑、平板电脑、互联网连接在内的"基本

数字篮",以弥合数字性别鸿沟。"基本数字篮"概念的提出,表明国际组织和政府充分意识到互联网连接对女性赋权的重要性,提出一揽子解决方案来全面跨越互联网连接的性别鸿沟。在推进数字技能教育平衡方面,最具代表性的案例是联合国妇女署联合非洲联盟委员会和国际电信联盟实施了非洲女性可编程倡议,对非洲女孩重要的编程和技术技能进行培训。2018—2021 年,非洲女孩可编程项目完成了第一阶段,向超过 600 名女孩传授了数字知识和技能,赋予她们追求 ICT 领域教育和创新的机会。

7.1.2 弥合数字时代的性别鸿沟不能忽视企业的力量

在数字时代,数字技术的普及应用衍生出诸多新业态、新模式,这一方面为女性创造了增量就业岗位和事业发展空间,另一方面也为弥合性别鸿沟带来了诸多挑战。而企业作为新模式、新业态的创造者和应用者,其在推动数字经济创新发展及影响性别鸿沟方面发挥着重要作用,因此,在探讨数字时代性别鸿沟的弥合问题时,不可忽略企业在这一问题领域的重要功能。本书搜集分析了3 个代表性企业作为典型案例,重点分析其在数字时代背景下弥合性别鸿沟所做的有益举措和经验。

企业案例研究发现,以爱库存和喜马拉雅为代表的数字经济企业分别以自身的独特方式为女性发展和弥合性别鸿沟加持赋能。其中,梦饷集团旗下的爱库存平台通过搭建网上基础设施平台、分销电商定位吸引女性参与创业,打造社群运营模式发挥女性社交优势。妇女社群具有爱分享、活跃度高、善沟通的天然优势,能够比较精准地发现客户的潜在需求,从而抓住创业契机,开拓新的创业领域。喜马拉雅作为全球最大的音频内容平台企业,通过优质音频内容为女性提供知识、信息和精神慰藉。数以千万的女性在这里保持收听习惯,帮助女性获取信息和新知识,为女性提供陪伴、精神慰藉和精神食粮。美克生在能源生态环境保护事业的双碳赛道上充分发挥女性的引领作用,为女性提供丰富的就业机会和清晰的职场路径,从而消除女性职场刻板印象,利用多种激励机制帮助女性实现自身价值最大化,营造良好的职场生态,在技术进步和数字化转型中挖掘更多的女性力量。

综上所述,无论是数字经济企业,还是高新技术企业,其在弥合数字时代的性别鸿沟方面具有十分重要的作用。可以预见的是,弥合性别鸿沟,需要政企齐发力,社会多元共治,才能达到理想的效果。

7.2 未来展望

7.2.1 数字时代的性别鸿沟将始终伴随数字技术的更新迭代与普及应用

当今数字时代,数字技术的更新迭代、普及渗透深刻影响和改变了人们的价值观念、行为方式和生产生活。在生产侧,数字技术的普及应用衍生出各类新模式、新业态,社会分工在数字技术的外生冲击下将持续发生重大调整和更新迭代。而这背后必然会对不同性别群体的社会分工地位和数字技能的掌握与获取产生差异性影响,并最终作用于性别鸿沟的扩大或缩小。在治理侧,以互联网、大数据、云计算、人工智能、移动设备等为代表的数字技术,为推进社会治理现代化提供了新的治理工具,然而数字技术本身并不足以保证社会治理的合法性、合理性和有效性,政府等社会治理主体在应用数字技术开展治理活动时,应当更加注重治理红利在不同维度群体中的公平性与合理性,其中就包括不同性别群体共享社会治理数字化转型红利的内涵要求。对此,政府等社会治理主体必须走出工具理性的迷失、技术主导的误区,回归技术为社会治理服务的逻辑起点。

7.2.2 近期应更关注数字技术创新供给对性别鸿沟的影响

随着数字经济新赛道的逐渐清晰,"元宇宙"化将成为数字经济未来发展的重要方向。由于当前元宇宙相关的各项技术尚未能够满足元宇宙未来所要达成的应用效果要求,即当前的数字技术并未在元宇宙领域形成令人满意的产业化应用与实践,因此,未来一段时间内,基于元宇宙发展方向的数字经济将更加侧重于数字技术的不断创新与更新迭代,即更加注重新技术的供给。因此,未来可预见的时间内,对性别鸿沟造成显著影响的数字化因素仍将是数字技术侧,即数字技术的研发攻关与试验等供给侧经济活动,而这有可能延续技术类岗位对女性的歧视和偏见。未来在弥合数字时代的性别鸿沟时,提升女性的数字技能,促进女性在数字技术岗位就业,打破数字技术岗位的性别歧视仍将是主攻方向。

7.2.3 未来应更加重视多元数字化应用场景对性别鸿沟的影响

在数字技术的产业化应用达到成熟期之后,或者说在数字技术足以支撑基于元宇宙的各项应用场景,且各类应用场景能够满足社会大众的精神和物质需求之后,数字时代的数字经济活动将由技术侧向应用场景侧偏移,即届时的经济主体将更加注重应用场景的开发和供给,全新的沉浸式体验场景将极大丰富。届时,网络空间内将释放出更多基于个体自主创作的个性化应用场景,数字技术的应用和各类场景将可能具有更强的性别包容性,其对性别鸿沟的影响和效应有待进一步分析和论证。

7.2.4 企业在弥合性别鸿沟方面的影响力将持续增强

伴随着区块链等去中心化数字技术的快速普及和更新迭代,将来的数字时代,在社会治理等多个领域都将呈现出去中心化的发展趋势。未来的社会治理将更趋多元主体共治的特征。因此,就性别鸿沟的弥合而言,在去中心化的大背景、大趋势下,企业等多元主体的力量将进一步凸显,政府的中心化治理地位将进一步削弱。未来的性别鸿沟弥合及其他社会性问题将更加依仗企业、社会组织等分散式多元主体的共同参与。

附录
UNIDO 报告《性别、数字化转型和人工智能》

实现性别平等、增加女性权能,是实现联合国可持续发展目标(SDG)和包容性可持续工业发展(ISID)的基本组成部分。在实现可持续发展目标9的同时,联合国工发组织持续通过各种行动和倡议支持妇女,为实现可持续发展目标5做出贡献。

《弥合数字时代的性别鸿沟》一书是对弥合数字时代性别鸿沟这一议题的一次积极探索。通过分析其内涵和表现剖析鸿沟,结合国际与国内进行经验借鉴,并且在元宇宙的创新视角下进行了展望,进而结合联合国工业发展组织(UNIDO)聚焦性别平等的 EQUIP 10 提出应对方案。此书是 UNIDO 上海 ITPO 办公室在性别议题上的优秀前沿研究成果。

近日,联合国工业发展组织同步发布了了《性别、数字化转型和人工智能报告》(详见下文),再次强调性别是数字化转型和人工智能发展过程中必须重视的议题。联合国工业发展组织希望通过该报告,引起社会各界在数字化转型背景下对性别议题的再度重视,倡议在八大关键领域中采取行动,共同构建一个性别平等的数字时代。

本书将该报告作为附录,希望给广大读者进一步的启发。

总干事　序言

性别、数字化转型和人工智能

数字转型和人工智能（AI）为我们带来了几乎无限的可能性。然而，即使在今天，我们也能看到，科技发展在很大程度上对女性和弱势群体存在偏见。我们不能接受这样的现状！当我们在思考、规划和实施数字转型和人工智能的问题时，性别视角必须居于核心地位。

如果没有刻意的选择，人工智能不会凭空消除偏见。当前最好的算法所依赖的数据，也反映了我们希望摆脱性别不平等的现状。在联合国工业发展组织（UNIDO），平衡和消除性别偏见是项目的重要组成部分。数字化转型和人工智能的技术飞速发展不能成为忽视性别问题的借口。我相信，为了在人工智能和数字化转型中实现性别平等，我们必须采取必要的干预措施并做好准备。

为建设这样的未来，我们需要在所有发展领域付出努力。这需要我们在力所能及的范围内纠正不平等，特别是在数字领域。然而，当性别数字鸿沟在国家、社会甚至家庭之间广泛存在时，我们又该如何确保性别的平衡和无偏见的人工智能或数字化转型发展呢？

我们可以在一些发展趋势上发挥影响力。想要揭露减少女性作为数字技术的用户、开发者和学习者的机制，需要以提高性别平等意识为出发点。通过底层设计，数字化转型的性别包容潜力必须得到发挥。在能力建设方面，人工智能和数字技术应该要首先面向女性。通过这种方式，我们不仅可以增加女性的参与度，更重要的是还能提升女性在算法及其开发、采用和进一步应用方面的必要技能。

在此背景下，联合国工业发展组织提出了我们所能采取的行动。我希望通过这个出发点，能够引起大众对性别议题的关注并着手弥合性别鸿沟。我坚信，通过我们的关注和努力，我们可以应对挑战，迈向一个更加光明、平等的未来。

格尔德·穆勒（Gerd Müller）

联合国工业发展组织总干事

概要

在数字、生物和物理领域,快速变化的技术发展正在改变工作场所、人际关系和贸易网络。第四次工业革命(4IR)创造了就业和商机,却也淘汰了一些岗位和活动。

性别偏见和刻板印象阻碍了女性作为数字技术用户、学习者和开发者的参与。

数字化得到了加速(尤其在新冠疫情后),但并非所有人都平等地从第四次工业革命所创造的机遇中受益。

女性和女童接触到数字技术的可能性更小,且在技术领域中,她们在学生、教研人员和企业家群体中的代表性较低,尤其在人工智能领域,这一差距更为显著。

数字技术可以为女性创造领导、参与和受益于技术发展的机会。然而,如果没有正确的政策支持,数字技术可能会强化性别刻板印象,使得女性无法融入经济和社会。

本报告基于对 5 个区域中超过 150 个倡议的研究,提供了关于进一步促进数字转型中性别平等和女性赋权的优先事项和切入点的建议。

弥合性别鸿沟是一个人权问题,同时也带来了经济和社会效益,从扩大市场和挖掘人才,到解决日益严重的技能短缺、提高财务绩效、增加创新活动,以及避免在社会中加剧地位和权力的不平等。

报告分析了全球有关促进和加强性别变革战略和新兴数字技术倡议的政策和举措的现状,重点关注人工智能。除人工智能领域,报告还关注以下技术领域:增材制造、大数据、云计算、网络安全、物联网(IoT)、分布式总账技术、机器人技术、无人驾驶车辆系统和量子计算机。

本报告对非洲、亚太地区、拉丁美洲和加勒比海地区、东欧、西欧和其他国家内超过 150 个倡议进行了研究。研究涵盖了案头调研、国际组织和民间社会组织所提交的意见,以及与关键利益相关方的访谈,发掘了优秀实践案例。

报告介绍了行动的主要领域和共同方法,并以对倡议的案例研究为特点,包括国际组织为了解技术领域的性别鸿沟而对研究进行的资助、开发银行对由女性领导的企业的支持、学术机构和私营部门在技能发展方面的合作,以及民间社会团体为数字包容边缘群体而开展的扶持。

为弥合在数字技术的使用、知识与发展方面的性别差距,八个关键行动领域如下:

 1. 缩小编码技能之外的性别技能鸿沟

在性别视角下培养技能主要聚焦于编码能力。然而,这就面临着无法解决其他相关领域的性别鸿沟的风险,这些领域中的性别差距更为广泛(如云计算领域),或者正在扩展(如数据分析、人工智能等领域)。因此,在制定技能培养措施时,应基于对劳动力市场具体动态和技能增量性的充分了解,对其范围进行专门化。

 2. 以终身学习的方法促进性别变革

女性终身都在数字技术领域内面临着参与障碍。在跨学科、跨职业和跨部门的数字素养、再培训和技能提升的需求日益增长的情况下,这些障碍使女性有一定风险失去数字转型相关机遇。因此,数字技能发展倡议应采取终身学习的方法。

 3. 将促进性别平等的路径应用于技术驱动的研究、设计和创新领域

促进性别平等的路径不仅关乎公平和正义,更能为更广泛的受众创造更优质的知识、产品和服务。在报告所识别的挑战中,人们越来越需要解决数字技术(特别是人工智能系统)中的潜在歧视问题。因此,在技术的开发和应用中,包括人工智能系统的开发和应用,应努力在技术和领导层职位以及团队内实现多样性,同时培养跨学科的能力,如对性别歧视作用机制的深刻理解。

4. 促进多方利益相关者的合作

在数字转型中,性别偏见和歧视以不同的新旧形式显现,各利益相关者在解决这些问题中都发挥着作用。例如,私营部门和研究机构在解决技术驱动的研究、设计和创新中的性别偏见方面起到关键作用。与此同时,民间社会组织也卓有成效地使人们开始关注数字技术对边缘群体的负面影响。因此,要想消除数字技术领域的性别差距,就需要采取多方利益相关者共同参与的方法。

 5. 在产业和创新战略中将性别议题纳入主流

数字转型中女性和男性参与度的差异呼吁在产业和创新战略中将性别议题纳入主流,即评估和解决计划行动对不同性别群体的影响。特别是在研究各倡议时发现,多个领域缺乏具有性别视角的措施,例如对企业技术采用的支持、创新周期后期技术扩展的资金支持等。

 6. 绿色化和数字化同步转型

数字化可以成为推动产业向更加循环低碳的方向转型的一大关键因素。然而,能源和基础设施领域存在着类似于数字技术领域中的性别鸿沟。循环经济和气候友好产业领域同样由男性主导,特别是在技术和领导职位方面。忽视这些相互关联的性别鸿沟可能会加剧现有的不平等问题。

 7. 持续加强创新生态系统和基础设施

为女性提供更多机会,也意味着需要持续加强创新生态系统和基础设施,特别是在发展中国家。政府可以在发展创新体系和基础设施时采取促进性别平等的方法。例如,可以在资助研究和创新项目时加入性别平等条件,采用促进性别平等的公共采购策略(促进性别平等的采购策略)等。

 8. 持续缩小信息差距

在解决技术领域的性别鸿沟时,公司、国家和国际统计中性别分类数据的匮乏是政策制定者面临的主要挑战之一。借鉴数字平台的经验,与私营部门合作,可以更好地了解先进数字技术的使用及潜在的裨益。本调研还表明,有必要更好地了解科技公司内部的性别平等措施。

如需获取全文,请点击链接：https：//hub.unido.org/node/12112

Chapter |
Research Background

China has entered digital age, and the rapid development of a new round of modern information technology, such as big data, the Internet of Things, artificial intelligence and block-chain, has become a new driving force for social and economic development. At the same time, there has been a new imbalance in many aspects, such as "access to digital tools, mastery of digital technology and participation in the digital world", namely, the "digital divide". The digital dividend in the 5G era has not been balanced among different gender types, and the gender divide in the digital age still exists.

1.1 Concept and Characteristics of the Digital Age

In the *Outline of the 14th Five-Year Plan (2021 – 2025) for National Economic and Social Development and Vision 2035 of the People's Republic of China (the Outline)* released in March 2021, China proposed the strategic planning of "accelerating digital development and building a digital China". The *Outline* also mentioned, "We will welcome the digital age, activate the potential of data factors, and leverage digital transformations to drive overall changes in production methods, lifestyles, and governance." *The Outline* made it clear that China has left post-industrialization age and informatization age and entered into digital age.

1.1.1 The Origin of the Digital Age

From the international perspective, the report entitled "Age of Digital

Interdependence" issued by the United Nations in June 2019 and the *Government Decision on Promoting Innovation in the Digital Age* issued by the World Trade Organization in November 2020 highlight the distinctive theme of the digital age.

From the perspective of science and technology and social development, informatization is the early stage of digitalization. The information age arrived with electronic computers and modern communication technologies, which are characterized by "information isolated island" constructed separately. In essence, digitalization is the higher level of informatization, which is manifested as "interconnection of everything, data sharing, platform enabling, information leading, and business collaboration". The rapid development and wide application of Internet of Things, big data, artificial intelligence, block-chain and other digital technologies have further accelerated the process of digital iteration and transformation.

The application of digital technology has given birth to a new digital age, which is advancing from the information field to all areas of human life. As a partner of "Digital France" "Digital Israel" and "Digital India", Cisco has a deep understanding of the connotation of the digital age, and has made a time distinction between the digital age and the information age. It believes that the 1990s to 2010 is the "information age", and that people will step into the "digital age" from 2010 to 2030.

1.1.2 The Connotation of the Digital Age

The digital age affects people's social production and social relations, especially social ethics and spiritual culture. ①

At the social production level, data has become an important factor of production, and the digital economy is booming. In the digital age, digital labor, as a kind of complex knowledge labor, takes data as the means of production, and

---

① 李华君.数字时代品牌传播概论[M].西安：西安交通大学出版社,2020：1-6.

creates value by consuming a certain amount of labor time and labor in cyberspace.[①] The multiplier benefit brought by new technology will be 5~10 times the scale in the information age. The digital age has brought a chance to reshape the production and distribution of the whole society, contributing to the reconstruction of the global economy and power.

At the social relations level, social relations are moving towards complex "aggregation and dispersion", from "virtual society" to "mirror society". The digital age has deconstructed the traditional social relations linked by blood and geography. The great flow of information can enable strangers to quickly gather in cyberspace and form a virtual community. People gradually find their own "tribal groups" in the collision of multiple minds, and relationships in the real society are increasingly transplanted in the network virtual space. With the progress of digital technology, people's activity tracks can be captured and input into the network database. The "mirror world" gradually replaces the "virtual society" and interacts more closely with the real world.

At the social ethics level, social ethics is more diversified and differentiated. In the digital space, social ethics exists in the form of conflict and tolerance. The more personalized, pluralistic and fragmented social forms have spawned different network groups, and these different circles live in the internet in a conflicting and harmonious manner. *The 2018 Tencent Post 00s Research Report* released by Tencent shows that the post 00s advocate the values of "equality" and "inclusiveness", are more accustomed to and good at expressing their feelings and views, and are more willing to accept others' differences.

At the spiritual and cultural level, knowledge acquisition is more convenient and knowledge updating and iteration speed has been accelerated. In the digital age, network digital culture has developed rapidly. People can quickly obtain a large amount of knowledge and information through the internet, which promotes the rapid iteration of knowledge and international communication of culture. At the

---

① 吴欢,卢黎歌.数字劳动与大数据社会条件下马克思劳动价值论的继承与创新[J].学术论坛, 2016,39(12):7-11.

cultural and ideological level, resources, environment, ecology, human future, individual survival and ego, ideal values, gender awareness and other topics have received more attention.

1.1.3　The Characteristics of the Digital Age

President Xi Jinping said in the congratulation letter to 2019 China International Digital Economy Expo: "The robust advancement of scientific and technological revolution and industrial transformation, as well as fast growth of the digital economy, have profoundly changed people's way of production and life, and brought far-reaching influence on the economic and social development of countries, global governance and progress of human civilization."[1] The characteristics of the digital age are as follows.

The digital economy adds new momentum to the development of the world economy. According to the data released in the *White Paper on the Global Digital Economy* (*2022*), in 2021, the added value of digital economy of 47 major countries in the world reached 38.1 trillion US dollars, with a nominal year-on-year growth of 15.6%, accounting for 45% of their GDP. Among them, the developed countries took up a larger share, with a scale of 27.6 trillion US dollars in 2021, accounting for 55.7% of their GDP; but the digital economy of developing countries is growing faster, with a growth rate of 22.3% in 2021. The value of China's digital economy reached 7.1 trillion US dollars, ranking second in the world, accounting for 39.8%[2] of its GDP. The basic component of digital economy is digital industrialization, and the main battlefield is industrial digitalization. The deep integration of digital industrialization and industrial digitalization has changed the structure and efficiency of allocation of factors and resources, and has produced a revolutionary impact on economic growth and social lifestyle.

[1]　Xinhua. Xi sends congratulatory letter to China International Digital Economy Expo [EB/OL]. (2019 - 10 - 11) [2023 - 02 - 01]. http://www.xinhuanet.com/english/2019 - 10/11/c_138463653.htm.

[2]　陈维城,孙文轩.2021 年中国数字经济规模达 7.1 万亿美元[EB/OL].(2022 - 07 - 29)[2023 - 02 - 01].https://baijiahao.baidu.com/s?id = 1739696825942008930&wfr = spider&for = pc.

Digital life makes life more convenient and intelligent. Digital life is a way of life based on the Internet and a series of digital technology applications. It uses a series of scientific and technological means to improve the quality of our life. With the increasing spreading of Internet technology applications, the Internet has comprehensively changed the way of life of all mankind. The latest scientific and technological means rely on the digital tools of the unified virtual network to support a convenient, comfortable and high-quality digital life mode.

Digital governance provides impetus for the modernization of the national governance system. Digital governance dynamically connects the government, market, society and individuals in a data based way, further forming a digital age community with multiple interactions and collaborative evolution of all parties, and promoting the healthy and orderly development of the digital society. The application and development of digital governance endow the country with "digital national capacities", in which the abilities to absorb information, manage data and make accurate decisions empower the national economic work.

1.2　Development of the Traditional Gender Divide

Nowadays, most young people have formed certain digital awareness and acquired basic digital knowledge. However, due to the influence of gender inequality from traditional culture, the renewal and development of cultural concepts and norms in the whole society do not fully coincide with the rapid digital transformation in the 5G era. On the contrary, it exerts a more subtle influence on men and women, in terms of their acceptance and use of digital technology, as well as their participation in the digital world.

1.2.1　The Historical Origin of the Traditional Gender Divide

Although human society has entered the 21st century, gender inequality between men and women is still an important manifestation of inequality of human society, which is particularly prominent in developing countries and regions. In the human history, the transformation from hunting to agricultural society is an important node. First of all, the male labor force in agricultural society has a comparative advantage over female in the agricultural production mode of ploughing and planting, which leads to a pattern in which men engage in outdoor agricultural production activities and women engage in production activities within the family. In addition, women spend a lot of time taking care of their children and have fewer opportunities to engage in other agricultural production activities, so the authority of men is strengthened in social concepts. This early social division of labor in agricultural society determined the different economic and social status and roles of men and women. The result was then strengthened into social concepts, which in turn led to the current gender inequality between men and women in various countries.

Nevertheless, the social status of women is not unchanging. In addition to the influence of cultural and religious beliefs, the formation and evolution of people's concept of equality between men and women are also in the process of development and improvement. On the one hand, historical factors will produce lasting impact on current people's behavior and ideas; on the other hand, with the change of social structure and economic development, the emergence of some new industries and occupations that can leverage female labor force has gradually improved the status and role of women in the economic society.

1.2.2 Impact of the Traditional Gender Divide

Influenced by traditional cultural concepts, parents tend to have different future development expectations for their sons and daughters. Traditional social and cultural norms regard digital fields, including digital technology related majors and jobs in schools and workplaces, as "exclusive to men". Parents have less support for girls to choose digital related majors, believing that they are more suitable for learning and working in social sciences domain. This ultimately leads to women's lack of confidence in digital professional fields and low participation in digital related occupations. According to the relevant data of the Program for International Student Assessment (PISA2015), 15 year old girls are less likely than boys to "imagine working in science and engineering fields in the future". ①

The traditional labor division of different genders does not support women to fully devote themselves to their career development. Especially for women in developing countries, the possibility for them to work in digital technology field has been reduced by an invisible factor—it is harder for them to master digital technology because they have to stay at home or take short-term and unstable jobs. Because women need to bear more family responsibilities entrusted to them by society, they lack sufficient time and energy to receive continuing education and training, which creates hidden obstacles for them to further improve their digital skills and deeply participate in the digital economy, indirectly hindering their career development at a higher level in the digital career field.

Stereotypes from traditional gender concepts limit women from remarkable development in the top field of digital industry. At the management level in the digital field, the proportions of men and women in senior positions are seriously unbalanced. For example, in the mobile industry, women are 20% less likely than men to hold senior leadership positions globally. The severe development problems faced by women in the digital professional field, to a certain extent, will further reduce their learning willingness and career aspirations in the digital professional field.

1.3　Global Efforts and Practices to Bridge the Gender Divide

Although new technology revolution and traditional cultural restrictions have constrained women's development in the digital age to a certain extent, global organizations are also taking active and effective measures to bridge the gender divide, promote women's self-development and expand the inclusiveness of the digital world.

1.3.1　Relevant Policies, Funds and Cultural Guarantees Issued at National and International Organization Levels

The United Nations Industrial Development Organization (UNIDO) has been

---

① OECD. PISA 2015 Results (Volume I): Excellence and Equity in Education[EB/OL]. (2016 – 12 – 06) [2023 – 02 – 01]. http://dx.doi.org/10.1787/9789264266490-en.

following gender equality issues for a long time, and takes gender equality and increasing women's empowerment as a core task. UNIDO released several policy and strategic reports on gender equality and women's empowerment, and in its series of consultative tools "Improving the Quality of Industrial Policy (EQuIP)" jointly developed with the German Development Cooperation Organization (GDC) and the German Society for International Cooperation (GIZ), UNIDO formulated the "Gender Equality in Manufacturing Development" tool to provide international policy advice to the government in this regard.

The action plan of "Global Partnership for Gender Equality in the Digital Age" jointly launched by UN Women, International Telecommunication Union (ITU), International Trade Center (ITC), United Nations University (UNU), etc. has developed a "Gender Digital Inclusion Map", which is used to widely collect and consult the practical actions of countries around the world to bridge the "digital gender divide", and to explore and share the best practices. The "Gender Digital Inclusion Map" asks all countries to form a "community of shared future" in the process of bridging the "digital gender divide", and narrow the gender divide in the access, use and in-depth participation of digital technology through the sharing, learning and mutual reference of excellent cases.

The OECD has proposed a series of policies and action plans aimed at introducing gender analysis, providing more equal education and employment development plans, and gathering attention to the gender divide in low-income and relatively underdeveloped areas. At the Digital Economy Ministerial Conference held in Germany in 2017, G20 members formulated "A Roadmap for Digitalization: Policies for a Digital Future", which incorporated a gender perspective and supported the development of digital financial service projects suitable for women, providing more platforms for women's in-depth participation in the digital world.

The "Digital Skills Training for Women" action program, launched by Germany, aims to bridge the gender divide in low-income and developing countries in the digital age. Its specific goal is to increase women's opportunities to participate in the digital world, including education and employment opportunities.

Through the collection and dissemination of knowledge, practice and policy recommendations to bridge the digital gender divide, different stakeholders are urged to jointly help more women enter and deeply participate in the digital economy.

1.3.2   Universities and Enterprises Join Hand to Launch Cooperative Projects and Learning Platforms

Many countries have established cooperation projects between schools and technology companies to provide women with opportunities to contact the real digital world in the workplace, and gradually cultivate their interest in digital technology during visits and exchanges. For example, Microsoft and the Australian Business Community (ABCN) jointly launched the "DigiGirlz" project and Career Days, aiming to give high school students a chance to contact the high-tech world. Among them, the "DigiGirlz" project has held various digital seminars to cultivate the interest of high school girls in digital technology and enable them to fully know about careers in the field of digital technology. This has broken the boundaries between schools and workplaces to some extent, and has greatly stimulated individual interest in digital technology.

In the 5G era, the rapid change of technology has become the new norm, and the total amount of knowledge has expanded unprecedentedly. Only lifelong learning can prevent the gender divide from further expanding in the digital age. In this context, UN Women has developed an innovative learning platform— "virtual skills school", which is committed to providing comprehensive support services and flexible training mechanisms for professional women. Through the construction of a lifelong learning system, the digital skills of female individuals could be continuously improved, so as to help more women obtain further education and employment opportunities.

1.4   Concept of Gender Equality

The traditional gender divide is rooted in the traditional cultural concept of gender inequality. To bridge the gender divide, the most important thing is to reach a consensus on gender equality.

1.4.1 Definition of Gender Equality

The United Nations Industrial Development Organization (UNIDO) defines gender equality as "the equality of men and women in rights, responsibilities and opportunities", which does not mean absolute equality, but ensures that the interests, needs and priorities of women and men can be equally valued in the design and implementation of industrial policies.

1.4.2 Significance of Gender Equality

Gender equality and economic empowerment of women are a key strategy for a country to reduce poverty, increase income and reduce social inequality. The implementation of UNIDO's gender advisory tools [1]in many countries and regions has confirmed the following views:

1) Gender equality plays a significant positive role in promoting regional economy and education

Gender equality can promote economic progress. Due to the difference between men and women in risk management strategies, more gender-balanced enterprises have higher productivity and efficiency, more comprehensive decision-making, and better innovation ability. Women's characteristics, such as more environmentally friendly awareness, more in-depth and sustainable career perspective, faster and more flexible business acceptance and more moderate and efficient communication ability, will play a greater role in the industrial development process under the trend of digital and technological integration. Increasing the proportion of women in companies, including management positions and boards of directors, can significantly improve performance.

It is conducive to education promotion and poverty reduction. Economic empowerment to women has a direct influence on universal education, that is, it

---

[1] The details of the tool will be highlighted in the next section.

can generate a stronger effect than the government-led large-scale conditional cash transfer project to encourage girls to go to school. Women are more inclined to invest in communities and future generations, and attach more importance to the education and health of girls and boys. This has greater spillover effects than making decision from men's perspective and can once again promote sustained economic growth and contribute to more lasting well-being.

2) Gender equality has a unique potential to be played in promoting national industrialization transition

Gender equality in manufacturing industry, that is, the fair distribution of female workers in all sectors and activities, so that women can get the same wages as men and enjoy the same working environment, will help women to obtain the skills and experience necessary to maintain future economic competitiveness, actively promote industrial technology change, and improve the productivity of agriculture and service industries.

Gender equality can promote innovative research and development. The idea of strengthening women's participation in manufacturing and R&D may attract more women. More than 90% of the R&D in the private sector occurs in the manufacturing industry. Ensuring women's fair participation in this sector also means that they will contact or participate in R&D activities.

Gender equality can strengthen investment in education. Women tend to invest more income in education. During the period of industrial transformation, women pay more attention to improving their children's STEM (science, technology, engineering, and mathematics) literacy and nurturing gender equality.

Gender equality can bring employment opportunities. In terms of liberating productivity, manufacturing can promote gender equality more than other industries. Innovation in manufacturing and production of consumer goods, such as dishwashers and other household appliances, can reduce or eliminate women's unpaid housework and nursing work, allowing them to have more flexibility. Innovation and technological progress have created new jobs that rely less on muscle strength, generating more female friendly employment opportunities and fields.

1.5 Connotation and Practical Results of UNIDO Gender Equality Advisory Tools

The trend of digital and integrated global industrial development requires that industrial policies must consider the comprehensive social, environmental and economic prospects, and effective industrial policies should aim at promoting inclusive and sustainable industrial development processes. UNIDO, the German Development Cooperation Organization (GDC) and the German Society for International Cooperation (GIZ) have jointly developed a more effective series of tools for global industrial policy support, namely, the "Improving the Quality of Industrial Policy (EQuIP)" series of advisory tools, aimed at supporting policymakers in developing and underdeveloped countries to formulate and design evidence-based strategies for inclusive and sustainable industrial development, so as to enhance the local industrial management capacity and enable them to have a greater voice in strategic design, policy formulation and international industry participation in development, and to improve international partnership. "Gender Equality in Manufacturing Development" (hereinafter referred to as EQuIP10) is an important part of the series of advisory tools.

1.5.1 Connotation of UNIDO Gender Equality Advisory Tools

EQuIP10, as an international advisory tool, can help government understand the extent and way of women's participation in the manufacturing sector, and identify opportunities and challenges for women's fair participation in industrial transformation. By analyzing the women's current participation in manufacturing and structural transformation and the key factors, the tool can help decision-makers to understand how the selected industrialization path promotes gender equality, make policy deployment and resource allocation from the gender equality dimension, and enable women and men to have equal opportunities to participate in social structural transformation.

(1) Key problems that EQuIP10 hopes to solve: increasing women's

participation in manufacturing; the difference between women and men in terms of wages, quality and employment types in the manufacturing industry and the direction of future guidance; guiding the trend of women's participation in manufacture industry, as well as the policy implementation and guarantee measures in this regard during structural transformation to the manufacturing industry, technology intensive sectors and more effective production processes; local key determinants to promote women's participation in the manufacturing industry, and formulation of targeted measures to make policies and resources more preferential for women; measure the degree and quality of local women's participation in manufacturing industry, and ensure continuous monitoring, evaluation and implementation of measures.

(2) Analysis path of EQuIP10: Policymakers first need to have a clear understanding of the current situation and trends of women's participation in manufacturing industry and its sub sectors, so as to formulate policies, strategies and interventions to unleash the potential of women and enable them to benefit equitably from the sector, while contributing to the country's inclusive and sustainable industrialization, social equality progress and overall economic growth.

Figure 1 − 1 shows the development path of women's participation in the manufacturing industry in all stages of industrialization. Analysts and decision-makers can use this to comprehensively analyze and examine the women's participation in manufacturing industry, so as to ensure that they can have a clear understanding of the complex gender equality issues in domestic manufacturing industry, which in turn can enable them to use this information to formulate gender equity strategies in the process of industrialization transformation.

Figure 1 − 2 is an analytical framework for measuring gender inequality in manufacturing industry. Through this analytical framework, analysts can locate each relevant factor and adjust the allocation of policy resources to measure gender inequality in manufacturing industry.

The first part of the framework helps researchers understand the background of gender inequality in manufacturing industry by assessing the basic indicators of gender balance in the labor market and the gender distribution in the three major

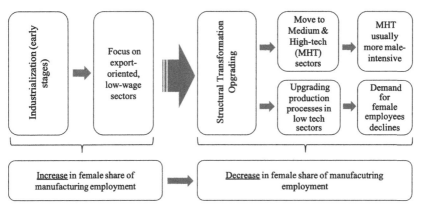

Source: United Nations Industrial Development Organization.

Figure 1 − 1   **The development path of women's participation in manufacturing industry in all stages of industrialization**

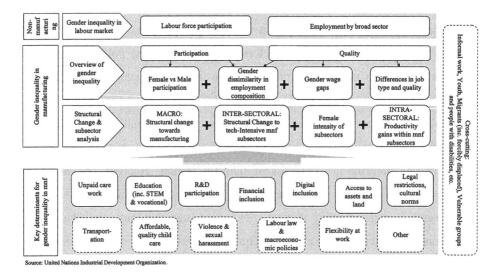

Source: United Nations Industrial Development Organization.

Figure 1 − 2   **An analytical framework for measuring gender inequality in manufacturing industry**

economic sectors (agriculture, industry and services). It assesses the basic indicators of gender balance in the labor market and the gender distribution in the three major economic sectors (agriculture, industry and services).

The second part of the framework describes the background of gender equality in manufacturing industry, which provides policymakers with an overall concept of the extent and types of gender inequality in manufacturing industry in the country.

The framework takes into account both the quantity and quality of women's participation in the industrialization process, because simply increasing women's employment in the manufacturing industry through typical sweatshop work is not considered gender equality or equity.

The third part of the framework is about structural changes and analysis by sector. Structural transformation is the pillar of industrialization and the core of the tool. However, due to the de-feminization of manufacturing employment, the relationship between structural transformation and female employment in manufacturing industry is not always positive. In order to measure this trend, it is necessary to analyze the issue of women's participation in the structural transformation from macro to interdepartmental micro perspectives.

The last part of the framework analyzes some key determinants affecting women's participation in manufacturing industry, including the extent to which women are more involved in unpaid care than men. This affects their overall tendency to engage in paid productive employment, and it is a key determinant.

(3) The indicator system of EQuIP10. The EQuIP10 tool has been widely used and developed since it came out. It also proposes a complete indicator system, which is adopted in Germany, Vietnam and other countries. The indicator system is shown in Table 1 - 1:

Table 1 - 1   The Indicator System of EQuIP10 Illustration

Level I indicators	Secondary indicators
Background	Proportion of women in the total labor force
	Proportion of female employment in agriculture, industry and service industry
Overview of gender equality in manufacturing industry	Percentage of women employed in manufacturing industry
	Gender diversity index in manufacturing industry
	Gender pay gap in manufacturing industry
	Proportion of women in management positions

(Continue)

Level I indicators	Secondary indicators
Overview of gender equality in manufacturing industry	Proportion of women in different ranks
	Gender differences in minimum pay
	Proportion of informal employment by gender
Structural adjustment and manufacturing industry segmentation	Structural adjustment of gender balance in basic manufacturing industry
	Structural adjustment of gender balance in medium and high-end science and technology fields
	Female employment density in manufacturing sector
	Changes in productivity and female employment density in subdivisions
Key determinants	Proportion of men and women in unpaid nursing work
	Proportion of male and female labor force at different levels of education
	Proportion of women among graduates of science, technology, engineering and mathematics
	Proportion of women in vocational training apprentices
	Proportion of women in R&D personnel
	Proportion of men and women who open accounts in financial institutions
	Ratio of men and women obtaining loans from financial institutions
	Proportion of men and women who start business by using financing
	Gender gap in Internet use
	Ratio of men and women using mobile cash accounts
	Ratio of men and women using electronic payment in the past year
	Workplace rights
	Legal rights to own land and non land property
	Rights of women with paid work outside the family

1.5.2　Practical Results of UNIDO Gender Equality Advisory Tools

（1）Bahrain ITPO: The main work direction of Bahrain ITPO is to help women entrepreneurs in Arabian countries and the rest of the world overcome cultural and investment barriers. The EQuIP10 advisory tool provides a powerful tool for Bahrain ITPO to communicate with the government and implement its work. Bahrain ITPO, through its Enterprise Development and Investment Promotion（EDIP）program, provides training and guidance, encourages self employment and business startups, and initiates the development of online training courses to enable women to seize economic opportunities.

（2）Russia: The United Nations Industrial Development Organization （UNIDO）and the Government of the Russian Federation have cooperated in promoting women's empowerment since 2018. With EQuIP10 as the implementation tool, the two sides have set up a cooperation project to promote women's economic empowerment and entrepreneurship, and established a strong network of regional participants, including the government, the private sector and relevant civil society organizations. At the same time, the two sides carried out global promotion and publicity. UNIDO invited outstanding women economic empowerment advocates from all over the world to share their views and policy suggestions to promote global knowledge sharing, at the Second Eurasian Women's Forum in 2018, the International Economic Forum in St. Petersburg in 2017, 2018 and 2019, and the Second GMIS in 2019. In addition, there is an online training course launched in 2019, which aims to improve the business management skills of female entrepreneurs and managers in the digital field. The course is currently in trial operation.

Chapter II

Gender Divide in the Digital Age:
Connotation, Representation and Causes

The "gender divide" is present in the digital age in new forms, and its underlying reasons related to the digital age are also worth further discussion. This chapter will start from the connotation of the gender divide in the digital age, focusing on the three levels of its conceptual connotation and analyzing the new manifestations of the gender divide in the digital age, and explore the underlying causes. Through analysis, it is found that the digital age has brought new challenges to the bridging of the gender divide. It has given the gender divide a new multi-dimensional form of expression (also the main manifestation of the gender divide in the digital age in the subdivided areas). The underlying reasons remind us that we must bridge it through the co-governance of multiple subjects.

2.1 Main Connotation of the Gender Divide in the Digital Age

2.1.1 Conceptual Connotation and Historical Evolution of the Digital Divide

The gender divide in the digital age can be understood as the representation of the "digital divide" in the gender dimension. Therefore, to summarize the connotation, representation and causes of the gender divide in the digital age, it is necessary to first analyze the conceptual connotation and historical evolution characteristics of the "digital divide", so as to find out the manifestation of digital divide in terms of gender dimension and its influence, during the dynamic evolution and development of the "digital divide" in the context of the digital age.

In recent years, with the popularization and diffusion of digital technology and the rapid development of the digital economy, the "digital divide" has aroused concerns from various parties. According to the existing research, the "digital divide" has become one of the major factors that widen the global gap between the rich and poor. The concept of "digital divide" can be traced back to the 1990s. In 1990, Toffler, a famous American futurist, put forward the concepts of information rich, information poor, information gap and digital divide in his book *Transfer of Power*. He believed that the digital divide was a divide in information and electronic technology, which caused the differentiation between developed countries and less developed countries. In 1999, the National Telecommunication and Information Administration (NTIA) of the United States published a report entitled "Falling Through the Net: Defining the Digital Divide", which defines Digital Divide as the divide between those who have the tools of the information age and those who have not. At this stage, the discussion on the "digital divide" mainly focused on the development gap between countries and people caused by the difference in the accessibility of digital equipment and digital infrastructure, which is currently named as the "first stage digital divide" by the academic community.

Since the beginning of the 21st century, the popularization of informationization infrastructure has increased rapidly, and the penetration and integration of digital technology into social and economic sectors has become more and more profound. In this context, the seriousness of the "first stage digital divide" problem has begun to fade, and the "digital divide" problem has begun to show new symptoms and change trend. Under the background of narrowing difference in the accessibility of digital equipment and the major improvement of popularity of digital equipment, people's mastery of digital technology and the degree of application of digital equipment directly determine their income level and social status, due to the omni-directional penetration and influence of digital technology and digital equipment on economy, society and life. There are significant differences between different regions and groups in the application of digital equipment and the mastery of digital technology, which leads to the "second stage digital divide", namely, the difference among different groups in digital skill mastery and application. For example, while mobile payment technology improves payment efficiency and security, the elderly and some disabled groups have obstacles or difficulties in the application of mobile payment software due to their physiological defects or insufficient ability to learn to use new technologies and new things, which leads to a significant "divide" between different social groups in the application of digital technology and in benefiting from digital technology dividends.

With the deepening of academic research on the "digital divide", as well as the rapid penetration of digital technology in the production side, the continuous acceleration of the process of economic digital transformation has led the academic research on the "digital divide" from the first and second stages to the third stage, that is, considering the significant differences in individual income, education level, consumption level, social status and other outcomes of different social groups caused by the diffusion of digital technology in different economic and social fields. The connotation of the "digital divide" in the first two stages tends to explain the differences between different social groups in the accessibility and proficiency of the application of digital technology and their impacts, which means it focuses more on the "digital divide" on the demand side. In the third stage, the "digital divide" focuses more on the economic and social effects of the spontaneous diffusion and penetration of digital technology in the fields of economic production and life application, meaning it focuses more on the differential impacts the popularization and penetration of digital technology made on different social groups from the supply side.

2.1.2 Definition of the Concept of Gender Divide in the Digital Age

The above-mentioned three stages of the evolution of the connotation of the "digital divide" actually match with the historical development track of the digital economy.

Therefore, when defining the concept and connotation of the "gender divide in the digital age", we can understand it as the manifestation of the "digital divide" in different gender types. In addition, the "gender divide in the digital age" can also be understood as "digital gender divide", which means: the concept is getting similar to the concept proposed by OECD①. In 2018, OECD released the *Technical Report on Bridging the Digital Gender Divide*, which aims to identify, discuss and analyze a series of driving factors underlying the digital gender divide and point out that the "digital gender divide" is "gender differences in effective access to information and communication technology, digital skills and other aspects within and among countries, regions, sectors and socio-economic groups". The concept it put forward basically covers the first two stages of the "digital divide", but the interpretation of the third stage is not complete. Therefore, this paper believes that the connotation of the gender divide in the digital age should also be excavated and summarized based on the three stages of the "digital divide".

The "gender divide in the digital age" mentioned in this report can also be understood as "digital gender divide", which mainly includes three aspects: ① the divide caused by significantly different accessibility to digital device for different gender types; ② the divide caused by significantly different mastery and application proficiency of digital technology of different gender types; ③ the divide and significant difference between different gender types in terms of employment, income, education and social status, caused by the expanding, penetrating and popularization of digital technology in various sectors in the economic production and social life domains.

2.2 Main Manifestations of the Gender Divide in the Digital Age

Combined with the conceptual connotation of the three levels of the "digital

---

① On January 29th, 2020, OECD released *The Role of Education and Skills in Bridging the Digital Gender Divide* and used the term "digital gender divide" within the report.

gender divide" mentioned above, this paper believes that the gender divide in the digital age continues to have the following specific manifestations.

2.2.1 The Accessibility of Digital Resources for Different Gender Types Is Obviously Different, the Digital Resources Accessed by Different Gender Types Are Very Unbalanced

According to data from international level, the digital gender divide is widening worldwide. The latest research report issued by the International Telecommunication Union (ITU) — *Monitoring Digital Development 2019: Facts and Figures* reports that: By the end of 2019, only 48% of women in the world had access to the Internet, and in 92% of countries and regions around the world, women had far less access to the Internet than men, which to some extent reflected the serious gender difference in the accessibility of current digital infrastructure. In addition, in terms of gender equality in national Internet services, less than a quarter of countries have basically achieved gender equality in Internet services. According to the evaluation data of ITU, and in terms of gender differences in Internet use, the gender divide in developing countries is larger than that in developed countries, and the divide between the two has not yet shown a significant convergence trend, which suggests that the gender difference in the accessibility of digital infrastructure such as the Internet has a significant negative correlation with the economic development level of the country or region: the higher the economic development level, the smaller the divide in the accessibility of its digital infrastructure among different gender types, and vice versa.

With the popularization and application of digital technology, the gender differences in the "digital access divide" have been gradually eliminated, but there are still differences between men and women in the form or way of using digital equipment: men surf the Internet more frequently and carry out more activities on the Internet (such as for games); women use the Internet more for social activities, such as sending messages and photos in the circle of friends.

2.2.2　Significant Gender Difference in Digital Innovation Achievements and Digital Skill Improvement

In October 2018, OECD released the report *Bridging the Gender Digital Divide*, which disclosed: Between 2010 and 2015, less than 9% of the invention patents of G20 members came from women. In terms of information and communication technology (ICT) inventions, this proportion has dropped to only 7%; all-female-team was even rarer, accounting for only 4% in terms of patents granted. According to relevant OECD data: Among the graduates of major STEM colleges and universities in G20 countries, women only account for a quarter, and the proportion of these women engaged in major STEM work is lower than that of men. The digital dividend in the 5G era did not achieve a balance between different gender types, but aggravated the "digital gender divide" to a certain extent, which is rooted in the gender inequality in STEM education. The report warns that at the current growth rate, only by 2080 would gender equality be achieved to some extent in the innovation field.

Digital skills refer to the digital capabilities necessary for individuals to adapt to the digital society. Gender stereotypes, gender role division, etc., have a subtle impact on men's and women's acceptance and use of digital technology, as well as the two group's participation in the digital world, thus causing gender segregation in the digital career field. In school education, women's participation rate in majors closely related to digital technology like science, technology, engineering and mathematics (STEM) is low, so is their graduation rate from these majors. Instead, the possibility for them to drop out or change majors is high. Women are less interested in STEM and are more inclined to study a non-STEM subject.

2.2.3　Seriously Inadequate Protection for Women's Digital Identity and Privacy

Digital space provides a platform for women to participate in political and social life, speak up bravely and show themselves, and it also provides a safe space for elderly women, women of sexual minorities, disabled women and migrant women to share, communicate and connect with each other. However, the security of digital identity in cyberspace is still vulnerable, especially for women. For example, the vulnerability of digital identity security has been confirmed by the cases of drivers working for car-hailing companies. They choose the criminal object according to user information and then steal and disseminate private photos or videos of women, and threaten to disclose the real identity or other privacy of women. This exposes women to the violence of digitalization or digital technology, which spreads fast and wild. And the anonymity of digital space reduces the cost of such violence and the risk of being punished.

2.2.4 Gender Inequality in Employment Being Aggravated by the Development of Digital Economy

According to the *2019 Report on Gender Differences in China's Job Market*, among the top 15 high paid jobs in 2018, women accounted for less than 30% of the total, except for strategic consulting and securities analysts which ranked the 14th and 15th (as shown in Figure 2 – 1). At present, women account for less than 20% (or even single-digit percentages) of the most popular AI and big data related jobs in the technology field, such as machine learning, deep learning,

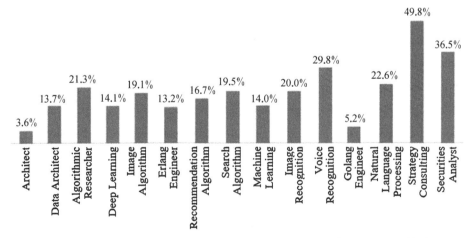

Figure 2 – 1   Proportion of women in the top 15 high paid positions in 2018

Data source: BOSS Direct Employment (a Chinese job search platform) Research Institute & Vocational Science Laboratory.

image recognition, architects, etc. These high paid jobs are all highly-skilled jobs emerging with the development of the digital economy and unfolding of the digital age. The low participation rate of women in such high paid technical digital jobs makes the pay difference increasingly obvious. At the same time, in recent years, with the constant penetration and development of the digital economy, the dividends of business models in various fields have weakened, industry giants have turned to technology driven, and the salaries of senior technical posts have continued to soar, further strengthening the salary advantages of high-income men in related fields.

2.2.5 Tagging of Gender Identity in Digital Space and Low Existence of Female Digital Space

Digital space is a new field for shaping the role of gender, and it is also an important part of social gender construction. However, few women participate in digital technology development and decision-making, which makes gender identity construction in digital space present the characteristics of lack of women's subjectivity and distorted digital gender identity construction. For example, due to the absence of female workers in the field of artificial intelligence, developers tend to project gender stereotypes onto robots, set robots that explore outer space, rescue humans, engage in scientific research and other work as male, and set robots that engage in communication and service work as female. It is not difficult to see the stigmatization of female images, in the current time when online short videos have gone viral. The extension of old gender stereotypes will aggravate gender inequality.

2.3 Main Causes of the Gender Divide in the Digital Age

2.3.1 Gender Stereotypes and Traditional Ideas Hinder Women's Participation in Digital Economy Employment and Entrepreneurship

The development of digital economy has improved the relative disadvantage of women in work, expanded the specific value of women in the labor market, and brought more and more forms of social labor suitable for women's participation. However, women's participation in employment and entrepreneurship in the digital economy is still affected by informal institutions such as culture and customs. The traditional gender role concept has a significant negative effect on women's labor participation. The division of family responsibilities and the work-family conflict mechanism make women assume more family responsibilities and their work roles weakened. Even in the digital economy, women can balance their family roles through flexible employment or telework, but women still face the dilemma of obtaining "legitimacy" for employment and entrepreneurial identity. In particular, women workers in rural areas and remote areas are more affected by the traditional gender system, and barriers created by traditional gender concepts still exist, hindering women's participation in employment and entrepreneurship in the digital economy.

2.3.2 Women's Work-Family Balance Pressure Is Greater than That of Men, Which Hinders Them from Enjoying Digital Dividends

The protection of the rights and interests of workers in new forms of employment still needs to be improved. In the development of digital economy, the boundary between online work and offline life has become more blurred, and the protection of the rights and interests of workers in new forms of employment needs to be improved. Such blurring of boundaries may damage women's arrangement of work activities and family activities. Currently, the labor participation rate of women in China is significantly lower than that of men. The job responsibilities brought by the digital economy will bring greater challenges to women's employment. The digital economy has brought about stronger competition, transparency and consumer choice changes. In the digital economy, women can improve the family-work balance and become family providers through digital platform entrepreneurship, telework or new employment forms. The increase of women's income will also provide a better living environment for their family members and improve their happiness. However, family life requires women to make efficient use of their personal working hours, which puts forward higher requirements for women's self-management. In the process of employment and entrepreneurship in the digital economy, women still bear a large amount of unpaid work in their families, and therefore need to properly deal with the contradiction between family harmony and career development.

2.3.3   Gender Bias of Digital Technology Is More Conducive to Men's Promotion of Social Division of Labor

Digital technology will produce significant gender bias during its continuous progress. In other words, digital technology progress has a significant difference and bias in enhancing the marginal output of male and female workers. From the current perspective, although digital technology progress has provided more opportunities and platforms for women's employment and development in the process of promoting economic digital transformation, it can still be found that current digital technology progress is more biased towards male workers. This is mainly presented in two aspects. First, in the progress, popularization and application of digital technology, more male workers participate in the fields of high value-added jobs such as digital technology R&D and design, as well as the design link of digital technology and industrial integration. Women's participation is limited by knowledge structure, traditional social concepts and occupational labels. Second, in the process of digital transformation of the economy, the development of high-end manufacturing industries, which is driven by the development of industrial Internet, still prefer hiring male workers to fill in the need for high-skilled workers. In the process of digital transformation, women are more involved in the low-skilled labor fields derived from the development of consumer Internet, such as live shows and promotion and sales, which leads to the differentiation of male workers and female workers in the employment field in the digital process. Without considering the external policy intervention and guidance, women are more likely to be locked in the low-end (employment field).

2.3.4 The Digital Penetration Prefers the Service Industry, and the Low Level of Digitalization in Manufacturing Industry Restricts the Bridging of the Gender Divide

In China's digital economy, the proportion of industrial digitalization has exceeded 80% of the overall scale of digital economy, making itself an important part of the digital economy. However, at present, China's industrial digitalization shows significant differences among different industries. The level of industrial digitalization in the service industry is significantly higher than that in the manufacturing industry. According to the measurement results of WIOD database input-output table, the level of industrial digitalization in China's manufacturing industry segments is mostly less than 20%, which is significantly lower than that in the service industry segments. According to the data of China Industry Research Network, the digitalization level of the service industry is the highest among the three industries. In 2020, the proportion of digital economy in service industry is 40.7%, higher than 38.6% of the total economy, 21.0% of industry and 8.9%[1] of agriculture. As the manufacturing industry has always been a field where male workers gather for employment, female workers are limited by their own physiological characteristics (physical strength, fertility requirements), and tend to choose the service industry when choosing careers. Therefore, the level of digital transformation in the manufacturing industry directly determines whether women's participation in the field of social division can be further enriched and expanded in the digital age. The improvement of the digital level of manufacturing industry will improve the adaptability of women to manufacturing jobs to a certain extent, and will also change the social impression of connecting traditional manufacturing industries with blue collar jobs. For example, the use of digital mechanical equipment makes the manufacturing industry no longer hold high demands on the stamina and strength of employees. At the same time, the manufacturing posts originally engaged in manual labor have begun to move closer

---

[1] Data source: Zhongyan, https://www.chinairn.com/hyzx/20220105/153131234.shtml.

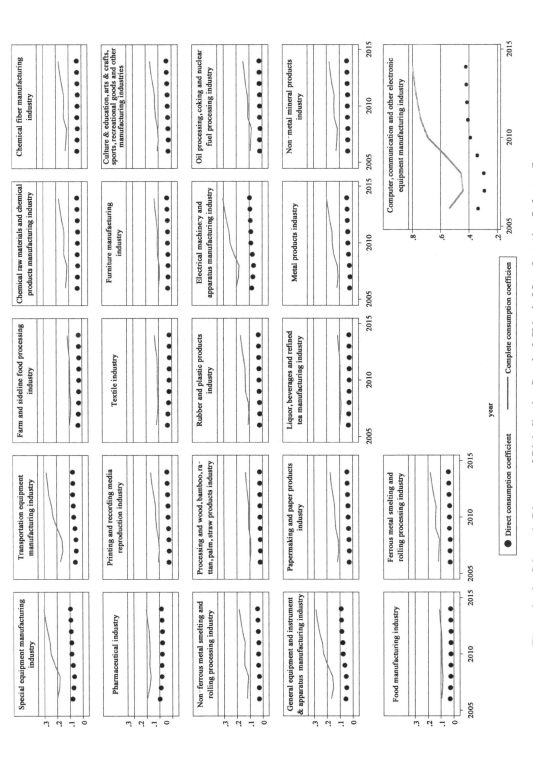

Figure 2 – 2 Schematic Diagram of Digitalization Level of China's Manufacturing Industry Segments

Data source: authors' calculation and drawing based on WIOD database input-output table.

to the technical field of digital mechanical equipment operation, making the labor environment and social evaluation of workers more decent, which will eliminate women's prejudice against manufacturing posts and improve their preference for manufacturing posts and further expand the industry field where female employment is possible. However, the low level of digitalization in China's manufacturing industry will severely hamper the above mechanism. Therefore, it is necessary to accelerate the digitalization in the manufacturing industry and open up a wider industry space for women.

2.3.5 Incomplete Governance Rules of Cyberspace Make Women's Cyberspace Rights More Vulnerable to Infringement

The incomplete governance rules in cyberspace are an important reason for the violation of women's security and rights in cyberspace. And because women are in a weak position, they are more vulnerable to cyber attacks and rights violations than men in cyberspace. A study by *The Economist* in 2020 found that "38% of women in the world have experienced online violence directly". According to this study, 85% of people have witnessed cyber violence against women, and young women are more likely to experience cyber violence.

Chapter III
Gender Divide in the Digital Age
in Shanghai

With the vigorous development of Shanghai's digital economy, a large number of digital economy related enterprises such as online education, online medical care and online entertainment have emerged, providing a lot of opportunities for women's career development. At the same time, women are also facing new workplace pressures and challenges in the digital age. To this end, the central government and the Shanghai government have issued various policies to protect women's employment rights, promote the development of women in science and technology, and support women to start businesses.

3.1 Development Background of the Digital Age in Shanghai

Backed by the strong support and promotion of the government, Shanghai's digital economy has developed rapidly, with increasingly rich forms of digital economy and more and more digital technology application scenarios. A large number of leading enterprises in the digital economy (especially daily-life service enterprises) have taken root in Shanghai, showing a positive development trend.

3.1.1 Promotion of Shanghai's Digital-Economy-Related Government Policies

In recent years, with the rise of digital economy in the global scope, local governments around China have encouraged and promoted the rapid development of digital economy. The Shanghai Municipal Government has also complied with this development trend, and has made arrangements in advance. Since 2020, it has issued a series of policies to promote and standardize digital transformation and development, and made specific arrangements for the significance, development goals, overall requirements, action plans, safeguard measures and other aspects of urban digital industrialization and industrial digitization, so that the development direction of Shanghai's digital economy is gradually clear and the development path is gradually visible. All these measures have greatly boosted the development of the digital economy.

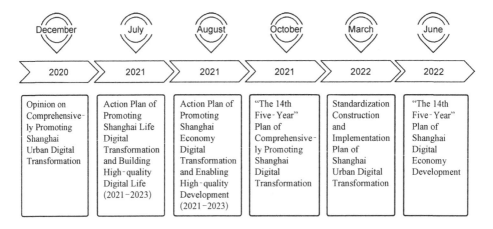

Figure 3 - 1   Relevant Policy Documents on Digital Economy Issued by Shanghai Municipal Government in Recent Years

Data source: The authors' collections.

The *Opinions on Comprehensively Promoting the Urban Digital Transformation in Shanghai*, issued in December 2020, clarified the significance and goals of comprehensively promoting the urban digital transformation of Shanghai in a new development stage. It proposed the general requirement that "by 2025, Shanghai will achieve remarkable results in comprehensively promoting urban digital transformation, form a basic framework for the construction of an international digital city, and build a world-class digital industrial cluster with world-class digital infrastructure and leading digital economy in the country; and to become an international digital city with world influence by 2035". At the same time, it also put forward the general task of "three insistings"—"insisting on overall transformation, insisting on all-round empowerment and insisting on revolutionary remodeling".

The *Action Plan for Promoting the Digital Transformation of Shanghai's Life and Building a High Quality Digital Life* (*2021 - 2023*), issued in July 2021, emphasized the creation of a digital enabling ecology, promoted intelligence technology to benefit people's basic livelihood, improve people's livelihood quality, and to be utilized in ensuring people's basic livelihood, and proposed to strengthen data empowerment, talent training, publicity, promotion, international exchanges and other safeguarding measures. The *Action Plan for Promoting the Digital Transformation of Shanghai's Economy and Enabling High Quality Development* (*2021 - 2023*), issued in August 2021, comprehensively elaborated the connotation and requirements of industrial digitalization from the aspects of new manufacturing mode, new business formats, new financial technology, new science and technology innovation ecology, new shipping hub, new agricultural experience, new data elements, and new digital infrastructure.

The *14th Five-Year Plan for Shanghai to Comprehensively Promote Urban Digital Transformation*, issued in October 2021, emphasized on promoting the digital transformation of Shanghai's economy, life, governance and other aspects through key work such as improving urban infrastructure, building urban data hub system, and creating a common technology enabling platform for the city. The *Implementation Plan of Shanghai Urban Digital Transformation Standardization Construction*, issued in March 2022, proposed to improve the digital transformation standards in economy, life and governance by strengthening mechanism construction, technology collaboration, implementation and application and other safeguard measures. The *14th Five-Year Plan for the Development of Shanghai's Digital Economy*, issued in June 2022, set out the key tasks of Shanghai's digital economy development, including expanding new digital industries, cultivating new data elements, improving new digital infrastructure, building new intelligent terminals, strengthening new digital enterprises, and building new digital carriers, and emphasized safeguard measures from financial support, talent training, track mechanism, etc.

Since entering the 21st century, the digital economy has become the main force to promote the economic development at home and abroad, and it has become the consensus of all circles that the digital economy leads the accelerated economic development. At present, the global COVID-19 epidemic is intensifying repeatedly, and the urgency of digital economy development is highlighted. The transformation of new and old kinetic energy has been forced to accelerate. Shanghai's systematic recognition and construction of the digital economy have also been accelerated. Digital industrialization and industrial digitalization have been breeding new industries, new formats and new models. Since 2020, Shanghai has given a high-degree "setting tone" to promote the comprehensive digital transformation of the city. On the basis of years of accumulation of informatization, digitalization and intelligence, it has promoted the rapid growth and in-depth integration of digital kinetic energy, and accelerated the development of the urban digital age.

3.1.2 The Vigorous Development of Shanghai's Digital Economy

As a mega-city, Shanghai has a large population, strong mobility, and strong demand for living and production, which brings severe challenges to the construction and development, operation and governance of the city, and requires the upgrading of public service supply and security level such as education, medical care, and elderly care. As the strategic node of the domestic economic cycle and the strategic link of the domestic and international dual circulation, Shanghai should give full play to its advantages in talent, technology, market, etc., and more actively serve the national development. Therefore, Shanghai has the internal impetus and external pressure to promote the urban digital transformation. ①

Shanghai has made great progress in Internet applications, artificial

---

① 顾丽梅,李欢欢,张扬.城市数字化转型的挑战与优化路径研究——以上海市为例[J].西安交通大学学报(社会科学版).2022,42(03):41-50.

intelligence, new infrastructure and other aspects developed on the basis of the digital economy, and has become a new growth point during the COVID - 19 epidemic, providing an important driving force for the national economic recovery after the epidemic. ①

The digital economy accounts for a relatively high proportion of GDP in the composite cities represented by Shanghai. Shanghai leads the country in terms of digital economy scale. With advantages like rich digital talents, digital technology resources, sound digital infrastructure, complete policy support, the city plays a leading role in the development of China's digital economy. Shanghai's digital economy enterprises, talents and data reserves rank first in the country: Shanghai has many data application enterprises in commerce and trade, port, shipping, logistics, customs, commodity inspection, medical, finance, communication and other fields. The rate of Internet users in Shanghai is leading in the country. Its online shopping users and other indicators also rank among the top in the country. The city also accumulates massive data in digital fields such as smart communities, smart medicine, and smart transportation. In addition, Shanghai also has a solid foundation of information industry, rich digital economy formats, and many digital technology application scenarios. ②

The "14th Five-Year" Plan for the Development of Shanghai's Digital Economy put forward specific development goals: By the end of 2025, the development level of Shanghai's digital economy will remain at the top of the country, and the added value of digital economy shall reach 3 trillion Yuan, accounting for more than 60% of the city's GDP. The degree of industrial agglomeration and display will be significantly improved. High potential emerging digital enterprises will grow fast. The high-level digital consumption will continue to rise. The layout of new tracks of high-value digital industries will be basically formed, and the basic framework system of a International Digital City will be

---

① 张伯超、韩清.疫情影响下上海在线新经济产业发展状况研究[M]//沈开艳.上海经济发展报告(2021):聚焦在线新经济和新基建[M].北京:社会科学文献出版社,2021:25-40.

② 赵义怀.上海数字经济发展的现实基础、未来思路及举措建议[J].科学发展.2020,No.137(04):79-88.

formed. The establishment of this goal provides strong impetus and policy support for the further development of Shanghai's digital economy in the next stage.

3.1.3 Emergence of Digital Economy Enterprises in Shanghai

As an important part of the digital economy, the online new economy has experienced explosive growth during the epidemic, including online office, unmanned factory, online finance, e-commerce retail, online education, online medical care, online entertainment, etc. As the epidemic continues, a number of leading enterprises in the life service digital economy in Shanghai have presented amazing development potential and sustainable competitiveness in line with the needs of the times, including leading enterprises in the industry represented by the Ximalaya Inc., Idol Group Co., Ltd, etc.

The Ximalaya Inc., an audio content platform, founded in August 2012, has been developing since then. Its audio content has a total duration of more than 2 billion minutes, which need 4 000 years to finish listening. In 2021, the average monthly active users of the whole platform reached 268 million, with a year-on-year growth of 24.4%, of which the average monthly active users of mobile app reached 116 million, and the monthly active users from other channels like Internet of Things, the Internet of Vehicles and third parties reached 151 million. The average daily listening time of mobile app users is 144 minutes, and the total listening time is 1 744.1 billion minutes, accounting for 68% of the whole industry. The number of paid users and payment rate in the Ximalaya are increasing year by year. In 2021, the number of paid members was 14.4 million, a year-on-year increase of 52%, with the payment rate of mobile app users increased to 12.9%. From January to April 2020, when China was hit most by the COVID-19 epidemic, the business income of Ximalaya Inc. grew by 91.54% year on year, and the number of users and business increased sharply. After launching online courses during the epidemic, the number of daily active users of online education app increased by 20% ~ 100%.

Founded in December 2017, Idol Group Co., Ltd, as a decentralized new e-commerce platform for the world, is committed to supporting the development of digital economy through scientific and technological innovation, and contributing to the society in the field of new e-commerce by promoting consumption, reducing surplus production capacity, stabilizing employment and helping environmental protection. In November 2020, it has obtained Round C financing. At present, the enterprise has nearly 1 000 employees. Through nearly 3 million online store owners (90% of whom are female store owners), it has sold more than 10 000 brands of cost-effective goods to end consumers. Its monthly sales exceeded 1 billion Yuan, increasing the store owners' income by nearly 5 billion Yuan. From January to April 2020, the operating income of Idol Group Co., Ltd increased from 500 million Yuan to 1 billion Yuan, the number of store owners increased by 600 000, and the number of consumers increased by 6 million. ①

3.2　Opportunities for Women's Development in the Digital Age of Shanghai

In the context of the vigorous development of the digital economy, Shanghai's manufacturing and service industries have generated a large number of career opportunities for women, helping more women realize their desire to work flexibly and give consideration to their families. At the same time, they also help women improve their own ability and internalize lifelong learning into their lifestyle.

3.2.1　A Large Number of Jobs for Women in the Digital Age

Shanghai has the largest market size among all cities, the second largest population density, and the most complete industrial system in China. In recent years, Shanghai's digital economy has flourished, and the integration of industrial development and digitalization has been constantly improved. A large number of leading enterprises in the digital economy have emerged

---

① 张伯超,韩清.疫情影响下上海在线新经济产业发展状况研究[M]//沈开艳.上海经济发展报告(2021): 聚焦在线新经济和新基建[M].北京: 社会科学文献出版社,2021: 25－40.

from various industries in Shanghai, including industrial Internet, information technology, artificial intelligence, new retail, community e-commerce, online medical care and education, online finance and enterprise digital services, driving the diversified development of Shanghai's economy.

Relying on Shanghai's strong advantages in gathering talent, technology, capital, information and other resources, Shanghai's enterprises take root in China and radiate around the world, showing significant advantages in terms of both quantity growth and energy level improvement. According to the data of Shanghai Municipal Commission of Commerce, by the end of November 2021, there were 827 regional headquarters of transnational corporations and 504 foreign-funded R&D centers in Shanghai. Among the regional headquarters of transnational corporations in Shanghai, the world's top 500 enterprises account for up to 15%, such as Wal Mart, Apple, ZF Friedrichshafen AG, Saint Gobain, General Motors, etc.

Shanghai has become a strategic location attracting leading enterprises in the digital economy at home and abroad, including global technology giants such as Microsoft and Amazon, as well as domestic leading enterprises such as Alibaba, Huawei, Tencent, Baidu, etc., and emerging digital economy enterprises such as Ximalaya Inc., Aikucun, Xiaohongshu, and Bilibili. Through them, Shanghai attracted massive user groups nationwide and even worldwide, breaking the traditional geographical boundaries of the enterprise service, and generating a large number of valuable opportunities and jobs.

Since the outbreak of COVID−19, enterprises have become more aware of digital transformation. With the vigorous development of 5G, artificial intelligence, the Internet of Things, block-chain and other new generation digital information technologies and the acceleration of application empowerment, the digital application and transformation of Shanghai enterprises have a solid technical support. More and more enterprises have built their own "risk prevention system" through digital means, making their daily operations digitalized and run on the Internet and mobile platform. Among them, the pace of digital transformation and development of the manufacturing industry has been significantly accelerated, which has promoted the acceleration from "made in Shanghai" to "intelligent manufacturing in Shanghai". In 2022, Shanghai plans to promote the construction of intelligent factories of different levels and different categorizes, build more "new tracks" in digital economy, give license to about 100 "Shanghai intelligent factories", strive to create 4 ~ 5 "national benchmark intelligent factories", and move towards the world-class "intelligent city".

In this context, the demand for digital technology talents in Shanghai is growing day by day. According to the data of BOSS Research Institute, the demand for digital technology talents in Shanghai will account for 14.3% of the demand for digital technology talents in 2020. Only Beijing, Shenzhen, and Hangzhou has a higher demand. The rapid development of Shanghai's digital economy has greatly broadened women's choice of employment and entrepreneurship, which is conducive to activating women's employment potential and generating more jobs and entrepreneurial opportunities suitable for women in the digital economy, such as digital trade, e-commerce, live broadcast, online medical/education and other industrial opportunities that can vigorously display and give play to women's advantages. According to the *Research Report on Digital Economy and Chinese Women's Employment and Entrepreneurship* jointly released by Ali Research Institute and the Research Group of China Employment Form Research Center, the digital economy has created employment opportunities for 57 million of women.

The development and popularization of the digital economy has greatly improved women's ability to find jobs and start businesses, broken the restrictions and constraints of traditional employment models, and thus generated various new industries and occupations. It has improved women's opportunities to start businesses online and earn income part-time, and also helped them to give play to their strengths and potential, and realize their dreams and values in life. Take the Aikucun platform of Idol Group Co., Ltd as an example. The majority of its store owners are women. 10 million consumers and store owners have settled in, helping more than 2 million store owners to successfully start businesses and generate income. Another example is the Ximalaya platform. Nearly 400 000 of its 584 000 monthly Internet live anchors are women, accounting for 64.02%. Most of them are female white-collar workers born in the 80s, using their spare time to create and obtain material and spiritual wealth via the platform, which has also become their new lifestyle and even changed their life and destinies.

Digitalization has also lowered the employment threshold in some industries and generated some new jobs. For example, with the popularization and application of automatic sorting systems, terminal sorters and other sub industries with lower physical requirements continue to attract more women. The development of digital economy and information technology has also greatly improved the market efficiency of women's job search, even realized the "zero marginal cost" in job search and the highly optimized "person job matching" method widened women's access to jobs, and helped reduce the information asymmetry of job supply and demand and the gender differences in job search arisen from the asymmetry.

3.2.2 The Digital Age Is Conducive to Women's Balancing Family and Career

With the development of economy and the progress of society, women in Shanghai have significantly improved their education and professional titles. According to the educational background of women in Shanghai, there were about 4.07 million women with college degree or above in Shanghai in 2020, including 52 000 female doctors, 466 000 female masters, 2 113 000 women with bachelor degree and 1 441 000 women that graduated from junior college.[1] In the digital age, the employment positions and opportunities of these women with higher education and professional titles have been greatly expanded and improved. According to the data of the sixth and seventh population censuses of Shanghai, the employment rate of urban and rural women aged 18~64 in Shanghai rose from 59.3% in 2010 to 62.1% in 2020. Among them, women aged 25~44 are the main

---

① 国家统计局.中国人口普查年鉴—2020[M].北京：中国统计出版社,2022.

force of employment, and the employment rate of women in this age group is higher than 84%.

Obviously, the age range of the main force of employment at the age of 25 ~ 44 coincides basically with the child-bearing age range of women, which also brings more difficulties in balancing family and career for employed women. In terms of life model, due to factors such as social concept of gender and working schedule, compared with Japan and other countries, China's family division of labor model features the characteristics of "husband and wife both work outside and inside", so Chinese women's time distribution is characterized by "work-family-balance".[①]In an international metropolis like Shanghai, the opportunity cost for female employees to give up their jobs and take care of children is higher, and they are more likely to fall into a dilemma.

In fact, one of the important reasons why women in Shanghai are not employed is "giving birth or taking care of children", a factor that forces career women in the workplace to suspend their work. When it comes to taking care of babies, mothers still bear the main responsibility. Many women have sacrificed a lot of working time and even career opportunities to take care of their babies. Therefore, Shanghai women have a strong desire to achieve work flexibility, so that they can take care of their families.

With the rapid development of the digital economy, the opportunities for women to break the "work-family" dilemma under the traditional employment model and speed up the balance between the two are emerging. Especially since the outbreak of the COVID-19 epidemic, the online new economy has been rising faster, and the trend of digital industrialization and industrial digitalization has become increasingly evident. More enterprises have begun to try and promote telework. From January to April 2020, the average growth rate of new users of online telework App in Shanghai reached 580%. [②]

---

① 焦健,王德,程英.上海与东京就业人员时间利用特征比较研究[J].未来城市设计与运营.2022, No.1(01):34－41.

② 张伯超,韩清.疫情影响下上海在线新经济产业发展状况研究[M]//沈开艳.上海经济发展报告 (2021):聚焦在线新经济和新基建[M].北京:社会科学文献出版社,2021:25－40.

The epidemic also promoted the development of online new economic platforms and the rise of flexible employment patterns. For example, digital platforms such as Shanghai Ximalaya and Aikucun have attracted a large number of women to work in a flexible way, replacing the traditional full-time employment mode that used to restrict the time and place of employment. The scope and fields of such flexible employment are also gradually expanding, covering e-commerce, culture, education, medical care and other industries. Thus women's employment model becomes more friendly, and their employment opportunities have greatly increased. Practice has proved that the flexible employment model can effectively relieve women's employment pressure, stabilize the employment market, enable women to break through space constraints and time constraints, obtain more job opportunities, and achieve home office and flexible office, so as to better take care of their families.

In addition, the digital economy has contributed immeasurably to women's efforts to lighten their family burden and given them equal opportunities for development. Through the interactions between the Internet and the Internet of Things, the domestic service industry platform has flourished, constantly promoting the domestic work from "family" to "market". With the support of scientific and technological empowerment, women are gradually freed from the heavy housework, and the quality of family life has been significantly improved. The digital economy has also optimized the allocation of resources, so that all kinds of resources have their own place and are fully allocated, greatly improving the total factor productivity of the social economy, which also benefited women.

3.2.3　Digital Age Helps Improve Women's Comprehensive Literacy

The Chinese central government highly values the importance and development trend of residents' digital literacy in the digital age. In 2022, the *Work Focuses for Improving the Digital Literacy and Skills of the Whole People in 2022* jointly issued by the Cyberspace Administration Office, the Ministry of Education, the Ministry of Industry and Information Technology and other departments proposed to improve the digital work ability of workers and promote lifelong digital learning of all Chinese. According to the document, a number of digital learning service platforms shall be established to speed up the improvement of the digital literacy of all people from educating "digital aborigines", and create a learning environment and atmosphere of "everyone, always, everywhere". It is necessary to adapt digital learning to the needs of digital economy by using new technologies such as virtual simulation and augmented reality.

The Shanghai government also attaches great importance to the digital transformation of education under the vigorous development of the urban digital economy. It strives to build a digital service network for lifelong education covering the whole city, constantly improves the digital governance of education and the digital literacy of citizens, gradually realizes the accurate supply of educational resources, and creates a new vision of an inclusive and friendly digital life that benefits all. Thus, the city aims to further the formation of a new pattern of digital development of lifelong education that matches Shanghai's efforts to build an international digital city with world influence.

In 2021, Shanghai issued the *Implementation Plan for Digital Transformation of Education in Shanghai (2021 – 2023)*, proposing to build Shanghai into a national benchmark city for digital transformation of education by 2023, forming a batch of high-quality, replicable, and promotable experience cases and demonstration scenes of digital transformation of education. Specific requirements include: It is planned to actively explore the construction of "new environment, new system, new platform, new model, and new evaluation" of education digitization, and develop education to a higher level of balanced knowledge, high quality and diversity. It is planned to explore and develop exploration-driven learning and personalized learning based on artificial intelligence in basic/vocational/higher education fields, immersive and experiential teaching based on augmented reality and virtual reality technologies and remote multi-point collaborative teaching based on 5G; at the same time, to deepen the integration and innovation of online and offline education; vocational education focuses on integrating virtual simulation training resources and platforms based on vocational environment and work process, carrying out innovative research and practice of practical training teaching in the digital environment, building a practical training curriculum system that meets the needs of digital teaching, and supporting the construction of the national vocational education virtual simulation public training base (Shanghai).

In the digital economy environment, women's access to digital technology has been greatly expanded, the educational barriers have been broken by large, and the opportunities and abilities for women and girls to benefit from the digital transformation have been greatly improved. Girls are more likely to perform well in digital professional fields, such as science, technology, engineering and mathematics (STEM) and information and communication technology (ICT), so as to bridge the digital gender divide in these fields and comprehensively improve their comprehensive literacy.

The central government and the Shanghai government have put forward clear goals and policy paths for using the digital economy to improve the comprehensive quality of residents, which provides a very favorable condition for women to achieve self improvement, maintain lifelong learning, and improve cultural quality and internal cultivation in an all-round way in the digital age. The digital transformation of education has changed the limitation that the supply and demand of education services cannot be separated under the traditional socio-economic operation mode, and has broken through the low labor productivity characteristics of traditional education services, such as "synchronization" (teacher and student must be in the same space) and "non-storage" (the lecture cannot be saved). With the development of information technology, education services can be provided remotely at a very low cost, to name just one advantage. [1]For women, education services in the digital age can provide them with various educational services at low costs, which can not only meet the needs of stay-at-home mothers troubled by housework, who need to study at home, but also provide career women busy with work with part-time education that is tailored to their needs to

---

① 江小涓,罗立彬.网络时代的服务全球化—新引擎、加速度和大国竞争力[J].中国社会科学. 2019,278(02): 68-91,205-206.

study with fragmented time. Various online learning platforms and various knowledge and skills learning courses provided via both online and offline channels have brought abundant educational opportunities for women.

At present, a new round of technological change driven by big data and artificial intelligence (AI) frees people from heavy work and enables them to become more intelligent and powerful with the help and support of science and technology. Lifelong learning will become the new normal of people's life style. For example, through training programs provided by employers, or through personal channels, we will continue to learn new skills, improve our way of thinking, and upgrade and update skills through digital means to meet the needs of future career development. All kinds of scientific and technological means and tools in the digital age will help women maintain flexibility throughout their career, adjust their career direction in time according to changes in market demand, and cultivate their personal qualities.

It is worth mentioning that online audio platform Ximalaya Inc. has become more and more well-known in recent years. It built an Internet connection and interaction platform for content creators and users. Its rich content supply can meet the differentiated needs of users across all ages, identities and occupations, and has become an indispensable part of the daily lives of many female users. In 2021, the number of content creators on Ximalaya platform exceeded 13.51 million. The total number of audio produced in Ximalaya is 340 million, covering more than 100 types of extensive audio content. And 4.9 million of the total are audio books. Ximalaya Inc. has established a collection of integrated comprehensive copyright content resources, ensuring upstream copyright advantages, and continuously producing high-quality audio content. As of December 31th, 2021, Ximalaya Inc. has reached cooperation with about 160 head publishers, including CITIC Press, and established business cooperation with more than 140 head online literary platforms in China.

Ximalaya Inc. has a wide range of terminal application scenarios, which well meets the requirements of women to use fragmented time for learning and self improvement, breaks the restrictions of learning in terms of region, time, space, etc., fits in with the lifelong learning philosophy of learning at any time and any place by using fragmented time, and provides valuable spiritual food for women.

3.3 Challenges of Narrowing the Gender Divide in the Context of the Digital Age in Shanghai

In the context of the digital age, women are faced with various pressures and challenges while gaining development opportunities, including more fierce professional competition, widening gender income gap, and difficulty in obtaining entrepreneurial empowerment.

3.3.1 Women Face Even Greater Competition in Work

Since the start of the "competition for talents" in 2017, the attraction of talents in various regions of China has been concentrated in the fields of new infrastructure, high-tech industries, financial trade and modern service industries. Shanghai has a huge siphon effect for attracting domestic and global talents. According to the *2021 Talent Capital Trend Report* released by BOSS Research Institute, Beijing, Shanghai and Shenzhen rank among the top three in terms of talent attraction, and Shanghai's internal workplace competition pressure is much higher than that of other second and third tier cities. However, from the education level of Shanghai's permanent residents, women's overall competitiveness in the workplace is not optimistic. According to the *China Population and Employment Statistics Yearbook 2021*, only 38.5% of the female population in Shanghai urban areas have a junior college degree or above, which is not only lower than that of men in Shanghai (39%), but also lower than that of women in Beijing urban areas (48.8%).

In addition, in recent years, with the accelerated development of Shanghai from digital industrialization to industrial digitalization, digital technology has been deeply integrated with almost all industries. Enterprises are faced with the dual pressures of coping with the impact of the epidemic and accelerating the digital transformation. The requirements of enterprises on the quality of talents have also been significantly improved, and the vocational skills required for jobs have also changed dramatically. The demand for professional and technical posts driven by hard skills has increased significantly. The selection and evaluation of talents are more "skill driven". Talents with composite skills are more popular than job seekers with a single skill.

According to the data of BOSS Research Institute, in 2020, the number of posts requiring digital skills doubled among 13 occupations, including investment consultants, bio-pharmaceutical engineers, securities analysts, and user operation managers. A lot of positions have also raised requirements for women's digital skills, which undoubtedly brings down probability and adds up difficulty for women to stand out in the workplace crowded with a large number of talents.

According to the data of "Wutongguo" (a recruitment platform), women accounted for 52.04% of college students in 2020, but only 36.11% and 45.39% of college students majored in engineering and science respectively. Obviously, the low proportion of women in science and engineering disciplines will directly reduce the opportunities for women to engage in occupations related to digital technology in the future. The polarization of posts in the age of the digital economy will not be conducive to women's access to better career opportunities.

In addition, in the context of the vigorous development of the digital economy, cutting-edge technologies such as artificial intelligence often quickly replace simple jobs that are highly repetitive, require a lot of computing, and have low technical content. The proportion of women in basic posts in Shanghai is significantly higher than that of men, which is partly determined by the education level of women (see Table 3 - 1 next page). Obviously, the replacement of labor posts with artificial intelligence is more unfavorable to women, and women with low academic qualifications who lack competitiveness in the workplace are also more vulnerable to the risk of being replaced by digital technology.

Table 3 − 1　Number and Proportion of Population with Different
Education Levels by Gender in Shanghai

Sex	Statistic	Primary school	Junior high school	High school	Junior college degree or above
Male	No. (person)	898 956	2 720 336	2 099 209	3 875 357
	Proportion	9.06%	27.41%	21.15%	39.05%
Female	No. (person)	1 108 847	2 422 125	1 906 317	3 688 817
	Proportion	11.57%	25.28%	19.89%	38.49%

Data source: *China Population and Employment Statistics Yearbook 2021.*

3.3.2　The Gender Divide in Income Levels in the Digital Age Is Easier to Widen

During the vigorous development of the digital economy, the most direct beneficiaries are the software, communications, Internet and other industries whose major business is "new infrastructure". As shown in Figure 3 − 2, from 2014 to 2020, the gap between the average wage of the information transmission, software and information technology service industries and other industries among the private sector employees in Shanghai has been further widened. The former takes a big lead over the others in the service industries. These achievements were all made possible through Shanghai's vigorous efforts in developing digital economy in recent years.

However, according to the *Shanghai Statistical Yearbook 2021*, in 2020, the number of employees in information transmission, software and information technology service industry only took up 5.9% and 17.3% respectively of all industries and service enterprises in Shanghai[1], and the proportion of female employees was even less. At the same time, according to the *White Paper on the Development of China's Digital Economy*, there is a significant gender divide between the number of digital technology practitioners and their incomes. The

---

[1]　上海市统计局.规模以上服务企业按职业类型分从业人员期末人数(2020)[EB/OL].(2022 − 07 − 29)[2023 − 02 − 07].http://tjj.sh.gov.cn/tjnj/nj21.htm?d1 = 2021tjnj/C0217.htm.

report shows that in 2020, women accounted for only 17.9% of digital technology posts, and the gender ratio was seriously unbalanced. In the Internet/IT industry, the salary of men in technical posts is 16.5% higher than that of women.[1] It can be seen that the development of industrial digitalization and digital industrialization has provided more opportunities for men to increase their wages, and may further widen the income gap between men and women through industrial barriers.

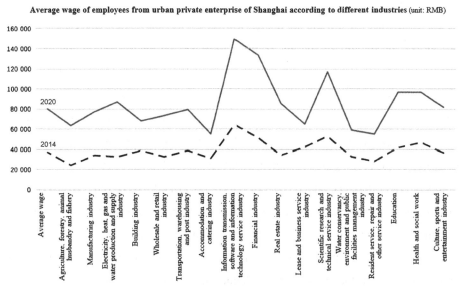

Figure 3 − 2   **Average Wages of Urban Private Employees by Industry in Shanghai in 2014 and 2020**

Data source: *China Statistical Yearbook*, http: //www.stats.gov.cn/tjsj/ndsj/.

Limited by their physiological and professional conditions, many women are engaged in labor-intensive industries, life services industry and other middle and low-end industries, such as hospitality/catering and wholesale and retail industries. In 2020, women accounted for 52.6% of the total number of self-employed workers in Shanghai, including 55% in the wholesale/retail industry and 49% in the hospitality/catering industry.[2] However, it can be seen

---

① 李秀萍.全国妇联：完善数字经济领域妇女劳动权益保障[N].农民日报,2022 − 03 − 10(4).

② 上海市统计局.上海市第四次经济普查主要数据公报（第一号）[EB/OL].（2022 − 07 − 29）[2023 − 02 − 08].http: //tjj.sh.gov.cn/tjgb/20200330/98f254db81fa405f95147551a548f9d4.html.

from the data above that the average wages of these industries in Shanghai are at a relatively low level among all industries, and the increase in recent 5 years is not remarkable.

Many industries (including catering and hospitality, retail and wholesale, leisure and entertainment, family service, education and childcare, etc.) where women are concentrated in Shanghai have a low degree of integration with the digital economy, and rely more on offline consumption, so they are more affected by the epidemic. According to data, from 2015 to 2020, the salary of "women industries" in Shanghai experienced ups and downs. It reached the highest value in 2017, then decreased to about 8 000 Yuan in 2018, following by a slight increase in 2019, and it again decreased to 8 071 Yuan in 2020, equal to 61.34% of the average salary in Shanghai. After 2017, the proportion of low-income jobs in Shanghai's female industry has increased year by year, especially in 2020, which is nearly 20 percentage points higher than that in 2019. Among them, the wages of family service, nursery and preschool education in 2020 were only 70% ~ 80% of that in 2019. [1,2]It can be seen that women are largely employed in industries that are difficult to benefit from the digital economy, so they face the risk that the gender divide in income will be further widened. When encountering the impact of exogenous adverse factors such as epidemic, the income risks will be overlapped, and women will be more likely to fall into economic difficulties when the economic resilience is insufficient. Shanghai women who are living at the forefront city of the digital economy are exposed to greater risks and pressures.

3.3.3 Inadequate Empowerment to Entrepreneurial Women by the Digital Economy

According to the *Questionnaire Survey Report on Entrepreneurial Women in*

---

[1] 城室科技.疫情下女性就业情况变得更糟糕了吗？[EB/OL].(2020-10-19)[2023-02-07]. https://www.thepaper.cn/newsDetail_forward_9584732.

[2] The data is based on the industry classification of recruitment websites, and matched with the female gathering industries (19 categories) screened by the population census to obtain 11 types of female gathering industries in Shanghai. According to the company, release date, description, salary and other information of the posts on the recruitment website, the overall female industry and 11 categories of female industries are analyzed respectively.

Shanghai of the Ziyulan Female Enterprise Development Plan hosted by Shanghai Haiyun Female Entrepreneurship & Employment Guidance Service Center in April 2022, among the companies owned by women entrepreneurs in Shanghai, education, training, scientific research, colleges accounted for the highest proportion (28.3%); the second was advertising, public relations, media, art (accounting for 16.98%). The industries closely related to the digital economy accounted for a relatively low proportion, of which IT, software and hardware services, e-commerce, and Internet operation only accounted for 7.55%; the pharmaceutical, biological engineering, medical equipment and device only accounted for 1.89%; bank, insurance, securities, investment band and venture capital industries accounted for 1.89% (see Figure 3 − 3).

Due to the limited ability of some female entrepreneurs to apply digital tools and technologies, especially the lack of initiative and comprehensive ability to use digital technology for business or economic purposes, the gender divide in profiting from the digital economy has also widened. Due to the low degree of

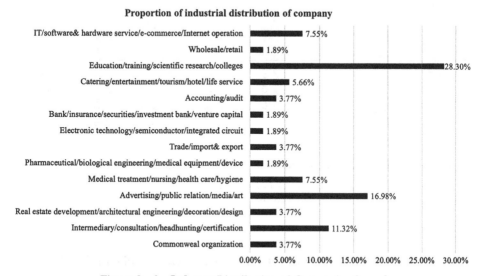

Figure 3 − 3　Industry Distribution of Companies Owned by Women Entrepreneurs in Shanghai

Data source: *Questionnaire Survey Report on Entrepreneurial Women in Shanghai* of the Ziyulan Female Enterprise Development Plan in April 2022.

digitalization, these female start-ups are not strong enough to withstand the impact of the epidemic. The negative impact of the epidemic on enterprises is mainly reflected in the decline in the number of customers, insufficient funds and increased costs. The questionnaire survey report shows that the degree of digitalization of the companies owned by female entrepreneurs in Shanghai is still at the primary stage, and the companies are in urgent need of digitalization transformation and upgrading in all aspects. The most demanding ones are digital marketing, digital customer service, digital management, etc. In addition, there are also some demands in supply chain/R&D/manufacturing digitization (See Figure 3 − 4).

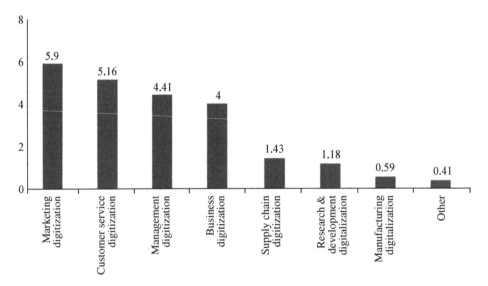

Figure 3 − 4   Digital Demand of Companies Owned by Women Entrepreneurs in Shanghai

Data source: *Questionnaire Survey Report on Entrepreneurial Women in Shanghai* of the Ziyulan Female Enterprise Development Plan in April 2022

3.4   Efforts Made by Governments at All Levels to Bridge the Gender Divide in the Digital Age

With the continuous development of China's social economy, the imbalance between women's demand for a better life and the insufficient development of women's career is still outstanding. For example, the social environment and policy support for women's employment need to be continuously optimized, and the policy and social support system for promoting family birth needs to be further improved. There is still a long way to go to further solve the problems troubling women's development and promote gender equality and high-quality and comprehensive development of women.

To this end, the central government and the Shanghai government have issued many policy documents around narrowing and bridging the gender divide in employment, entrepreneurship and other fields. They have made unremitting efforts for a long time to help women cope with challenges, get better opportunities for survival and development, and promote the balance between social equity and gender development in the rapidly developing socio-economic environment, especially in the changing digital age.

In July 2021, Shanghai released the *14th Five-Year Plan for the Development of Women and Children in Shanghai*, proposing the overall goal of "by 2025, the development level of women and children in Shanghai will be 'leading at home and advanced internationally', and the development level of women will stay stable at the level of moderately developed countries". The policies issued by the central government and the Shanghai government have continuously improved the employment and entrepreneurship environment for women in the digital age, providing favorable conditions for Shanghai to achieve the above goals.

3.4.1　Fully Protect Women's Employment Rights and Interests

The Shanghai government has issued a more detailed planning document for the protection of women's employment rights and interests. The *14th Five-Year Plan for the Development of Women and Children in Shanghai* proposed to promote women's employment and improve the quality of women's economic participation, and defined gender equality indicators in terms of employment rights, including the stability of the gender ratio of labor participation rate, the proportion of urban female employees at about 40%, and the reduction of the gender income ratio. To achieve these goals, Shanghai has proposed a series of measures, such as ensuring the institutional arrangements for women's employment, so that women enjoy equal employment rights; standardizing the employment behavior of enterprises, punishing the employers for employment discrimination, and gradually eliminating the occupational segregation of industry and gender; supporting women to return to work after childbirth, and encouraging employers to develop measures that will help workers balance work and family.

In order to focus on solving the problem of gender discrimination in employment, the central government specially issued relevant documents to guarantee women's equal employment rights, promote women's equal employment, and promote women's more extensive and in-depth participation in social and economic activities. In February 2019, the Ministry of Human Resources and Social Security, the All-China Women's Federation and other departments jointly issued the *Notice on Further Standardizing Recruitment Behavior to Promote Women's Employment*, which clearly prohibited gender discrimination in recruitment. The notice stipulates that in the process of drafting recruitment plans, releasing recruitment information and recruiting personnel, gender shall not be limited or given priority, women should not be restricted from seeking employment on the grounds of gender, and women should not be rejected if they prove to be qualified. The notice also stipulated that it is prohibited to inquire about women's marriage and childbearing plans, to take pregnancy test as an entry physical examination item, to set no-birth-promise as a precondition of employment, and to raise the employment standards for women in a differentiated way. In case of gender discrimination in recruitment, the notice orders such behaviors to be corrected, and the entity who conducts so will be fined, or his/her human resources service license shall be revoked according to law. At the same time, joint interview mechanism shall be adopted to correct gender discrimination in employment and resolve conflicts and disputes in a timely manner, and judicial relief mechanism shall be used to provide legal aid to women who suffer from gender discrimination in employment.

In recent years, the All-China Women's Federation has paid close attention to the protection of women's employment rights and interests in the age of the digital economy. At the Fifth Session of the 13th CPPCC National Committee in March 2022, the All-China Women's Federation submitted a sector proposal focusing on digital economy and women's development, proposing to broaden women's employment channels in the digital economy, improve women's digital employability, and improve the protection of women's labor rights and interests in the field of digital economy. The proposal encourages enterprises in such industries as online retail, mobile travel, Internet medical, and online live broadcasting to develop new jobs suitable for women, and establish a job grade system to open a new window for female college graduates to find jobs; improve women's digital employability and strengthen women's digital skills training; improve the incentive mechanism for female talents to participate in digital construction and promote the growth of high-level female talents; encourage employees of the digital economy to participate in social insurance, include women with new forms of employment and flexible employment into maternity insurance, and promote the introduction of policies to apply for maternity allowances on a pro rata basis. [1]

The Shanghai Women's Federation has also played an important role in promoting the protection of women's employment rights and interests. For example, during the Shanghai Two Sessions in 2021, the Municipal Women's Federation submitted a proposal to "revise and improve the *Provisions of Shanghai Municipality on Promoting Employment* to promote women's employment". The *Provisions of Shanghai Municipality on Promoting Employment* was formulated in 2005 and has not been revised thereafter. The *Employment Promotion Law of the People's Republic of China* was promulgated and implemented in 2007, and was revised once in 2015. There is a special chapter to regulate "fair employment", but there is no further detailed and specific provisions at the local level. The Municipal Women's Federation pointed out that great changes have taken place in Shanghai's social and economic development over the past decade, and many new situations have emerged in the employment situation of women. It is urgent to

① 李秀萍.全国妇联: 完善数字经济领域妇女劳动权益保障[N/OL].农民日报,2022 - 03 - 10 [2023 - 02 - 10].https: //baijiahao.baidu.com/s?id = 1726707945558606779&wfr = spider&for = pc.

introduce measures to promote women's employment that meet the current situation and requirements. At present, against the hidden discrimination of women after employment, there are difficulties in obtaining evidence and conducting supervision, investigation and punishment. In addition, the public service system to promote women's employment also has room for further improvement, such as the psychological and emotional needs of women in the three periods (pregnancy, maternity and lactation), and the vocational training needs of women with flexible employment. Therefore, it is necessary to make timely revision and improvement.[①]

In 2022, the Shanghai Women's Federation also spares efforts on promoting the Women's Action for Employment and Entrepreneurship to improve the level of employment services, help all women to find jobs and realize high-quality employment, and do a good job in "six stabilities" and "six guarantees". It specifically includes the following aspects. The first is to promote the employment and entrepreneurship of female college students. In this regard, it is planned to implement the "Seagull Plan" for female college students to take a career leap, to promote colleges and universities to establish and improve the "Seagull Bay" working mechanism, to launch "We are Waiting for People with Aspiration"— Employment Action Plan for 2022 graduates in cooperation with the Municipal Association of Women Entrepreneurs, to organize job fairs specialized for female graduates where over 100 enterprises participate and over 10 000 posts are provided, to provide employment guidance services for female college students, and to help female college students find jobs through multiple channels. The second is to promote employment stability and improve employment quality for women. In this area, it is planned to strengthen the training of new vocational skills in the digital field for women, to improve women's digital ability, and to enhance women's participation in employment and entrepreneurship in new digital industries, new business forms and new models; it also makes plan to promote

---

① 罗菁.维护促进公平就业,加强灵活就业群体保障! 上海今年将修订促进就业地方性法规[EB/OL].(2022-03-29)[2023-02-11].https://www.511db.com/shsldb/zc/content/017fd38ca47cc0010000df844d7e124a.htm.

regional coordination in terms of women's employment and entrepreneurship in the Yangtze River Delta, deepen exchanges and cooperation among women entrepreneurs in the Yangtze River Delta, and create more jobs.

Based on the above summary, the central government of China has defined many indicators of women's gender equality in employment, including labor participation rate, proportion of employees, income level, etc., and proposed to achieve the above indicators through strategies such as punishing employment discrimination, eliminating occupational segregation, and supporting women to return to the workplace after childbirth; the relevant ministries and commissions of the central government, starting from the recruitment stage, have issued a notice to promote women's employment, standardized recruitment behavior, and provided legal aid for women; the All-China Women's Federation has paid close attention to and focused on the digital economy and women's development, and strived to broaden women's employment channels and improve their employability; the Shanghai Women's Federation has also been committed to protecting and improving women's employment rights and interests for a long time, and has made an appeal for timely revision of the related documents and regulations that lag behind the development of the real society; in addition, the Shanghai Women's Federation has made efforts on cultivating women's ability, from campus to workplace, to get employed and promoting their participation in employment. It can be seen that, in order to help women cope with the employment challenges in the age of digital economy, governments at all levels have been paying attention to and actively responding to them. Through the introduction of various policies and regulations, they have continuously improved the protection of women's employment rights and interests.

3.4.2 Facilitate the Development of Female Scientific and Technological Talents

In November 2021, 17 departments, including the Shanghai Women's Federation and the Science and Technology Commission, jointly issued *Measures to Support Female Scientific and Technological Talents to Play a Greater Role in*

Shanghai's Construction of a Science and Technology Innovation Center with Global Influence, proposing 12 specific measures for female scientific and technological talents, including better leveraging the role of high-level female scientific and technological talents in science and technology decision-making and consulting, increasing support for the cultivation of high-level female scientific and technological talents, improving the international influence and activity of high-level female scientific and technological talents, promoting the implementation of policies related to retirement of high-level female scientific and technological talents, carrying out the "Women in Science and Technology Innovation Initiative" in depth, supporting female scientific and technological talents to participate in the construction of Pudong Leading Area, improving the scientific research vitality and social contribution of female scientific and technological talents, establishing and optimizing the evaluation and incentive mechanism for female scientific and technological talents, creating a fertility friendly working environment for female scientific and technological talents, strengthening the training of reserve female scientific and technological talents, and strengthening the basic work of female scientific and technological talents.

The *14th Five-Year Plan for the Development of Women and Children in Shanghai*, released in 2022, puts forward many indicators for gender equality in the development of technical talents: the proportion of female senior managers in high-tech enterprises shall be steadily increased, the gap between the proportions of male and female senior professional and technical talents shall be narrowed, the proportion of women selected for various talent projects and those undertaking scientific research projects shall remain balanced, the proportion of women among those who have obtained invention patents shall gradually increase, the contribution rate of women's human capital shall improve, and the ratio of reaching standard scientific literacy among female population shall keep up with that of the whole Chinese population. At the same time, the above plan also puts forward more practical policies and measures. The concept of gender equality runs through the whole process of education, promoting women's professional and technical learning, ensuring women's equal access to training of vocational skills, improving women's network literacy, building a science, education and cultural service system that is suitable for all stages of women's life course, continuously improving women's scientific literacy, comprehensively improving women's artistic and cultural literacy, and promoting lifelong education services for women.

In 2022, the Shanghai Women's Federation vigorously promoted the Women in Science and Technology Innovation Initiative, further stimulating the innovation vitality of Shanghai's female scientific and technological talents, and better playing the important role of female scientific and technological talents in accelerating the construction of a science and technology innovation center with global influence. In addition, the Shanghai Women's Federation held Women Scientists Summit of Pujiang Innovation Forum, continued to hold the AI Women Elite Forum of the World Conference on Artificial Intelligence, and participated in the "She" Forum of the World Laureates Forum. The Federation also promoted the implementation of policies for women's scientific and technological talents, strengthened policy research, created conditions for implementation, and did everything possible to create a child-bearing friendly working environment for women's scientific and technological talents; it carried out the "girls love science" training plan for cultivating scientific and technological reserve talents, which aims at exploring and studying the early-stage training mode for cultivating female scientific and technological innovation talents and the "girls love science" project, which guides and stimulates the scientific thinking and scientific interest of female students.

To sum up, the Shanghai Municipal Government attaches great importance to the important role of women in the development of science and technology, and has introduced various policies to help female science and technology talents better display their talents and contribute to society in the digital age. The relevant "14th Five-Year Plan" also sets clear targets for the proportion of female talents in science and technology, their contribution rate, qualification rate and other indicators, and proposes strategic measures in terms of training opportunities, lifelong education services, science, education and cultural services. The Shanghai Women's Federation has held various international forums and domestic summits to provide a stage for female scientific and technological talents to show "her power", boost the implementation of relevant policies and provide a favorable environment for women of all ages to grow and develop at the same time.

3.4.3 Cultivate Female Entrepreneurs and Support them at all Stages

The *14th Five-Year Plan for the Development of Women and Children in Shanghai* included "a stable gender ratio of men and women in entrepreneurial activities" as a main indicator of promoting women's entrepreneurship and employment and improving the quality of women's economic participation in Shanghai; and put forward the following measures. The first is to strengthen the support for women's entrepreneurship, which includes promoting women's entrepreneurship, publicizing women's entrepreneurship models, providing information and guidance for women's entrepreneurship in areas of financial support, investment and financing channels, and improving the institutional environment to promote women's entrepreneurship. The second is to guide women to integrate into the integrated development of the Yangtze River Delta and contribute their wisdom to the open scientific and technological innovation environment and emerging markets. The third is to encourage all kinds of mass entrepreneurship spaces and incubation platforms to provide more open and convenient services for female entrepreneurs and innovators. The fourth is to explore and establish an incentive mechanism for women's entrepreneurship, and increase support for women's entrepreneurship in high-tech fields such as the Internet and big data.

In 2022, the Shanghai Women's Federation pushed forward the "Women's Action for Employment and Entrepreneurship" project, which includes the implementation of the "Seagull Plan" for female college students to take a career leap, continuing to carry out the Shanghai Female College Students' Innovation and Entrepreneurship Competition, stimulating female college students' enthusiasm for innovation and entrepreneurship, and promoting entrepreneurship to drive employment. The project also encourages all districts to hold women's entrepreneurship competitions, explore and cultivate a number of outstanding female entrepreneurship projects and model cases, and provide precise services for the needs of "incubation projects" "accelerated projects" and "key cultivation projects" at different stages, as well as the difficulties and pain spots of female entrepreneurship.

In February 2016, Shanghai Haiyun Female Entrepreneurship & Employment Guidance Service Center (hereinafter referred to as "Haiyun"), the first female entrepreneurship and employment guidance service center in Shanghai led by the Women's Federation, was established. Over the years, Haiyun has been committed to providing systematic, innovative and practical guidance and consultation on entrepreneurship and employment knowledge and skills for full-time mothers, career women and female entrepreneurs, and helping women own independent careers and achieve sustainable growth. At present, Haiyun has formed core products and services such as "Chuangyi Family" and "Ziyulan" female entrepreneurship training course system, Private Advisory Board, Maker Roadshow, Female Entrepreneurship Interview, and Face-to-face Consultant, bringing together a community of thousands of excellent female entrepreneurs. Haiyun is providing more female entrepreneurs with continuous guidance, training, consultation and services.

Under the guidance of the Shanghai Women's Federation, Haiyun launched the care and assistance plan for start-up women in 2018 and 2019 to help entrepreneurial women solve practical problems through customized and problem-oriented workshops. The center also carried out projects such as the "lighting up" plan for women's entrepreneurship and the women's entrepreneurship competition. In cooperation with the female-themed Entrepreneur Harbor of China Construction Bank, the center successfully bridged access to inclusive financial loans, so as to ease the financial difficulties of enterprises during the epidemic. It continuously carried out empowerment training for female entrepreneurs running small and micro enterprises. Through the official channels of the Shanghai Federation of Industry and Commerce and the Shanghai Municipal Commission of Economy and Information, the center responded to the key epidemic-caused problems faced by small and micro enterprises owned by female entrepreneurs, and put forward constructive proposals.

Shanghai has clearly included the index of " female entrepreneurial activity rate" into the objectives of its 14th Five-Year Plan, and has proposed strategic measures from capital, system, environment and other aspects. The Shanghai Women's Federation provides guidance, consultation and continuous empowerment for female entrepreneurs to help them solve their problems in entrepreneurship, and carries out training programs for female college students in order to nurture female entrepreneurs and entrepreneurs with a forward-looking vision. It can be seen that Shanghai has made great efforts to provide strong support to women at all stages of entrepreneurship, helping them succeed on the road of entrepreneurship.

Chapter IV

Case Study of Bridging the Gender Divide in the Development of Shanghai's Digital Economy

In this chapter, we will present several carefully selected cases for thorough analysis, which will fully demonstrate the efforts made by enterprises to bridge the gender divide in the digital age. For example, by building its Aikucun platform into an online infrastructure platform and e-commerce distribution platform, Idol Group Co., Ltd aims to attract women to participate in entrepreneurship, and create a community operation model to give play to women's social advantages. Women's communities have the natural advantages of loving sharing, highly active and good at communication, and can accurately identify potential customer needs, so as to seize the entrepreneurial opportunities and open up new entrepreneurial fields. Ximalaya Inc., the largest audio content platform enterprise in the world, provides women with knowledge, information and spiritual comfort through high-quality audio content. The Ximalaya platform supports women from different careers to find a career they love, realize greater social value, and share the dividends of the digital age. Gathering women's voices and building a platform for communication, exchange and mutual assistance between women, Ximalaya delivers the concept of gender equality to the society, and helps women work together to bridge the gender divide. MS Energy fully leverages the leading role of women on the track of carbon peaking and carbon neutrality in the fields of energy, ecological, and environmental protection, provides abundant employment opportunities and clear career paths for women to eliminate gender stereotypes in the workplace, help women to maximize their own value through various incentive mechanisms, and create a positive work environment, discovering more female power in technological progress and digital transformation.

4.1 The Case of the Aikucun Platform of Idol Group Co., Ltd

Founded in December 2017, Idol Group Co., Ltd has experienced three stages: special sale, store owner and platform in the past five years. At present, Idol Group Co., Ltd is positioned as a B2R distribution e-commerce company. It has its own Aikucun App for store owners, consumer-oriented Xiangdian applet, and institutions-oriented Corporate Xiangdian SaaS. From the development history of Idol Group Co., Ltd, the first Aikucun platform was created from "store owners share product information in the community—the customers place order to the store owners—the store owners place order to the platform after receiving customer order". After placing an order to the platform, the store owner can draw a certain fee as commission, which brings income to part-time or full-time store owners. However, the disadvantage of this operation mode is that customers can't directly touch the purchase page, and the store owners need to purchase and ask for after-sales on behalf of the customer, which affects the operation efficiency of the platform. Therefore, Idol Group Co., Ltd has developed the Xiangdian platform, where the store owners on the platform can share the applet or H5 interface to community, and customers can directly place orders on the platform, making the operation more convenient. The upgraded Xiangdian platform is capable of exposing over 10 000 brands to over 100 million consumers through millions of store owners, which was only possible on the Aikucun platform. In 2021, Idol Group Co., Ltd upgraded its strategy to B2R distribution e-commerce (B refers to business, R refers to retailers and resellers, also known as store owners), and it has developed enabling tools such as distribution robots around R, further improving R's work efficiency. For the convenience of description, "Idol platform" will be used as a general term when it does not specifically refer to Aikucun or Xiangdian platform.

The vast majority of the store owners and consumers of Idol Group Co., Ltd are women, and the store owners take the Xiangdian business as their own small businesses or part-time jobs. Giving full play to the advantages of women's community sharing and communication ability, providing more women's employment opportunities, promoting urban and rural women's income generation, weakening the impression of women's stereotyped role as caregivers in the family, improving women's sense of self-identity, exploring new forms of women's rights and interests protection organizations and other aspects, Idol Group Co., Ltd is promoting the bridging of the gender divide in the context of digital economy development.

4.1.1 The Platform Helps Women Give Play to Their Advantages and Open up Women's Entrepreneurship Market

1) Positioning of distribution e-commerce to attract women to participate in entrepreneurship

Idol Group Co., Ltd has created the B2R distribution e-commerce model (see Figure 4 - 1), and B (supplier) is the upstream brand in the business model ecosystem. At present, Idol Group Co., Ltd has established cooperative relationships with more than 10 000 international and domestic brand merchants from all over the world, including Nike, Adidas, Estee Lauder, Li Ning, Dove, UGG, Shachi, Swiss, etc.. R (distributor/retailer) is a downstream distributor/ retailer in the ecosystem. Through the supply chain management solution based on SaaS store management software and tools and the integration of goods and services, the purchase warehousing, logistics, after-sales customer service, IT system and other elements are integrated into standardized services, connecting suppliers (B), R (distributors/retailers) and consumers (C).

R (distributors/retailers) can be divided into small R, medium R and large R according to their scale. Small R refers to small distributors, mainly individuals. Medium R refers to medium-sized distributors/retailers, mainly small and medium-sized institutions, which can contact and serve a medium number of consumers. Some of them are distributors and some are retailers. Large R refers to large institutions that can contact and serve a large number of consumers. Most of

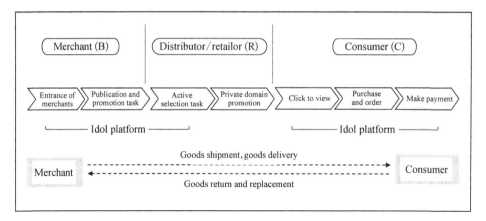

Figure 4－1　B2R Business Model of Idol Group Co., Ltd

the large R's are retailers and provide retail services directly to consumers.

At present, the about 3 million R's of Idol Group Co., Ltd, are mainly small R's, 95.5% of which are female store owners.

From the development history of Idol Group Co., Ltd, the Aikucun platform at the early stage of development focused on the inventory sales of clothing brands, and accumulated a number of female customers and female store owners. The reason is that women are sensitive to both brand quality and price advantages. The products in the platform are about 20% cheaper than the rest of online platforms on average, which attracts a large number of women to consume on the platform. Due to the convenience of flexible employment, according to statistics, 48.2% of store owners joined the Idol platform through friends' recommendation, and 41.5% became store owners from buyers. Compared with conventional workplace, Idol platform strengthens the sense of trust and be longings, which makes it easier for customers to become store owners.

After accumulating a large number of female consumers and store owners at the initial stage, the social networking advantages of women have been superimposed, which has brought continuous impetus to attract female consumers and store owners in the following development. At present, 95.5% of women consumers of Idol platform are also store owners. By 2021, more than 10 million consumers have settled in, and about 3 million store owners have been empowered to start businesses and generate income. As a new economic platform, Idol Group Co., Ltd makes full use of the online new economic model. During the epidemic, it provided more than 220 000 employment opportunities, becoming a model of promoting employment and entrepreneurship with the online new economic model, and an important platform to promote women's entrepreneurship and employment.

2) 8S empowerment provides women with entrepreneurial convenience

The community economy is the original product of the age of mobile Internet and the age of digital economy. It has changed the " people-goods-market " relationship and business model in the centralized traditional e-commerce age. The seller has the first-hand source of goods, which reduces the intermediate circulation process and costs, so it can attract women to participate in social and economic activities.

Specifically, Idol platform provides store owners with 8S empowerment: SaaS (software as a service), supply chain, skill, service, share value, social relationship, social value, and standard.

Among them, SaaS provides store owners with the required software, Apps and applets for store opening, customer management, order management, etc. Supply Chain refers to providing complete supply chain services for store owners through investment attraction, quality control, warehousing, logistics and other links. The store owners do not need to purchase, prepare and deliver goods, but have tens of thousands of brand goods at hand instantly. Skill training is to provide various skills training required by store owners, including community operation skills, commodity and brand knowledge, management training, psychological training, child rearing and family relationship maintenance. Service (customer service) is to provide after-sales service for all customers and help store owners solve customers' troubles in the after-sales process. Share value provides store owners with brand culture knowledge, commodity knowledge and other contents, and at the same time, store owners pass on common values to engage and develop others. Social relationship refers to the flexible employment model that allows store owners to have more time to return to society and social relations. It serves as a guarantee that enables women to have sufficient confidence to keep a closer relationship with their children, husbands and mothers-in-law and make neighborhood relations more harmonious. Social value (social status) refers to the fact that the flexible employment mode enables the store owners to obtain economic benefits and thus improve their status, and that they have achieved self growth as well as self value and achieved social status. Standard (industry standard) refers to the establishment of the new S2R2C e-commerce industry standard, which standardizes and promotes the development of the industry and enables store owners to develop healthily in a compliant and orderly industry environment.

3) Community operation model gives full play to women's social advantages

"Community" refers to a group with common goals or interests that can interact, collaborate effectively and act in concert. The core of community economy is to gather the power of netizens through the community to form productive forces with economic effectiveness. It emphasizes the collective power of the community, the productivity of the collective power and its economic effectiveness[1]. Community economy is a new model of "decentralized" e-commerce operation and a carrier that links people, information, services, content and goods.

Women ushered in a new round of development opportunities in the process of digital economy development. In the era of agricultural economy and the subsequent era of industry, human beings rely on physical strength to survive, and commerce also depends on physical strength to develop. In the current age of digital economy, women's social attributes, emotional communication advantages, and the power underneath social and communication capabilities have greatly promoted business.

Community economy provides more possibilities for women to start up business in the society. On the one hand, community members share common beliefs and values and are more willing to work towards the same goal. Processing natural advantages of sharing, proactive and communicative, the women's

---

① 彭兰.如何在网络社群中培育"社群经济"[J].江淮论坛,2020(03): 123 – 129+144.

community can accurately find the potential needs of customers, seize entrepreneurial opportunities and open up new entrepreneurial fields. The key to the development of community e-commerce lies in sharing and communication. At present, the average number of forward times per day of an Idol store owner is 95 and that of Idol Assistant is 490. At the same time, the community assists in women's entrepreneurship by providing them with a platform for mutual-learning and communicating. Through interaction, communication, collaboration and mutual infection, community members build up trust and dependence on the community, which in turn increases women's entrepreneurship rate.

4.1.2 The Platform Helps Women Achieve Self-growth and Improves Their Business Capabilities

1) Entrepreneurial service — "tool box" digital service

Idol platform is a global distribution e-commerce platform. The platform integrates supply chain, SaaS store software, operation, data, compliance training and other one-stop services to fully enable store owners to generate income and start businesses. The emergence of various e-commerce platforms provides new infrastructure for the digital economy, enables flexible employment for women, and boosts the development of the digital economy. In terms of data empowerment, Idol Group Co., Ltd has launched the "tool box" operation tool to achieve accurate matching of people and goods through platform's big data and artificial intelligence technology and outline the "customer portrait", which effectively reduced operation costs for female entrepreneurs, improved the input-output ratio, and accelerated the integration of online and offline business. Through the empowerment service provided by the platform, women entrepreneurs obtain "shortcut" for entrepreneurship, which shortens the time for identifying opportunities for seeking entrepreneurial resources and understanding new e-commerce entrepreneurial information, and realizes entrepreneurial revenue at a lower cost, thus creating value for the society.

2) Business training—"Idol Class" course services

In order to help rookie entrepreneurs quickly grow into business elites and emerging force, Idol Group Co., Ltd has created an online TV class for female entrepreneurs—Idol Class (since the store owners are addressed as "Aidou" on the platform, which sounds similar to Idol, the class was named as Idol as well), through which the female entrepreneurs can improve their comprehensive quality and ability, understand their future career development and growth path, and increase social identity and sense of belonging. At present, Idol Class has formed a relatively systematic curriculum, from basic training such as knowledge of the Internet and detailed operation of Apps for the novice to professional skills training in professional selection and marketing methods, from courses on building a healthy and positive attitude to emotional management courses, from training on standardizing workplace behavior and workplace etiquette to learning about policies and laws. Idol Class provides courses that meet the needs of store owners at each stage. Women who start businesses in Idol Group Co., Ltd said that it is very important to have learning ability in the process of starting businesses, and that the key to success is to learn, in the "Idol Class", how to manage customers hierarchically and classify product types, and fully leverage personal communication ability and community operation ability.

4.1.3 The Platform Supports Women's Economic Independence and Promotes Women to Start up Business and Generate Income

1) Urban women can relieve economic pressure by taking a self-employed part-time job

The survey[1] results show that about 70% of women interviewed of Idol Group Co., Ltd are part-time store owners. When answering "Why choose to become a professional practitioner of the platform", 83.4% of interviewees said "can increase income", which proves itself a dominating factor. The income obtained by the female interviewees is usually used for daily household expenses and their own pocket expenses. When using this part of income in shopping, they

---

① The survey was conducted by Professor Shen Yifei from the Family Development Research Center of Fudan University, entrusted by the Women's Federation of Pudong New Area, Shanghai, on the Idol platform.

feel more pleasing. Therefore, such income can alleviate their family economic pressure and improve quality of life.

In order to enable more women to achieve economic independence, Idol Group Co., Ltd has set two income targets, since income is the most concerned factor. The first one is food and clothing line and the other is happiness line. Idol store owners living in first tier and second tier cities can reach the food and clothing line when they earn 5 000 Yuan a month, and reach the happiness line when they earn 10 000 Yuan a month; the two figures for those living in third tier cities are 2 000 Yuan and 5 000 Yuan respectively. At present, 54% of the distributors have taken the Idol platform as a private small business, which not only solves their own employment problems, but also brings most of them a monthly income of 3 000 to 10 000 Yuan.

2) Effective sinking into rural market to increase women's income

Idol Group Co., Ltd has attracted about 3 million store owners, 95.5% of whom are women, 53% of whom are from first tier and second tier cities, and 47.09% are from third and fourth tier cities, counties, towns and rural areas. Idol platform spreads all over the country, with female store owners from Heilongjiang in the northeast, Hainan in the south and Xinjiang in the west. By 2022, the Idol platform has created nearly 5 billion Yuan of income, especially the rural store owners' income increased by 1 billion Yuan.

During the development of digital economy, due to the differences in resource endowments and technologies among regions in China, the market of third-tier and lower cities, counties, towns and rural areas is large but scattered. When providing digital services, the service cost is higher, and the platform economy is more difficult to operate. To help the rural revitalization, Idol Group Co., Ltd established cooperation with Xihe County in Longnan on agricultural products in 2022 to promote the economic independence of women in Xihe County, and provided women in Xihe County with more opportunities to participate in social activities. In 2021, Idol Group Co., Ltd organized the "Rural Revitalization Fine Goods Festival", and established enterprise village partnership with Sanghoyila（15）Village, Arele Township, Shache County, Kashi

Prefecture, Xinjiang, and Liuku Village, Liuku Town, Lushui City, Nujiang Lisu Autonomous Prefecture, Yunnan Province. The commodities of the "Rural Revitalization Fine Goods Festival" are mainly agricultural products from Xinjiang Shache, Yunnan Dali and Yunnan Nujiang. In addition to selling products on the platform, the Idol Group Co., Ltd live broadcast team also went to Yunnan and other places to perform on-site live broadcast to promote the local products. Idol Group Co., Ltd provides a long-term and sustainable Idol scheme through "one plus and one minus" and "one up and one down", in which "one plus" and "one up" refer to adding one store owner to each village, moving the rural agricultural products to upper link of value-chain, accurately matching the needs of farmers and consumers, and increasing the income of store owners; while the "one minus" and "one down" are to reduce the consumption cost a little, and at the same time let the industrial products go down to rural areas, so that consumers can get more cost-effective goods with less money. Idol Group Co., Ltd sold products at special prices that do not betray brand positioning, which can effectively promote the sinking of the sales market and bring employment opportunities for women living in third and fourth tier cities and rural areas.

4.1.4 The Platform Helps Women Find Jobs at Home and Balances the Gender Division of Labor

1) Realistic level — reducing the stereotype of female roles

First of all, balancing family and career is still an important obstacle to women's career development and a source of anxiety. In the contradiction between family life and participation in economic activities, the role of motherhood still leaves women in a dilemma. The digital economy can provide more new modes to meet the need of striking balance between family and work, and reduce women's inability to devote themselves to family care due to their career development, or their total withdrawal from the labor market due to family care. (Guan Jian, 2019). According to the survey of Idol platform, 96% of women in the platform are married, and 97.7% of them have children. However, more than 50% of women reflect that their spouses cannot share the responsibility of family care with them, which leaves them in the dilemma of taking care of their families and going out for employment. 63.9% of the women surveyed believe that they can freely arrange their time while running a business on the Idol platform, and 54.2% of the women think they can take care of their families at the same time. The development of digital technology makes the office space of enterprises freer from the restriction of geographical location, and home office has gradually become a new trend. This change can save commuting time and enable women to perform multiple work and life tasks at the same time. Besides, it can make full use of fragmented time to realize fast and flexible transformation of work and life roles. Flexible and free working methods are increasingly recognized by women and are becoming an important factor affecting women's choice of employment. Flexible time can solve women's work needs and balance the division of current family roles. Although the interviewed women cannot change the current division of labor in which they play more part as a care giver, flexible working hours can provide women with more work opportunities, realize their personal value and improve their family economic status on the premise of balancing the existing division of labor in the family roles.

Secondly, the development of the digital economy has also helped women reduce the burden on their families. The uses of Internet such as online shopping, placing takeout order and online payment of various bills can reduce the time of housework, enable women to devote more energy to work, and improve women's labor participation rate.

2) Spiritual level — promoting women's identification of self-worth

According to the survey, the job of store owners has a positive impact on the family life of the women interviewed. 52.6% of women surveyed said that the work of store owners had a positive impact on husband and wife relationship; 31.8% of women surveyed said that the work of store owners had a positive impact on parent-child relationship; 76.6% of women surveyed said that the work of store owners had a positive impact on self-identification; 46.0% of women surveyed said that the work of store owners had a positive impact on family status.

From the perspective of improving women's self-identification, a good store owner needs multiple abilities, such as interpersonal communication ability, customer demand identification ability, business promotion ability and video/picture shooting and processing ability. While promoting such an entrepreneurial work, it will enable women to enhance their sense of self-worth. Among the female store owners interviewed by Idol platform, 68.9% believed that the most outstanding significance of such a job was to enrich their lives, open up new career routes, enhance their sense of self-worth and learn new knowledge. Obtaining such a fulfilled sense of gain, 86.7% of the women will continue to work as store owners.

4.1.5 The Platform Explores the New Connotation of Women's Federation to Meet Women's Diversified Needs

The Shanghai Women's Federation closely follows the new development pattern, promotes high-quality development, provides services in the front line, and unites and mobilizes women to make contributions to the development of new technologies, new products, new formats and new models. Relying on the new economic e-commerce platform—Idol Group Co., Ltd, Shanghai Women's Federation has established the first platform women's federation in China, the Aikucun Women's Federation. Combined with the characteristics of the Idol platform, it is positioned as a platform women's federation.

The platform women's federation has the following organizational characteristics: ① In terms of participants, the platform women's federation is a women's organization for women participants in Internet platforms and women employees in enterprises. ② In terms of organizational form, the platform women's federation is a composite organizational system combining the online work network of women's federation and the offline organization network of women's federation. ③ In terms of leadership members, the executive committee members of the platform women's federation should be composed of women leaders, women employees and representatives of women participants in the platform supported enterprises. ④ In terms of institutional setting, the platform women's federation should build an integrated organization with mutual support between women's work and business work. ⑤ In terms of team building, the platform women's federation should build a cadre team composed of full-time, part-time and temporary.

In November 2020, Aikucun Women's Federation was officially established, a new type of women's federation for women participants in the platform and women employees of the enterprises, with the goal of promoting the healthy development of the platform and women's all-round development. Its specific work contents include: ① carry out online publicity and education, and explore the spiritual civilization path of online and offline interaction; ② give full play to the advantages of community economy, promote women's flexible employment and broaden the sales path of female entrepreneurs; ③ build a compound rights protection system, and do a good job in law popularization and rights protection for store owners; ④ establish the corresponding research mechanism and explore the working rules of women's federations under the new digital economy.

Store owners who started their own businesses in Idol Group Co., Ltd have a high awareness of gender equality as a whole. They believe that both genders should share the housework and agree that they have their own strengths. Relatively speaking, they do not agree with the view that "the development of the husband is more important than the development of the wife" and that "men should focus on society while women should focus on family". It can be seen that women in Idol Group Co., Ltd have a better awareness of gender equality and have a certain understanding of gender equality. In the context of a better awareness of gender equality, more women interviewed in Idol Group Co., Ltd hope that the Aikucun Women's Federation can carry out activities related to the protection of women's and children's rights and interests around employment information, public welfare activities, business training, childcare knowledge, etc. More than 90% of the women are willing to participate in the construction of Aikucun Women's Federation, and these women pay more attention to women's personal growth and employment activities.

4.1.6 Main Conclusions

1) Idol Group Co., Ltd lowers the threshold of flexible employment and provides women with digital technology empowerment

Idol Group Co., Ltd is a distribution e-commerce company that provides online digital stores and a full range of supply chain services for registered store owners, as well as online training on sales skills, product selection skills, community management, and platform customer service. These digital technologies are open to store owners at a low threshold. As long as the store owners have basic literacy and smart phone operation capabilities and are willing to invest a certain amount of energy and time, they can make full use of the digital technologies and services provided by Idol Group Co., Ltd and obtain considerable income. This is undoubtedly very helpful for female store owners to strengthen their digital technology empowerment.

2) Idol Group Co., Ltd breaks the time and space restrictions, allowing women to balance work and family

After establishing families, many women begin to live a tense life while switching between family and work. Especially after they have children, the limited time, energy and mental power often challenge women. Many women bear a lot of unpaid family work while taking the pressure of their own jobs. In order to better take care of their families, some women even choose to quit the workplace. You can even find women with higher education in these groups.

For women who take care of their families, the restrictions on time and space in the traditional workplace make them worry about returning to the workplace. The online flexible employment mode provided by Idol Group Co., Ltd can provide women with the way to balance family and career. While taking care of their families, many female store owners of Idol Group Co., Ltd can engage in their own digital distribution work at any time and place, and obtain economic income from it and spend on family consumptions. In this process, women have narrowed the income gap between themselves and men by means of digital economy, and even achieved a certain degree of income class leap through the digital platform.

3) Idol Group Co., Ltd formulates industry norms to protect the rights and interests of female store owners

As a leading distribution e-commerce enterprise, Idol Group Co., Ltd has strictly set the code of conduct and tax standards for digital distributors, which provides a safe career development environment for women engaged in digital distribution and is conducive to female store owners' long-term operation in the field of digital distribution. In Idol Group Co., Ltd, when the monthly income of the store owner exceeds 500 Yuan, the store owner must apply for the qualification of an individual business or enterprise, and pay taxes according to national regulations. This allows many full-time mom store owners to make tax contributions to social and economic development, demonstrating the power of "women are not inferior to men".

4) Idol Group Co., Ltd creates a platform women's federation to meet women's diverse needs in the digital age

Idol Group Co., Ltd serves about 3 million female store owners. In order to better meet the growth needs of female store owners, Idol Group Co., Ltd has established the first platform women's federation in China, the Aikucun Women's Federation. The Aikucun Women's Federation mainly makes efforts in six aspects, including the establishment of organizational system, online publicity and education, promotion of women's employment, balancing family and work, protection of women's rights and interests, and exploration of research mechanisms, to help women achieve breakthroughs in employment, entrepreneurship, rights and interests, ideological education, etc. in the digital age, and to help female store owners grow into better themselves, and make a unique voice in the digital age.

4.2   The Case of Ximalaya Inc.

Founded in 2012, Ximalaya Inc. is an online audio platform that grew up in the digital age. Its audio services cover user groups at different ages from 0 to 100.

It has accumulated 340 million pieces of audio content in 101 categories. In the first three quarters of 2022, Ximalaya had 282 million monthly active users on average across all scenarios. Ximalaya Inc. uses rich content related to knowledge, information, entertainment and other categories to accompany users and help them grow throughout their lives. It increases understanding and tolerance among people, and helps to develop a more diverse and inclusive society. As an accompanying media, Ximalaya Inc. has unique advantages in empowering women economically and psychologically. Women's voice is the main theme on Ximalaya. Women have achieved self-development through skill learning and voice entrepreneurship in Ximalaya; by expressing themselves and finding confidants, women have realized the exchange and collision of ideas. Ximalaya Inc. has become an important force to bridge the gender divide in the digital age.

4.2.1 Provides Women with Knowledge, Information and Spiritual Comfort

Tens of millions of women have kept listening to Ximalaya information and new knowledge. In the Ximalaya platform, female users are 47.6%, mainly post-80s women in the first and second tier cities. They like listening to audio book for entertainment, but also pay attention to childcare knowledge and personal growth knowledge. Ximalaya has selected a batch of audio content for women groups and created the XiBo Education platform to help women to learn. It also launched activities like "Super Emotion Festival" "Xi-Mother FreeDay" and other women specific activities, built exclusive communities for women, and provided basic elements for women of all walks of life and different ages to survive and develop in the digital age.

It provides women with companionship, spiritual comfort and spiritual nourishment. The female users in the Ximalaya platform cover women of different occupations, ages and regions, such as ordinary white-collar workers, assembly line workers, fast-food restaurant clerks, housewives, etc. The Ximalaya platform accompanied them with audio product, providing them with spiritual comfort, from which they find content and strength that can support them.

The digital age is also an age where people are prone to anxiety. Women who have long suffered from pressure of work and family care tend to have higher levels of anxiety, and female users' demand for spiritual nourishment to solve their life puzzles is increasing. According to Ximalaya's big data, relationship and breakup, marriage and family, and personal growth are popular categories highly demanded by female users. After nearly ten years of accumulation, the Ximalaya platform has collected millions of emotional albums to meet the emotional needs of female users. In October 2020, Ximalaya Inc. launched the first "Super Emotion Festival" activity, and invited its platform anchors and celebrities from all walks of life to participate. The activity initiated discussion of women's topic, shared women's growth experience, and helped with their personal growth.

4.2.2   Ximalaya Gives Full Play to Women's Advantages and Provides Women with New Career Opportunities

The Ximalaya platform gives full play to women's advantages in personal growth, parent-child, emotion, live audio broadcast and other content creation fields. The Ximalaya platform lets more women realize their self-worth through content creation and transmitting their voices. In 2021, Himalaya content creators reached 13.51 million, most of whom were women, far more than male streamers.

The Ximalaya platform empowers female creators. There are several hundred thousand active female creators in the Ximalaya platform every month, and the Ximalaya platform empowers these female creators from various aspects including using cloud editing and AI manuscript as tool empowerment; A+ audio publishing and the "Spring Sound Program" as resource empowerment; XiBo Education platform as education empowerment; and creating a female business department as the exclusive operation empowerment for female anchors.

The Ximalaya platform helps female creators to expand the industry chain of their content products by cooperating with other sectors. Young office workers account for nearly 50% of the monthly active female anchors of the Ximalaya platform, who take the creation on Ximalaya as a part-time job or business out of interest. The content created by female creators on the Ximalaya platform covers many fields such as parent-child, emotional life and personal growth, forming a diversified ecology. Especially in the fields such as parent-child, emotion and live audio broadcast, the scale and popularity of female creators are 20% ~ 30% higher than that of men all the year round. In order to further amplify the advantages and content influence of female creators, in October 2021, Ximalaya Inc. reached a strategic cooperation with China Women's Publishing House. The two sides mainly focused on copyright cooperation in content related to family education, women's social sciences and other categories, and are committed to creating high-quality and rich content for women to add value to their content.

4.2.3 Ximalaya Provides Women with New Vocational Education and Creates A System of "Integration of Industry and Education"

XiBo Education is the online education training and talent service brand established under Ximalaya Inc. With the brand mission of "no matter how small your life is, you can reveal your fragrance", XiBo Education explores in building a diversified vocational talent education system and provides users with lifelong vocational education and career planning services. So far, it has helped more than 2.51 million women access to new careers such as audio broadcasting. Coming from users, they are eager to speak up for themselves and are on the way to become a new force in the audio industry.

With the Ximalaya ecosystem as the core, XiBo Education cultivates women's new professional talents, so that women can adapt to new occupations and find new employment opportunities. XiBo Education adopts an online and offline teaching mode to enable students to broaden their interests, improve their professional quality and learn professional skills. Guided by the market demand and centered on ability cultivation, XiBo Education provides women students with new vocational education and new business education to complete the closed-loop from "study" to "employment", through Ximalaya official training programs such as "Voice Studio Training Camp" "Voice Book

Anchor Climbing Program".

XiBo Education has trained more than 3. 96 million students, and the proportion of women among monthly active students has reached more than 63%, much higher than that of men. Female trainees and contracted trainees are 26% higher than males. Among the more than 2.51 million female students in XiBo Education, more than 27% are mothers, nearly 34% are women aged 31~40, and nearly 43% are women in second-tier cities, hoping to learn new careers and find new opportunities.

Through flexible employment services, XlBo Education provides part-time opportunities for women and increases their sideline income. Despite the strict contract signing conditions in the Ximalaya platform, women accounted for 63% of the contracted trainees trained by XiBo Education. Through training, they realized their dreams, achieved self-breakthrough and gained both material and spiritual wealth.

On June 29, 2022, Shanghai Association of Women Entrepreneurs, together with XiBo Education, moved the offline job fair online and launched a special live recruitment session of "We are Waiting for People with Aspiration". The online job fair attracted more than 100 enterprises from Internet, medical, manufacturing, retail and other industries, and received more than 6 000 resumes. During the live job fair, the anchors and female entrepreneurs conducted online job recruitment and interacted with fans to solve the problems troubling female college students and women's secondary employment. This innovative way of live recruitment has opened up the online channels for women to seek employment, made the society focus more on women's employment, and helped more female job seekers connect with enterprises, fully reflecting the corporate social responsibility of Ximalaya Inc. to empower women.

4.2.4　Ximalaya Builds a Platform for Women to Communicate, Exchange and Help Each Other, and Make Female Voice Heard

Female ideas are exchanged and integrated to create a field atmosphere of

girls help girls. The female anchors on the Ximalaya platform include not just scholars, stars, media people, but also ordinary women. While striving hard for their own lives and careers, they also share knowledge, express views and inspire female users with their voices. Countless female users on Ximalaya have not only obtained high-quality content and creation, but also obtained companionship, comfort and the strength of growth. Female users tell their own stories and that of those around them to the creators, which is also a feedback to the creators. This kind of atmosphere where a creator is also a user, and users can also become creators, builds up a two-way incentive between women.

Ximalaya Inc. has set up a "Women's Business Department" within the company to work together with female anchors, creators and users to continuously create and release female oriented content and voice based on women's pain points in work, life and spiritual growth, and take "helping women to be better themselves" as Ximalaya's continuous engagement.

Speaking for women through public welfare activities, and making continuous efforts to promote the formation of an inclusive social atmosphere that advocates gender equality. Since the establishment of Ximalaya Inc., many excellent female anchors have grown up and set an example for users. Stories from female users were collected and spread. Through each of Ximalaya's female-oriented activities, female stories, voices and views were spread, so as to infect more people. Through integrating women's pain points and demands in life and career, Ximalaya has joined hands with female anchors, creators and women from all walks of life to speak for women, such as "Super Festival of Sentiment" "Her Tavern" "Xi-Mother FreeDay" and other brand activities, which have become industry benchmarks, with tens of millions of participants and hundreds of millions of views.

On the International Women's Day every year, the Ximalaya platform speaks out for promoting gender equality in the form of thematic activities, creates female role models and helps women grow. On March 8, 2020, Ximalaya released a public welfare poster of "honoring the power of women's voices" to show the contribution and strength of women to the whole society, pay tribute to ordinary but great women under the epidemic, and create female role models. On March 8, 2021, Ximalaya launched a special activity, named "Accompanied by You, Women's Growth Plan" to accompany and stimulate women's growth with high-quality content and spiritual nourishment. On March 8, 2022, Ximalaya launched a special activity, named "Hear Her Voice", to provide a voice channel for ordinary women to showcase themselves and convey the positive attitude that the voice of every woman is worth hearing. During the same period, Ximalaya Inc. released videos and declarations that express women's attitudes. Ximalaya focuses on the hot female topics in society, appeals to society to pay attention to the growth and development of women and to identify the value of women, and encourages women to break gender bias and live their own lives. In addition, Ximalaya organizes live broadcast and discussion on women's topics to provide voice channels for women. From March 8 to March 13, 2022, Ximalaya's live studio launched several live audio broadcasts and discussions on the theme of women's power. Users expressed their views on women's topics, and uploaded audio content to the Ximalaya platform, so as to raise society's attention to women's issues. Ximalaya also cooperates with famous brands to enlarge the voice of gender equality. Ximalaya Inc., together with L'Oreal Paris, launched the "I Say I'm Worth It" campaign to encourage every woman to recognize herself and live with confidence; together with Suning (a large family electronic product retailer), Ximalaya solicited audio works with the theme of "Women's Power is Worth being Seen" from all walks of life to record and publicize the contributions of women to family and society, and conveyed the concept of gender equality through audio.

4.2.5   Ximalaya Helps Women Share the Dividend of the Digital Age

Ximalaya helps women with different career starting points to find a career they love, and explores the commercial value of female anchors. Tens of thousands of grassroots women have grown up on Ximalaya, found their own career, accompanied and helped others with their voices, and realized their own values.

Ma Yinqing, a woman in Shanghai, is a visually impaired female anchor.

She worked as a host on the Ximalaya platform, and established an audio book broadcasting company to start her own business. Three quarters of Ma Yinqing's employees are visually impaired. Ma Yinqing broke the secular prejudice, and with an optimistic and sunny attitude and perseverance, she found a place for herself in the world of voice, and helped and inspired many visually impaired partners. In September 2021, Ma Yinqing was listed on the 2021 Forbes China 30 Under 30 list and was the only voice entrepreneur listed in 2021.

Voice anchor "Miss Good Morning" has developed from a rookie to an entertainment anchor, and has seized the opportunity to enter the field of audio book broadcasting. At present, she has nearly one million fans on Ximalaya, and her audio works have been played for over 610 million times. In 2017, Miss Good Morning set up a team, and established her own audio content studio. Its annual revenue reached millions of Yuan, making her one of the most commercially valuable anchors on Ximalaya in 2020.

Numerous female scholars, stars and media people have joined hands with Ximalaya to make female voices and tell stories about women. Many female anchors on Ximalaya, such as Li Yinhe, a sociologist, and Su Qin, an emotional expert, are outstanding women in their respective fields. On Ximalaya, they inspire and encourage others through audio content, enlighten the audience, and demonstrate the power of contemporary women. They are followed and recognized by their fans, and their careers have developed a second growth curve.

Ximalaya helps women realize social values and gain social recognition. Female creators on Ximalaya have created a number of albums with a cumulative play times of over 100 million, covering content related to children, emotions, music, entertainment and other categories, accompanying and helping countless listeners to grow, and affecting hundreds of millions of listeners. **Ximalaya helps women recognize themselves and become more fulfilled and confident.** When using Ximalaya, female users generally feel they are " gaining strength " "becoming fulfilled " " growing independent " " becoming confident " and "becoming a better person". In the process of learning and training, female students on Ximalaya gradually awaken their new professional consciousness. They constantly overcome themselves, lean closer to their ideal selves step by step, and realize greater life value through Ximalaya.

4.2.6　Main Conclusions

The online audio platform Ximalaya, which grew up in the digital age, provides women with rich knowledge products and helps them overcome the knowledge and information divide in the digital age. Such spiritual nourishment helps women alleviate their anxiety toward survival and establish an active and healthy lifestyle. The XiBo Education platform of Ximalaya Inc. provides women with new vocational education opportunities, enabling them to master new vocational skills in the digital age, find new jobs suitable for themselves, and bridge the gender career divide in the digital age. Ximalaya empowers female anchors and content creators, helps them to make full use of their advantages in content creation and supports women from different career starting points to find a career they love, realize greater social value, and share the dividends of the digital age. Ximalaya gathers women's voices and builds a platform for women to communicate, exchange and help each other. It delivers the concept of gender equality to society, and helps women work together to transcend the gender divide.

4.3　Digital Transformation Empowered by Women in Technology of MS Energy

Globally, women in technology have always been pioneers, innovators and participants in the cause of ecological environmental protection. During China's ecological civilization construction, women exhibit extraordinary innovation and leadership with their unique delicacy, carefulness and meticulousness in promoting energy transformation, power structure reform and high-quality green development of China's economy and society.

With the implementation of China's carbon peaking and carbon neutrality goals, energy reform has become the main battlefield, and electricity upgrading has become the main driving force. Whether it is energy, energy storage or power, careful, scientific and systematic implementation plans are required. Founded in 2018, MS Energy is a national high-tech enterprise focusing on "blood level" battery safety pre-diagnosis technology and providing customers with comprehensive solutions for green energy assets. Based on China's carbon peaking and carbon neutrality strategy, the company is a "dual unicorn" enterprise in the field of digital energy and energy storage security.

4.3.1　A Long Way to Go Before Achieving Carbon Peaking and Carbon Neutrality, and Women in Technology Shall Lead the Way

Ms. Wei Qiong, the chairman of MS Energy, is not only a female entrepreneur who highly values science and technology, but also a senior practitioner in the field of new energy, fully demonstrating the leading role of women in technology. Before founding MS Energy, she participated in the preparation of major industry reports such as the electric power planning of the "13th Five-Year Plan" and Shanghai Municipal Government Information. She was responsible for more than 16 major projects such as electric power research, infrastructure, and technological transformation. She engaged in the preparation, construction and operation of more than 10 regional landmark key new energy projects, and played a leading role in promoting the national green energy reform and traditional power reform. After the establishment of MS Energy, Ms. Wei Qiong gathered outstanding talents from the world and led MS Energy to complete a number of major development breakthroughs in the fields of scientific and technological innovation, business, finance and team building.

1) Give full play to the advantages of women in technology, and achieve a number of industry-leading technological breakthroughs

MS Energy creates a fair platform and environment for female employees, gives full play to the advantages of women in technology, and stimulates everyone's internal goals to grow together with the company's goals. Every man and woman can achieve self drive, self appreciation, and self evolution. More than 30% of MS Energy employees are female, including managers and front-line employees in key positions such as algorithm engineering, project management and marketing.

By giving full play to the strength and advantages of women in technology, the MS Energy scientific research team independently developed the battery safety Prognostic Safety System (PSS), which can detect potential battery problems 15 days in advance and prompt for preventive measures, realizing "prevention before fire", exclusively solving the problem of battery safety, the pain point of the energy storage industry, and ensuring the safe and stable operation of energy storage assets. At present, PSS has been successfully applied to many demonstration energy storage power stations in China, such as the UK Minety battery storage project, the largest overseas energy storage power station built by China, Nanjing Jiangbei Power Station, the first largest energy storage power station to be used in a cascade manner in China on the grid side, and Huaibei Anhui Energy Storage Power Station Phase I, the largest energy storage project in Anhui. This product fills the market gap in the domestic energy storage field. In 2021, the PSS system, as an application part of an important research and development project, won the first prize of the National Grid Science and Technology Progress Award, which is one of the most valuable awards in science and technology in the national power industry. In addition, it also won the second prize of the Invention and Entrepreneurship Award of the China Association of Invention and the second prize of the Science and Technology Award of the China Electrotechnical Society.

2) Utilize the influence of women in technology to link commercial and financial resources, and help science and technology to become self reliant

Using their communication skills and strong resource integration ability, women in technology help MS Energy build a solid competitive barrier for its development, make active exploration in promoting and practicing green and low-carbon development, and become an important "her force".

In order to ensure the R&D development of MS Energy and inject capital momentum into enterprise innovation, under the leadership of Ms. Wei Qiong, MS Energy has made full use of the influence of women in technology in linking commercial and financial resources. Since March 2021, MS Energy has obtained five rounds of risk investment from angel round to round C. Investors include Sequoia Capital, Source Code Capital, Junlian Capital, Hong Kong New World Group, Granite Global Ventures and other top investment institutions. The total amount of financing has reached hundreds of millions Yuan, and has been supported by a number of prestigious investment companies to build a 10 billion level special green energy fund to comprehensively help green low-carbon strategy and serve the Scientific and Technological Powerhouse strategy.

4.3.2 Eliminate the Stereotype of Women in the Workplace and Improve the Sense of Gain of Women Employees in the Digital Transformation

The digital transformation causes the work with high physical labor intensity, high repeatability and high risk gradually to be replaced by equipment. Creative work has gradually become the mainstream of jobs in enterprises. As a high-tech enterprise, MS Energy gathers the strength of women, balances the workplace ecology, and provides all men and women with more creative and rewarding jobs, so that both men and women can fully release their value and build an ecosystem where they can perform their own duties, drive themselves and make progress together.

Scientific and technological innovation is a competitive field based on intelligence. More and more women are based in high-tech industries, and with strong anti pressure ability, careful overall thinking ability, and excellent R&D breakthrough ability, they demonstrate the irreplaceable nature of women in technology. In the recruitment of talents, MS Energy does not set limits on gender, but pays attention to the balance between men and women in the team, and provides rich employment opportunities for women. In terms of talent cultivation, MS Energy provides equal resources and mechanisms to stimulate the team to grow together; in terms of the use of talents, the company is achievement-oriented and provides women with a large number of performance opportunities and display stages. At present, 30% of MS Energy female employees are in high-level manager positions.

4.3.3 Establish a Learning Incentive and Intellectual Property Protection Mechanism to Help Women Maximize Their Self-worth

1) Implement the "scholarship" system, build a learning organization, and help women grow

In order to better help men and women to grow together, MS Energy has established an employee scholarship system, which provides one-time bonus and monthly subsidy based on different levels of professional skills learning, and takes the learning achievements as an important basis for salary adjustment, promotion and evaluation, so as to encourage employees to actively recharge themselves and improve their knowledge reserves and working ability despite busy and fulfilled work.

The implementation of the "scholarship" system has effectively promoted the construction of a learning culture inside MS Energy, created a positive organizational atmosphere, and enabled female employees to eliminate worries about learning and growth in the workplace and their financial pressure. Thus they can devote more energy to their own skills improvement, and broaden their career development channel. Inspired by the "scholarship" system, the female employees of MS Energy realized more efficient production, more breakthrough innovation, and common growth of themselves and the company by carrying out skill learning and actively transforming their learning achievements.

2) Implement the "intellectual property" incentive policy to encourage women to participate in scientific and technological innovation

MS Energy promotes the protection of intellectual property and strengthens women's awareness of intellectual property protection. In order to improve the company's scientific research and innovation capability and intellectual property management level, MS Energy released the *Incentive Measures for Intellectual Property Application* in July 2022, encouraging all employees to participate in the writing, application and management of patents, software copyright and other intellectual property rights. The implementation of this system effectively encourages more women to participate in scientific and technological innovation, guarantees women's scientific research achievements, provides very important long-term value for women's career promotion and future development, and plays a significant incentive role in the scientific research of MS Energy. Up to now, the company has accumulated more than 300 intellectual property rights and invention patents, of which a considerable part was completed by women.

4.3.4 Build a Comfortable and Caring Workplace Environment to Provide Female Employees with All-round Job Security

MS Energy has always upheld and improved the protection mechanism for the rights and interests of female employees, with the purpose of "making them feel secure, warm and comfortable", to provide female employees with an excellent working environment and job security.

1) Attach importance to the introduction of high-tech talents and help female talents settle down

In the process of talent introduction, MS Energy broke the gender bias, treating men and women with equal opportunities and fair treatment. As a result, a large number of female talents that studied abroad and graduated from domestic colleges and universities joined MS Energy. MS Energy closely follows the settlement (Hukou) policy in Shanghai, actively strengthens communication with the government, strives for more settlement quotas for female employees, helps more female employees successfully settle down in Shanghai, and eliminates the worries of women's development in Shanghai. In 2021, MS Energy actively applied to the relevant departments of Songjiang District Government for adopting the applicable principle of "talents in key fields of high-tech industrialization" of the talent introduction strategy of Shanghai to the company. As a result, MS Energy successfully helped the first batch of talents to settle down in Shanghai, made it possible for its female employees' children to study in Shanghai, and improved the balance between their family and work.

2) Provide women with equal promotion channels and flexible job transfer mechanisms to meet their career development needs

The proportion of female talents in MS Energy is getting higher and higher, and female employees have shown excellent business and leadership skills. The equal promotion mechanism allows female employees to participate in senior position competition through a clear path, opening up unlimited space for female career development.

Based on the change of their own cognition and the need to balance work and life, employees usually want to adjust the job content while keeping their work stable. MS Energy provides employees with a flexible job transfer mechanism, so that women can not only find their own position in the workplace, but also ensure the realization of value.

3) Provide women with comprehensive employment security to better balance family and career

MS Energy stipulates that female employees can enjoy a variety of holidays, including statutory holidays, annual leave, marriage leave, maternity leave, parental leave, sick leave, personal leave, etc., as well as regular free physical examination, holiday care, birthday care, etc., to provide women with all-round life care. In the early, middle and late stages of female childbearing, MS Energy pays close attention to the physical and mental health of female employees, provides them with competitive remuneration, guarantees their career development, and makes adjustment preparations for the return of female employees after childbirth, so as to help them return to the workplace more quickly.

4.3.5　Main Conclusions

MS Energy gives full play to the leading role of women in technology on the carbon peaking and carbon neutrality track, realizes industry leading technological breakthrough, linking technological innovation with financial resource, and helps enterprises stand at the forefront of energy technology. In talent recruitment, training and promotion, MS Energy gathers women's strength, provides women with rich employment opportunities and clear career promotion paths, eliminates women's stereotype in the workplace, and balances the workplace ecology. By using incentive mechanisms such as "scholarship" and "intellectual property", MS Energy helps women release their potential, improve their R&D capability, upgrade their skills and maximize their self-worth. By providing female employees with a reassuring and caring workplace environment, MS Energy enables women to choose their own career development channels based on their own advantages and potential, so as to achieve the unity of employee growth and company development, the unity of company development and market demand, and explore more "her power" in technological progress and digital transformation.

Chapter V

International Experience or Lessons on Bridging the Gender Divide in the Development of Digital Economy

Bridging the gender divide in the digital economy age is a shared challenge for all of humanity, requiring collaborative efforts from all countries in the world and all sectors of society. It's important to adopt a global perspective rather than confining the understanding to a single city or nation. By drawing insights from the experiences of other countries, we can more effectively promote gender equality and empower women in the digital age. This chapter will examine the international community's understanding of gender equality in the digital era, analyze cases of international organizations and enterprises worldwide working to bridge gender gaps in various aspects, and sum up the international experiences in bridging the gender divide in the digital age.

5.1 International Community's Understanding of Gender Equality in the Digital Age

Opportunities and challenges coexist in the digital age. The development and application of digital technology make human production and life more convenient, and also bring a wide range of digital dividends. Although digitalization has created new production and living spaces, the distribution of digital elements among the population is uneven, and people's mastery of digital tools varies. Some groups do not fully enjoy the digital dividend, and inequality related to digitalization has emerged. In the digital age, gender inequality remains a major challenge to achieving inclusive and sustainable development.

5.1.1 Approach Female Digital Inclusion

Achieving gender equality is essential to promoting inclusive and sustainable development in the digital age. Women should not be left out of the digital age. Instead, women should fully participate in economic and social activities in the digital age and fully integrate into the learning, development and application of digital technology. Gender equality is an important driving force for promoting inclusive and sustainable development in the digital age. Only if women were able to participate in and integrate into the digital world equally, could they make due contributions to digital transformation and technological innovation.

Digital inclusion approaching women is an important aspect of promoting inclusive and sustainable development. In recent years, the international community has fully realized the importance of gender equality for achieving inclusive and sustainable development in the digital age, and accelerated the global pace of bridging the digital gender divide. In September 2016, "EQUALS", a global partnership for gender equality in the digital age, was jointly launched by the International Telecommunication Union (ITU), the UN Women, the Global System for Mobile Communications Association (GSMA), the International Trade Center (ITC), and the UN University. It is committed to promoting gender equality in the field of technology and striving to bring women the same Internet connectivity, skills development and career opportunities that men enjoy. In 2017, during Germany's presidency of the G20, G20 member countries joined hands with the United Nations Educational, Scientific and Cultural Organization (UNESCO), the UN Women, ITU, and OECD to launch the G20 "eSkills4Girls" initiative, which has taken an important step towards "digital inclusion of women and girls". Its goal is to increase the participation of women and girls in the digital world on a global scale, and improve relevant education and employment opportunities. In September 2020, the United Nations Development Programme (UNDP) and the UN Women launched the COVID − 19 global gender response tracking to analyze the economic and social security measures provided by countries for women and ensure that the impact of COVID − 19 is addressed in a gender equal manner.

As an important platform to promote women's economic empowerment, UNIDO follows on women in the context of digital development. Fully aware of the importance of promoting gender equality and women's empowerment in achieving inclusive and sustainable industrial development, UNIDO is committed to addressing gender inequality in industry and promoting inclusive growth. UNIDO's Strategy for Gender Equality and the Empowerment of Women 2020 − 2023 clearly states that "the essence to achieve inclusive and sustainable industrial development and sustainable development goals (SDGs) lies at gender equality and women's empowerment".

UNIDO advocates a people-centered approach to promote inclusive and sustainable industrial development through digitalization, so that all people can benefit from industrialization and digitalization. In June 2021, with the financial support of the Government of Finland, UNIDO has launched its new "UNIDO Guide to Gender Analysis and Project Gender Mainstreaming", which takes UNIDO's Country Programmes (CPs), Programmes for Country Partnership (PCPs) and other important projects as examples to illustrate that industrial development projects can be designed with gender equality as the goal, and that the mutual promotion between industrial development and gender equality will be realized in the end.

5.1.2 Build A Systematic System to Bridge the Digital Gender Divide

Bridging the digital gender divide requires systematic efforts of international organizations, governments, enterprises and non-profit organizations. International organizations promote the international community to reach a consensus on gender equality, which serves as a bridge and link to promote cooperation among governments, enterprises and non-profit organizations. Globally, developed countries are at the forefront of digital technology development and digital transformation, while developing countries are lagging behind in digital promotion.

International organizations have introduced effective measures taken by developed countries to promote digitalization into underdeveloped regions, enabling outstanding global enterprises to help underdeveloped regions improve Internet infrastructure, and playing an important role in promoting the global popularization of digital education and digital skills training.

Governments are responsible for formulating gender equality action plans and coordinating the efforts of different sectors. Different countries are at different stages of digital development. The main tasks they face in promoting gender equality in the digital age are different, and there are also some differences in their implementation strategies. For example, less developed countries pay more attention to the construction of Internet infrastructure and the popularization of mobile Internet devices, while developed countries pay more attention to the growth of women digital skilled talents and give play to women's role in scientific and technological innovation.

Enterprises stand on the front line of digital transformation, and promoting gender equality, which also reflects corporate social responsibility, is conducive to the long-term development of enterprises. In terms of digital technology development orientation and the formulation of digital technology standards, ICT enterprises should maintain gender sensitivity, establish gender neutral awareness, and timely identify and solve gender discrimination in technology development. Enterprises in the non-ICT field should actively integrate gender perspective into employment and talent training, customize career planning for female employees, and help female employees prepare for digital transformation by supporting skills upgrading (upskill) and cultivating new skills (reskill), so as to promote gender equality and inclusiveness in the profession field.

Compared with the government and enterprises, non-profit organizations (NPOs) gather women in different fields of society, which can better respond to the needs of women in the digital age. NPOs unite with international organizations, governments and enterprises to promote women's empowerment, so that women's rights and interests can be more fully protected and more development opportunities can be obtained. For example, NPOs such as Girls Who Code and Code First Girls cooperate with all parties to carry out digital skills training for women, build women's communities, promote women's empowerment in the digital age, and narrow the gender digital skills gap, which have made important contributions to changing gender inequality in the field of technology.

5.2   Bridging the Gender Divide in Internet Access and Use

5.2.1   Equal Access to the Internet Is the First Step to Bridge the Digital Gender Divide

The Internet is an important infrastructure in the digital age, and everyone should have equal access to and use of the Internet. Globally, because of social prejudice, women have less access to Internet devices and fewer opportunities to make full use of the Internet than men. Some women cannot be covered by the Internet because they live in remote areas with underdeveloped digital infrastructure. Some women cannot afford the access to the Internet because their families are poor. For various reasons, women are excluded from the digital world and are unable to connect with the Internet, resulting in limitations on their access to knowledge, information, education, medical and financial services, which has a negative impact on their personal development, as well as the inclusive and sustainable development of the whole society. Therefore, removing the barriers preventing women's access to and use of the Internet and reducing gender inequality in access to and use of Internet resources are the key steps to bridge the digital gender divide and move towards digital equality.

5.2.2   International Experience and Cases

Equal access to digital technology is the first step towards gender equality and empowerment of all women and girls. In today's world, smart phones are the most convenient and widely used Internet tools. Broadband with high transmission speed brings smartphone users better Internet experience. The cooperation between the government and the private sector to provide women with smartphones and high-speed broadband at lower prices or free of charge is the most effective way to narrow the gender divide in Internet access and use.

1) Case of international organizations: Basic Digital Basket

In developing countries, gender inequality in Internet connectivity is caused by incomplete Internet infrastructure, low Internet coverage, high price of mobile broadband, and social prejudice against women's access to digital technology. In 2021, UN Women, the International Labour Organization (ILO) and the Economic Commission for Latin America and the Caribbean (ECLAC) put forward the concept of "basic digital basket", that is, to provide "basic digital basket" that includes mobile phones, laptops, flat-panel computers and Internet connectivity for women who do not have Internet connectivity, so as to bridge the digital gender divide. The introduction of the concept of "basic digital basket" shows that international organizations and governments are fully aware of the importance of Internet connectivity to women's empowerment and propose a package of solutions to comprehensively bridge the gender divide of Internet connectivity.

2) Case of enterprises: Microsoft Airband Initiative

Whether women have adequate connectivity to Internet is the direct manifestation of the digital gender divide. In recent years, important Internet technology enterprises in the world have supported less developed countries and regions to accelerate Internet infrastructure construction and reduce Internet access costs, playing an important role in promoting Internet coverage, which reflects the social responsibility of enterprises in bridging the digital divide and the digital gender divide. Microsoft Airband Initiative is committed to bringing the Internet to more women around the world, enabling women to have equal access to and use of digital technology services, and bridging the digital gender divide.

5.3 Bridging the Gender Divide in Digital Skills Education

Popularizing digital literacy for girls matters to the future of digitalization.

Adolescence is the best time to develop women's digital potential. Today's girls who study in the digital technology field are the future female talents to engage in the technology industry. In the past, due to social prejudice, family and social investment in girls' education, especially in the STEM field, was insufficient, resulting in only a small number of adult women graduating from STEM today. In the future, if we want more women to enter the STEM field and leverage their potential in the STEM field, we should first change today's education model and put gender equalization of digital education in an important position to narrow the digital gender divide.

5.3.1 The Importance of Universal Digital Education for Girls

The empowerment of women in the digital age is the first and foremost empowerment of education. Due to the limitations of social expectations and inherent norms, the proportion of girls entering STEM or ICT related learning and vocational fields is significantly lower than that of men. In fact, girls' interest in learning and exploring STEM fields is no less than boys', and girls' learning ability is no inferior to boys'. As long as society breaks the biased cognition of girls' learning technology and provides girls with the same learning resources and platforms as with boys, girls' performance in the scientific field, will be more outstanding. Encouraging and supporting girls to receive digital literacy education provides guidance for their future career, which not only helps to break the digital gender divide, build a female digital talent pool, but also creates a more inclusive and sustainable world in the future.

5.3.2 International Experience and Cases

Breaking the gender divide in digital education is the direction of national efforts. In the past, local schools limited educational resources and training bases for girls. In the digital age, with the emergence of online education platforms, educational resources, including tutors and teaching materials, have been shared globally. Even girls in poor and backward areas have the opportunity to access the best course resources in STEM fields through online education platforms, interact with excellent teachers, and learn together with teenagers from other regions. This is an important opportunity to bridge the gender divide brought about by the development of digital technology. Using digital technology tools to overcome the digital gender divide will not only effectively change the future of women, but also imperceptibly change the inherent social prejudice against women's access to technical education and work in the technical field.

1) Case of international organizations: African Girls Can Code Initiative

Africa is the region with the weakest digital infrastructure and relatively backward digital literacy. UN Women, together with the African Union Commission (AUC) and the International Telecommunication Union (ITU), implemented the African Girls Can Code Initiative to train African girls in their programming and digital skills. In 2018—2021, the first phase of the African Girls Can Code Initiative was completed, which taught digital knowledge and skills to over 600 girls and gave them the opportunity to pursue ICT education and innovation.

In 2022, UN Women, AUC, ITU, the United Nations Educational, Scientific and Cultural Organization (UNESCO), the United Nations Economic Commission for Africa (UNECA) and the United Nations International Children's Emergency Fund (UNICEF) utilized their respective expertise to launch the second phase of the African Girls Can Code Initiative (AGCCI) in Tanzania. The second phase is committed to teaching 2 000 African women and girls aged 17~25 digital knowledge and skills in 4 years, providing them with opportunities to step into the ICT sector in the future.

2) Case of enterprises: IBM (STEM for Girls)

The "STEM for Girls" initiative launched by IBM India is committed to improving STEM education for girls, paving the way for girls' future careers from computer programming, digital skills learning, vocational guidance, social skills learning, etc. At the same time of STEM education for girls, educators and parents are also trained, so as to further change the society's view and understanding of girls receiving technical education.

5.4 Bridging the Gender Divide in Digital Skill Jobs

Women can be both users of digital technology and promoters of digital technology development. At present, the inadequate development and utilization of female workers' digital skills have hindered the development of women's innovative potential, and also caused gender occupational division and gender wage gap.

The gender divide in digital skill jobs requires enterprises to join hands with female employees. Gender equality and gender tolerance in the workplace determine the career development of female employees. If the enterprise can give women equal career development opportunities from the perspective of gender equality, pay attention to the skill investment of female employees, and support female employees to return to the workplace smoothly after childbirth, it will actually achieve a "win-win", which not only guides and supports the career development of female employees, but also has a positive impact on the long-term development and cultural shaping of the enterprise.

5.4.1 Women's Employment and Inclusive Workplace in the Digital Age

Under the traditional economic conditions, women's workplace dilemmas are mainly manifested in the unequal opportunities to enter the labor market, the unfriendly working environment for women, the difficulty in balancing the work and family responsibilities in the workplace, and the heavy resistance to women's career development. In the digital age, the application of automation technology saves manpower, and requires workers to have the ability to program and control digital equipment. Women do not have an advantage in this regard. In textile, clothing, food processing and other labor-intensive industries where female employment is more concentrated, the risk of "machine replacement" is higher. Confronted by the dual challenge of workplace difficulties and lag of digital skills, it is more difficult for women to survive and develop in the workplace.

The COVID − 19 epidemic has made the employment environment for women more fragile. On the one hand, as the epidemic has accelerated the digital transformation, women performing routine tasks on the assembly line are exposed to a higher risk of unemployment. On the other hand, due to the quarantine measures forced by the epidemic, the burden of childcare and housework in the family increased, further squeezing women's labor time investment, and some women were forced to leave the workplace. In the post epidemic age, it is more urgent to establish an inclusive, sustainable and resilient digital age.

5.4.2 Establish Lifelong Learning and Skill Improvement System

In the traditional economy, women are mainly employed in non-STEM fields. In the digital age, technological progress represented by automation and artificial intelligence will significantly change enterprises and future jobs, and workers' digital skills will have an important impact on enterprises' labor productivity and competitiveness. Women who cannot keep up with the requirements of digital skills will face the risk of being replaced by automation and eliminated from the labor market. Therefore, helping women to build their abilities and develop their skills is an important aspect of empowering women in the digital age.

1) Case of international organizations: ILO's skill development project for women in STEM fields

It is an important part in women's empowerment to help women obtain equal employment opportunities and improve employment quality through digital skills training. In 2017 − 2021, the International Labour Organization (ILO) cooperated with J.P. Morgan Chase Foundation to launch a 4-year working skill development project for women in STEM fields in Indonesia, Thailand, and Philippines. The project aims to empower women by improving their acquisition and utilization of relevant technical skills and soft skills in STEM fields.

The project designs and provides targeted skills development plans, employability training plans and courses according to women's working ability characteristics and their career development needs. For female graduates receiving vocational education, pre-employment technical skills and employment skills training are provided to help them enter STEM related fields for employment. For women who are not fully employed in primary posts in STEM, their skills are to be upgraded to help them achieve higher quality employment in STEM and expand their career prospects. For women working in STEM fields with medium-level skills, high-level technical skills and management skills training are provided to promote them to higher positions.

2) Case of enterprises: LinkedIn Learning online learning platform

With the rapid development of digital technology, women should keep learning and be ready to update their skills at any time. Enterprises actively invest in lifelong learning and actively support women to upgrade skills and learn new skills, which will help women acquire new skills to adapt to the digital economy. In recent years, with the promotion of digital technology, education and training have moved from offline to online, and LinkedIn Learning and other learning platforms are widely available. The platform provides a large number of professional skill learning and training courses for learners to study on their own. The platform also cooperates with enterprises to help professionals improve their skills. The extensive application of online learning platform breaks the time and space constraints of learning and training, helps learners to choose learning content independently and flexibly arrange learning progress, reduces learners' learning costs and enterprises' training costs, and helps women to bridge the divide of digital knowledge and skills to a certain extent.

5.4.3 Support Women to Balance Family and Career in All Aspects

Traditional ideas hold that women should bear the main responsibility of childcare and family care, resulting in women's less time and energy investment in career than men. Helping women realize the balanced development of family and career, is conducive to developing their career potential and the development of enterprises and society. Family-friendly policies and flexible working arrangements are important aspects in promoting gender equality. However, the implementation of family-friendly policies and flexible working arrangements requires the joint efforts of the government and enterprises.

1) Case of international organizations: family-friendly workplace certification

UNICEF Australia, together with other partners, has jointly developed a set of family-friendly workplace certification standards to provide guidance for building family-friendly workplaces, which not only protects the rights and interests of women and children, but also promotes gender equality in the workplace. Enterprises that have obtained family-friendly workplace certification not only create conditions for women to balance their professional and family responsibilities, but also build an inclusive and diverse workplace culture, which is conducive to attracting and retaining female talents, as well as improving the social fertility rate.

2) Case of enterprises: Google Next Innings Program

Women may leave their jobs for a period of time due to childcare and family care during their career. When the family affairs are settled, they hope to return to the workplace again. In the digital age, with the updating and iteration of technology and the rapid flow of job roles, these women will face certain difficulties in returning to the workplace. Women need some support from enterprises or organizations to guide them to learn new skills on the original basis, and to adapt to new roles and obtain job opportunities.

Helping women maintain a harmonious relationship between family care and labor employment is a direct reflection of gender inclusiveness and social responsibility of enterprises. It is also conducive to attracting and retaining women talents, giving full play to the creativity of female talents, further enhancing the competitiveness and cohesion of enterprises, and winning social praise for enterprises. Take Google as an example. Google provides a 6-month paid training program "Google Next Innings Program" for women who want to return to the workplace. This program is specially provided to women who have taken more than 6 months leave and have at least 3 years of work experience, so as to provide transition and buffer for women to return to their posts. The program is equipped with experienced professionals for guidance, and trainees can get the opportunity to communicate with experts. As the training program is paid training, it can better motivate women to participate in training and eliminate women's concerns about the cost of training opportunities. With the guidance of the most experienced professionals, female trainees can learn new skills in the most effective way and return to the forefront of technology. At the end of the training period, the enterprise also provides women who receive training with the opportunity to re-enter full-time work. The program has formed full path support for women's reintegration into the workplace, encouraging more women to join the technology industry and retaining more female talents for the technology industry.

5.1.1   Encourage Women to Become Leaders and Innovators in the Digital Industry

Female leaders are role models of women groups, and the diversified, equal and inclusive workplace is the soil for cultivating female leaders. However, from a global perspective, the proportion of female leaders is still significantly lower than that of male. Especially in the technical field, women face more obstacles than men in their career development, which is not conducive to giving full play to the value and contribution of female talents to innovation and sustainable development. The gender divide in career development must be broken.

In terms of encouraging and supporting women to become leaders, enterprises must have a clear attitude and action plan to ensure that female employees have equal opportunities for career development and leadership positions with practical actions. These practices will promote the emerging of female talents and female role models, and better utilize women's advantages in technological innovation and management. It will also help the society gradually eliminate the prejudice against women leaders and entrepreneurs and form a more diversified, equal and inclusive society.

1) Case of international organizations: UNIDO digital business competence training program for female entrepreneurs

UNIDO highlighted the important role of women as entrepreneurs in achieving digital gender equality, and strengthened support for women entrepreneurs in capacity building. UNIDO has developed an online training course, named "Digital Business Innovations for Women Entrepreneurs and Managers", which mainly includes digital technology foundation, digital marketing, digital project management, e-commerce and other contents, and is committed to helping women capture the benefits of digital technology development.

2) Case of enterprises: HP Catalyst@ HP project

The gender imbalance in the technology field and the gender inequality in the career development path in this field do exist. But changing this situation and establishing a diversified, equal and inclusive career development environment will drive innovative thinking and solutions, which is the key for enterprises to gain competitive advantage in the digital age.

HP is a leading enterprise in the technology industry, and embracing diversity and inclusiveness is an important principle for HP's development. In 2021, HP proposed that by 2030, the proportion of women in leadership positions would increase from about 30% at present to 50%. In practice, HP has made many meaningful explorations in building a diversified and inclusive workplace and a career development environment conducive to women. HP launched the Catalyst@ HP project to support the career development of employees that lack representatives in technical and leadership positions (including female employees). The project requires participants to pair up with senior executives, who are responsible for supervising the career development of participants. Through the learning model of integration of training, practice and sharing, the project not only helps women and other project participants master the core skills of career development, but also helps them to successfully promote or enter new positions.

5.5 Develop Platform Economy to Enable Women's Employment and Entrepreneurship

5.5.1 Platform Economy Opens up New Space for Women's Employment and Entrepreneurship

The economic empowerment of women by platform economy is mainly reflected in two aspects. First, the emergence of e-commerce platforms has enabled women merchants to gain greater market development space, more efficient connection with customers and access to more commercial resources, which is conducive to fully tapping women's commercial potential and promoting women's economic independence. Second, the "part-time job economy" creates flexible employment options for women, supports women to maintain balance in work and family care, improves women's employment participation and economic capacity, and helps to improve the welfare of their families.

However, women's economic empowerment through the development of platform economy still faces some difficulties and obstacles. The inherent prejudices against female entrepreneurs still exist in current society. Women still face many entrepreneurial challenges, and female flexible workers are also being discriminated either intentionally or unintentionally. Women engaged in part-time job economy cannot get sound and perfect labor security on the labor employment platform, and the rights and interests of female workers are damaged by longer working hours and lower wages, which are all aspects that need to be improved and perfected in the future.

5.5.2 International Experience and Cases

1) Case of international organizations: UNIDO and IFAD use digital platforms to enable agricultural product value chain

In June 2021, UNIDO and the International Fund for Agricultural Development (IFAD) launched a project focusing on women and youth to enhance the fruit value chain through a digital platform, which is mainly implemented in Vietnam's Dong Thap Province and Ben Tre Province. Through the cooperation with local farmers to develop an intelligent agricultural model, the project connected small farmers with fruit wholesale and processing enterprises, opened up the value chain of Vietnamese agricultural products such as pomelo and mango, and empowered women and young people through digital platforms.

2) Case of enterprises: Facebook "SheMeansBusiness" project

Platform economy creates new business development space for women. And digital enterprises use platform resource advantages to support women to engage in online business operation, which is an important way to empower women economically in the digital age. The "SheMeansBusiness" project launched by Facebook is dedicated to helping female entrepreneurs engage in platform business operation, which can reach more consumers and avoid the high cost of running physical stores. Through the platform business operation training for female entrepreneurs, the project teaches women how to create a business operation homepage, how to conduct digital marketing, and how to communicate with consumers, so as to help women improve their platform business operation skills and integrate their commercial enterprises into the digital economy. By providing guidance with advanced financial knowledge and financial management methods, the project helps women entrepreneurs to master scientific operation and management methods and improve business operation resilience. The project has covered women in Asia Pacific, Europe, Latin America, Africa and other regions.

5.6   Summary of International Experience in Bridging Gender Divide in the Digital Age

5.6.1   The Voice and Response to Gender Equality in the Digital Age Are Stronger

All countries in the world are actively preparing for the digital transformation, but the digital transformation has not naturally eliminated gender inequality, and women are still at a disadvantage in the digital age. If we can realize that the gender divide in digital economy participation, digital education and digital skills has a negative impact on economic and social development, and take systematic and targeted measures to enable women and girls, so as to bridge the gender digital divide, we will benefit not only women and their families, but also facilitate digital transformation, and create greater development space and opportunities for mankind.

Digital empowerment of women is the core of achieving female digital inclusion. Whether it is the coverage of digital infrastructure, the configuration of digital elements, or the distribution of digital dividends, it should be considered and planned from the perspective of gender equality to ensure that the opportunities brought by digital transformation are equal and the dividends of digital transformation are shared.

5.6.2 The Main Experience in Bridging Gender Divide in the Digital Age

Digital inclusion of women is an important component of the digital inclusion framework. That the government, enterprises and social organizations put bridging the gender digital divide on the important development agenda is a positive attitude to enter the digital age and is conducive to the transformation of human society to an inclusive and sustainable digital age.

In terms of methods to promote gender equality, we should pay attention to adjusting measures to local conditions, while promoting the cooperation between international organizations, government departments, the private sector and social institutions, so as to accelerate the pace towards the goal of gender equality. In terms of specific content of gender equality promotion, we shall systematically promote the following aspects: providing women with digital equipment, popularizing digital literacy education for girls, and supporting women to keep up with the pace of digital transformation in entrepreneurship and employment.

First, the basis for bridging the gender divide in the digital age is ensuring that all women and girls have access to the Internet. The accessibility and affordability of the Internet shall be improved, so that all women and girls have accessible Internet access equipment and affordable broadband Internet. Only by connecting to the Internet can women and girls enter the digital world, obtain more and more extensive information, get better education and achieve higher income. Therefore, this is the first step to achieve gender digital equality.

Second, the long-term strategy to bridge the gender digital divide is popularizing digital literacy education among girls. Digital literacy education is a long-term investment. If women had built up interests in STEM and reached certain digital literacy during their adolescence, they would be future talents working in the area, which means the talent pool for the future development of digitalization would be enlarged. To enable women to enjoy equal digital education opportunities with men requires the joint efforts of schools, families and society. In the school curriculum, we should take the initiative to change the curriculum with gender bias. In terms of curriculum content and teaching methods, gender discrimination should be avoided and gender mainstreaming should be promoted. In terms of quality expansion outside school, girls should be given more opportunities to participate in practice, and girls should be encouraged to pursue digital technology content of interest. As the promoters and leaders of education, parents, teachers and society have an important impact on girls' digital education. Through lectures, training and other ways, parents, teachers and society can gradually reverse their prejudice against girls' digital education. Relevant parties shall work together to create a favorable education environment for girls, which will better support and help girls to obtain adequate digital literacy education.

Third, helping female entrepreneurs and employees prepare for digital transformation is the most direct way to reduce the negative effects of the gender digital divide. The negative impact of the gender digital divide on the economy and society is mainly manifested in the loss of female labor force and the waste of female innovative talents. The career performance and career development prospects of female workers in the digital field are not as good as those of male workers. This is not only related to women's family care responsibilities, but also to the inherent prejudice of society towards women's career development, as well as the lack of career development opportunities provided by enterprises for women. This also means that to bridge the divide between gender in the digital field's career performance and career development prospects, it is necessary to help women balance the relationship between family and work, provide women with broad career development opportunities and create a social environment suitable for women's entrepreneurship and employment.

First of all, in helping women balance career and family relations, the government and enterprises can make certain arrangements in terms of public policy and enterprise human resource management respectively. The government could actively develop public childcare, provide flexible childcare options for families, provide childcare subsidies for families, reduce the burden of childcare and family care for women, and advocate and promote men to assume the responsibility of childcare and family care from the social level, thus reducing women's worries for family so that they can focus more on career development. In helping women balance career and family relationships, enterprises should establish a diversified and inclusive corporate culture internally, while carefully considering the characteristics of female employee's work, and promote flexible working systems to allow flexible working arrangements such as telecommuting. Tailor career development plans for each female employee and give them necessary encouragement and support, which will minimize the loss of female employees, attract and retain female talents, and enhance the resilience of enterprise development.

Secondly, enterprises play an important role in providing women with equal and inclusive career development environment, and allowing women to enjoy equal rights to participate in the labor market and career development opportunities with men. In addition, an equal and inclusive workplace environment should be built and reflected in both the internal system design and the soft environment of the enterprise. Enterprises shall provide women with equal opportunities for career entry, on-the-job skills training and promotion. They shall not discriminate against women in recruitment and promotion because of pregnancy and childbirth. Instead, women shall be provided with equal opportunities for on-the-job skills learning and training. Necessary ability training shall also be provided for women workers to return to work after childbirth. Enterprises shall also establish family-friendly working models, such as flexible working system, telecommuting, etc., so as to provide a more friendly office environment for women, especially working mothers. A reasonable gender ratio shall be set for enterprise leadership positions. Enterprises shall create a corporate culture of gender equality and inclusiveness, regularly evaluate and audit the gender equality measures and results, and timely correct deviations.

Moreover, a business environment suitable for women's employment and entrepreneurship shall be created. The digital age has brought women new opportunities for employment and entrepreneurship. The government and enterprises shall provide women with new vocational education and new business education to adapt to the digital age, so that women can learn new skills and complete skill upgrading through open learning platforms and economically affordable skills training. Thus women's new vocational awareness will be awaken, after which they will actively grasp new career opportunities. Equal opportunities for entrepreneurship and development shall be provided to women entrepreneurs. Moreover, governments and enterprises shall provide women entrepreneurs with training of digital business ability and business management ability, help build a community of women entrepreneurs, and enable women to have more space in the field of employment and entrepreneurship, so as to better tap their potential and utilize their advantages.

Chapter VI

Prospective Analysis of Bridging the Gender Divide under the Trend of Metaverse

Metaverse is regarded as the representative of the next generation of space Internet and the main development direction of the future digital economy. In essence, Metaverse is a process of virtualization and digitalization of the real world, which requires massive transformation of content production, economic system, user experience and physical world content. This chapter will make a preliminary analysis of the impact on gender divide when the real world is marching toward Metaverse.

6.1 Concept and Development Orientation of "Metaverse"

6.1.1 Concept of "Metaverse"

Metaverse is a virtual world that is linked and created by scientific and technological means, mapped and interacted with the real world, and a digital living space with a new social system. Parallel to the real world, reaction to the real world and integration of various high technologies are the three characteristics of the future Metaverse. In essence, Metaverse is a process of virtualization and digitalization of the real world, which requires massive transformation of content production, economic system, user experience and physical world content. However, the development of the Metaverse is a step-by-step process. Supported by shared infrastructure, standards and protocols, it is formed by the continuous integration and evolution of many tools and platforms. It provides immersive experience based on extended reality technology, generates a mirror image of the real world based on digital twin technology, builds an economic system based on blockchain technology, closely integrates the virtual world with the real world in economic system, social system and identity system, and allows each user to produce content and edit the world[1]. According to Zuo Pengfei (2022), Metaverse will affect human life and economic and social development from the following aspects: first, further improve social production efficiency in terms of technological innovation and cooperation mode; second, create a series of new technologies, new formats and new models and transform traditional industries; third, promote the cross-border derivation of cultural and creative industries and greatly stimulate information consumption; fourth, reconstruct the working and life style, and a lot of work and life will take place in the virtual world; fifth, promote the construction of smart cities and innovate social governance model[2].

6.1.2 Main Development Direction of Metaverse

At present, the discussion on the Metaverse has not settled down to a conclusion, but it is undeniable that the current technology level is far from reaching the development stage of moving social life into Metaverse. And this means that it is impossible to fully predict the main application scenarios of social and economic development under the background of the future Metaverse, neither the complete blueprint of new models and new formats. Therefore, most governments of major countries and ecological leading enterprises take Metaverse as their development orientation, and vigorously support and develop supporting technologies and related industries based on Metaverse in the current and foreseeable future. That is, in the government and industry levels, the current driving force for the development of Metaverse is still mainly at the technical and

---

① 胡喆,温竞华.什么是元宇宙? 为何要关注它? ——解码元宇宙[EB/OL].(2021 - 11 - 19) [2023 - 02 - 10].https://baijiahao.baidu.com/s?id=1716854014749625905&wfr=spider&for=pc.

② 胡乐乐."元宇宙"解析[EB/OL].(2022 - 04 - 06)[2023 - 02 - 01].https://baijiahao.baidu. com/s?id=1729338881562621670&wfr=spider&for=pc.

industrial ends. Since this research focuses on the gender divide in the context of the digital age, this section will focus on the analysis of the industrial and technological ends where governments and enterprises of various countries are focusing on, and discuss their potential impact on the gender divide, the application scenarios of the future Metaverse in multi-dimensional fields such as society, life and economy after it reaches the mature stage, and their impact on the gender divide. This chapter will make a preliminary analysis with a cautious attitude.

As a "new technology on the horizon", the accurate definition of "Metaverse" is still at the stage of "coexistence of differences and consensus", but the industry generally recognizes that "Metaverse" is the representative of the space Internet, an important development direction of the next generation of Internet, a comprehensive upgrade of the digital industry in the Internet age, and something that will trigger disruptive innovation in certain areas. In terms of promoting industrial development, the greatest value of the "Metaverse" lies in "promoting reality from virtuality". A larger, more immersive virtual digital world is built through digital technology to feed back the development of the "industrial Metaverse", that is, to enable reality by means of expanded reality, digital simulation, digital primitives and other technical means to reduce costs and improve efficiency. The accelerated development of the Metaverse will accelerate the urban digital transformation, promote the realization of high-quality economic development, encourage the industrial development orientation of "promoting reality from virtuality", empower all kinds of real economies, solve all kinds of practical problems with virtual simulation, cross space integration, digital sand table deduction, etc., and reduce the cost of social production, operation, governance and decision-making.

From the perspective of the industrial chain and core technology elements involved in the Metaverse, it can be roughly divided into the link layer, interaction layer, computing layer, tool layer and ecological layer. Specifically, the link layer mainly covers the new generation of digital infrastructure supporting the operation of the "Metaverse". It includes

computing power, storage, sensors, power supply and communication chips, which are the core of the new generation of intelligent terminal hardware. Together with 5/6G, IoT and other network transmission software and hardware, they form the infrastructure supporting the operation of the Metaverse. According to industry estimates, the development of "Metaverse" will drive 5 ~ 10 times the growth of bandwidth traffic, which is the main direction of 5G+ application in the future. **The interaction layer mainly covers a new generation of intelligent interactive devices that provide users with immersive experience**, which includes VR/AR/MR technology, holographic influence technology, brain-computer interface and sensing technology. With the breakthrough of new display technology and the formation of device miniaturization solution, VR/AR technology is close to maturity and will enter the zero point of large-scale commercial use. Brain-computer interface/holographic display technologies are still in the pre-research stage. **The computing layer mainly covers the new generation of computing platform that provides strong support for "Metaverse" applications**, including cloud computing, edge computing, artificial intelligence, blockchain, etc. According to industry judgment, the development of "Metaverse" faces a huge computing power gap, which will promote the mainstreaming of new distributed computing architecture of "cloud+edge". **The tool layer mainly covers the new generation of digital tools that provide the key "bridge" technology for building the "Metaverse"**, including content production tools, bottom-level graphic visual engine, digital twins and virtual-reality interaction tools. **The ecological layer mainly includes a new generation of digital ecology and applications driven by the "Metaverse"**, including office, social, entertainment, medical, intelligent manufacturing, simulation and other scenario applications.

6.2　Short-term and Long-term Impacts of the Metaverse on Gender Divide

As mentioned above, most governments and ecological leading enterprises in various countries are now laying out and contributing to the new race track of the Metaverse from the technical and industrial sides. Up to now, except for the field of e-sports, there are still few mature application scenarios based on the guidance of the Metaverse. It can be seen that the Metaverse is still in the stage of technical improvement, and its future application scenarios are still highly uncertain. This section will analyze the possible impact of the development of Metaverse on the gender divide from short-term and long-term perspectives. The short-term perspective focuses on the technical and industrial dimensions that governments and enterprises of various countries are trying to make efforts on. The long-term perspective focuses on analyzing the impact on the gender divide from the perspective of application scenarios.

6.2.1 Short-term Impact: Gender Bias at the Technology Improvement Stage May Exacerbate the Gender Divide

Under the unprecedented global competition and the trend of "overtaking by changing lanes" in the digital economy, the "Metaverse", as an important direction facing the future, has a huge prospect and has the potential to subvert the existing digital industry. However, at the present moment, the technologies and application scenarios related to Metaverse have a rather long way to go before they can support the completely developed Metaverse. For some time to come, all countries in the world will continue to make efforts in the relevant technology of the Metaverse and lay out their technological development strategies related to the Metaverse industry. From a global perspective, the United States, as the birthplace of the concept of "Metaverse", began to lay out as early as 2015 under the leadership of META, Microsoft, Google and other enterprises, and has gathered major leading enterprises and key core technologies in Europe. To sum up, the US is leading the way. Japan focuses on the production of content. The ROK tends to promote the application on the government side. It can be seen that in the foreseeable future, the development of the Metaverse will focus on tackling key problems and R&D on the technical side. Therefore, the impact of the Metaverse on the gender divide in the short term shall be analyzed from the technical side.

The technical side of the Metaverse may lead to more intense gender bias. In the process where governments all over the world make efforts to lay out the Metaverse industry and its related technologies, the Metaverse may deepen the gender divide from the technical side in the foreseeable future due to the inherent gender bias in the information technology and financial fields, as the Metaverse related technologies are all in the forefront of information technology, synchronized with block-chain and other technology fields with financial attributes. **Therefore, this section takes the cryptocurrency technology under the computing layer blockchain technology of the Metaverse industry as an example for analysis.**

Cryptocurrency technology and gender divide. Cryptocurrency has long been expected to act as an equal force in many areas, including gender bias. The technological innovation in the cryptocurrency field aims to ensure an open, peer-to-peer interaction form, which in principle does not depend on the identity of the participants. Obviously, we should expect this to become an equal force to counter identity discrimination. However, the reality is quite different. According to almost all available indicators, cryptocurrencies are largely male dominated. The specific reasons are as follows:

The gender bias is deep-rooted in finance and technology sectors. Women are still in a weak position in the financial sector and the higher the position, the greater the gap. The proportion of women in leadership positions in financial companies is only 21.9%, which will reach mere 31% by 2030 according to the predicted speed. Therefore, it is little progress in long term.

The number of women working in science and technology is also disproportionately low, and the gap is even larger in leadership positions and senior positions. Although women accounted for 28.8% of the workforce in the technology industry, they held only 5% of the leadership positions. Even with the consistent growth rate, it will take 12 years for the science and technology industry to achieve gender equality.

These inequalities have deep-rooted causes. For example, the long-standing cultural prejudice has led many women to give up studying STEM (science, technology, engineering and mathematics) subjects, which is the root cause to continuously limit the number of women who desire to work in the technology industry. In the UK, women account for only 35% of STEM students in higher education — down to 19% in engineering and technical subjects. Moreover, the problem is not only that fewer women can obtain the qualifications required to enter the industry. The proportion of women leaving the technology industry is also much higher than that of men, partly because they have to endure gender discrimination in the workplace.

In recent years, there have been many major initiatives to correct this serious imbalance. Nevertheless, much remains to be done. We certainly have reason to believe that the innovation of cryptocurrency technology may be part of the solution. The development of cryptocurrency is inseparable from the pursuit of open and anonymous digital interaction, which is both technical and moral. The purpose is to avoid centralized control and authentication based checks by centralized institutions, which have the right to decide who can or cannot participate. By hiding the user's identity, blockchain based transactions should theoretically provide a fair competition environment, where everyone can participate freely.

Despite this hope, cryptocurrencies so far seem to have inherited many of the gender biases of the technology and financial industries, rather than eliminating them. The contradiction between the possibility and reality of cryptocurrency may be most obvious in the NFT field. NFT market can enable emerging artists to display their works in a way impossible in the past, which is expected to add diversity to the male dominated art world in history. However, artificial intelligence company Limna recently revealed that only 29% of NFT artists are women, which is similar to the gender divide in the traditional art market.

A study by LongHash in 2018 shows that only 14.5% of blockchain startups have female team members, and only 7% of senior management positions are held by women. At the same time, since the birth of the cryptocurrency industry, the so-called "cryptocurrency brothers" culture has prevailed in the industry, which has always hindered women's participation. The 2018 North American Blockchain

Conference proves this issue. Although more than 80 speakers gave speeches of 10 hours in total, only 3 of them are women. Although the cryptocurrency industry is fully capable of avoiding these discriminatory traps according to its original intention, men still remain dominant.

6.2.2 Long-term Impact: The Future Application Is Expected to be the Main Battlefield to Bridge the Gender Divide

In the future, the continuous progress and improvement of Metaverse related technologies will further strengthen the development of Metaverse related products and the rapid popularization of multi application scenarios. Local governments will certainly accelerate the integration and innovation of digital technology, application scenarios and business models; expand the deep application of Metaverse in business, education, entertainment, cultural tourism and other fields; promote the upgrading of the quality of consumption, and open a new entrance to the digital world of immersive experience and cross space integration. After the development of the Metaverse reaches the above stage, each scenario enhanced by the Metaverse technology will become the main battlefield to bridge the gender divide, thanks to the popularization and application of multiple application scenarios.

First, many application scenarios in the Metaverse will no longer have gender bias. For example, in the commercial field, the Metaverse technology will accelerate the promotion of innovation in the commercial circulation field, meet needs of new scenarios, new experiences, and new consumption, and achieve online and offline integration and symbiosis. At that time, local governments and enterprises will encourage and take the initiative to create virtual full scene navigation applications in various venues, parking places, etc., to improve the experience of indoor navigation, commercial shopping guide, parking and locating cars. At the same time, various commercial complexes will realize transformation, and further innovate the shopping experience on Metaverse. Integrate immersive, digital human and other technologies to optimize online shopping experiences such as live-streaming e-commerce and virtual stores. All major commercial entities will expand new business operation concepts and create a new consumption experience via integrating virtual and reality by superimposing virtual landmarks, virtual promotions, interactive games, holographic advertising, etc.

Second, specific Metaverse applications will break the inherent gender threshold and promote gender equity at the application level. For example, in the field of manufacturing, the Metaverse will further promote the digital transformation of the manufacturing industry, accelerate the merging of virtual reality integration technology and production and manufacturing scenarios, and empower industrial intelligent manufacturing. Production collaboration tools shall be promoted. The mature application of Metaverse technology will support the application of virtual production collaboration platform integrated with extended reality, multi-dimensional simulation (CAD/CAE/CFD), robot and other technologies in the industrial manufacturing field, and realize visual real-time collaboration of product simulation design, test verification and optimization. In the future, various digital twin factories will continue to emerge. The digital twin project will build a high-precision, highly reproduced, interactive virtual mapping space, carry out modeling and simulation and sand table deduction of the whole industrial manufacturing process, break the data island, and achieve collaboration of all processes and production process reengineering. AR + intelligent manufacturing shall be developed. It is necessary to promote the application of AR and 3D visualization technology in operation and maintenance inspection, remote maintenance, asset management, and other areas, so as to improve the efficiency of production and operation and maintenance. These new applications will break the strong male employment color in the manufacturing industry in the past, and male manufacturing jobs that rely more on physical strength may be partially replaced by female practitioners. With the accelerated popularization and application of Metaverse technology, the gender threshold in the manufacturing industry will bridge the divide and difference between men and women caused by different physiological structures.

Chapter VII
Research Conclusions and Future Trends

7.1 Main Conclusions

The arrival of the digital age has a significant impact on the production relations, social relations, culture and social ethics of the whole society. In the context of the digital age, the wide application and popularization of digital technology has promoted the rapid development of the digital economy. The gender bias of digital technology and the asymmetry in the penetration field have made the gender divide in the digital age present a new trend of evolution. In the context of the digital age, the latest manifestations of the gender divide mainly include the following aspects: First, there are gender divide in the accessibility of digital resources, the digital resource accessed by different gender groups is quite unbalanced. Second, there is a significant gender difference in digital innovation achievements and digital skill improvement. Third, protection for women's digital identity and privacy is seriously inadequate. Fourth, the development of the digital economy has aggravated gender inequality in terms of employment levels. Fifth, the tagging of gender identity in digital space and women's sense of existence in digital space is low.

The impact of the digital economy on the gender divide is also characterized by multifaceted and comprehensive features. On the one hand, the gender bias of digital technology makes it easier for men to use digital technology and digital skills to improve their social status. On the other hand, however, digital technology provides women with incremental job opportunities through empowerment and business mode innovation, meanwhile promoting women to use digital technology to balance their careers and families. To sum up, the arrival of the digital age brings both challenges and opportunities to bridge the gender divide.

7.1.1 Governments Are the Top Designer to Bridge the Gender Divide in the Digital Age

In the context of the digital age, bridging the gender divide is a negative externality of the market. Therefore, the government is required to play the role of "visible hand", make up for the market failure caused by the popularization and application of digital technology at the gender level through policy regulation and behavior regulation, and ensure that different gender groups can share the digital dividend as much as possible to achieve comprehensive development. The domestic and foreign governments focus on improving the extent of women's participation in different industrial divisions, improving women's wages and employment environment, and strengthening policies to guide women's employment and protect women's rights. The specific analysis is as follows.

1) Domestic governments: actively planning policy frameworks and useful initiatives to bridge the gender divide

Domestic governments mainly attempt to bridge the gender divide in the digital age in the following aspects.

First, by fully protecting women's employment rights, women's frictional unemployment caused by the rapid development of the digital economy could be reduced as much as possible. For example, the Shanghai government has issued a more detailed planning document for the protection of women's employment rights and interests. The *14th Five-Year Plan for the Development of Women and Children in Shanghai*, released in 2022, proposed to promote women's employment and improve the quality of their economic participation, and clearly designated employment-rights-related gender equality indicators. In order to focus on solving the problem of gender discrimination in employment, the central government issued relevant documents to guarantee women's equal employment rights, promote women's equal employment, and promote women's extensive and in-depth participation in social and economic activities.

The second is to facilitate the development of female science and technology talents. In November 2021, 17 departments including the Shanghai Women's Federation and the Science and Technology Commission jointly issued *Measures to Support Female Scientific and Technological Talents to Play a Greater Role in Shanghai's Construction of A Science and Technology Innovation Center with Global Influence*, proposing 12 specific measures for female scientific and technological talents. The *14th Five-Year Plan for the Development of Women and Children in Shanghai* put forward many indicators for gender equality in the development of technical talents: The proportion of female senior managers in high-tech enterprises shall be steadily increased, the gap between the proportions of male and female senior professional and technical talents shall be narrowed, the proportion of women selected for various talent projects and those undertaking scientific research projects shall remain balanced, the proportion of women among those who have obtained invention patents shall gradually increase. In 2022, the Shanghai Women's Federation vigorously promoted the Women in Science and Technology Innovation Initiative, further stimulating the innovation vitality of Shanghai's female scientific and technological talents, and better playing the important role of female scientific and technological talents in accelerating the construction of a science and technology innovation center with global influence.

The third is to cultivate female entrepreneurs and support them at all stages. For example, The *14th Five-Year Plan for the Development of Women and Children in Shanghai* released by the Shanghai Municipal Government included "enable a stable gender ratio of men and women in entrepreneurial activities" as a main indicator of promoting women's entrepreneurship and employment and improving the quality of women's economic participation in Shanghai. In 2022, the Shanghai Women's Federation pushed forward the "Women's Action for Employment and Entrepreneurship" project, which includes the implementation of the "Seagull Plan" for female college students to take a career leap, continuing to carry out the Shanghai Female College Students' Innovation and Entrepreneurship

Competition, stimulating female college students' enthusiasm for innovation and entrepreneurship, and promoting entrepreneurship to drive employment.

2) International organizations and governments of other countries: strengthen the equal use of the Internet and pay attention to the balance of digital skills education

International organizations and governments of other countries focus on promoting the bridging of the gender divide by promoting the equal connectivity of the Internet and its universal application among genders. In addition, international organizations also attach great importance to improving the digital skills of women in the digital age, and pay attention to the balanced development of digital skills education between genders. In terms of equal use of the Internet, the most typical case is that in 2021, the UN Women, the International Labour Organization (ILO) and the Economic Commission for Latin America and the Caribbean (ECLAC) proposed the concept of "basic digital basket", that is, to provide a "basic digital basket" including mobile phones, laptops, tablets and Internet connectivity for women who do not have Internet connectivity, as an attempt to bridge the digital gender divide. The introduction of the concept of "basic digital basket" shows that international organizations and governments are fully aware of the importance of Internet connectivity for women's empowerment and therefore have proposed a package of solutions to comprehensively bridge the gender divide of Internet connectivity. In terms of promoting the balance of digital skills education, the most representative case is that UN Women, together with the African Union Commission (AUC) and the International Telecommunication Union (ITU), implemented the African Girls Can Code Initiative to train African girls in important programming and technical skills. In 2018 – 2021, the first phase of the African Girls Can Code Initiative was completed, which taught digital knowledge and skills to over 600 girls and gave them the opportunity to pursue ICT education and innovation.

7.1.2   The Power of Enterprises Shall Not Be Overlooked in Bridging the Gender Divide in the Digital Age

In the digital age, the popularization and application of digital technology has spawned many new forms of business and new models, which, on the one hand, has created incremental jobs and career development space for women, and on the other hand, has brought many challenges to bridging the gender divide. As the creators and users of new models and formats, enterprises play an important role in promoting the innovative development of the digital economy and influencing the gender divide. Therefore, when discussing the problem of bridging the gender divide in the digital age, we cannot ignore the important functions of enterprises in this field. This study collected and analyzed three representative enterprises as typical cases, focusing on their beneficial initiatives and experiences in bridging the gender divide in the context of the digital age.

The enterprise case study revealed that the digital economy enterprises represented by Ximalaya Inc. and Aikucun empowered women to develop and bridge the gender divide in their own unique ways. For example, by building the Aikucun platform into an online infrastructure platform and e-commerce distribution platform, Idol Group Co., Ltd aims to attract women to participate in entrepreneurship, and create a community operation model to give play to women's social advantages. Women's communities have the natural advantages of loving sharing, highly active and good at communication, which can accurately identify potential customer needs, so as to seize the entrepreneurial opportunities and open up new entrepreneurial fields. Ximalaya Inc., the largest audio content platform enterprise in the world, provides women with knowledge, information and spiritual comfort through high-quality audio content. Tens of millions of women have kept listening on the platform as a habit, which helps them acquire information and new knowledge. The platform also provides women with companionship, spiritual comfort and spiritual food. MS Energy fully leverages the leading role of women on the track of carbon peaking and carbon neutrality in the fields of energy, ecological, and environmental protection, provides abundant employment opportunities and clear career paths for women to eliminate gender stereotypes in the workplace, help women to maximize their own value through various incentive mechanisms, and create a positive work environment, discovering more female power in technological progress and digital transformation.

To sum up, both digital economy enterprises and high-tech enterprises play an important role in bridging the gender divide in the digital age. It is foreseeable that it requires the government, enterprises and all sectors of society to work together and make contribution to achieving desirable results.

7.2   Future Outlook

7.2.1   The Gender Divide Will Always Be Accompanied by the Updating, Iteration and Popularization of Digital Technology in the Digital Age

In today's digital age, the updating, iteration, popularization and penetration of digital technology have profoundly affected and changed people's values, behavior, production and life. On the production side, the popularization and application of digital technology has led to various new models and formats. Social division of labor will continue to undergo major adjustments and updates under the exogenous impact of digital technology. And these changes will inevitably have a different impact on the social division status of different gender groups and the mastery and acquisition of digital skills, and ultimately affect the expansion or narrowing of the gender divide. On the governance side, digital technologies represented by the Internet, big data, cloud computing, artificial intelligence, mobile devices, etc., provide a new governance tool for promoting the modernization of social governance. However, digital technology itself is not enough to ensure the legitimacy, rationality and effectiveness of social governance. When the government and other social governance bodies apply digital technology to carry out governance activities, more attention shall be paid to the fairness and rationality of the governance dividend among different dimensional groups, including the innate requirements for different gender groups to share the digital transformation dividend of social governance. In this regard, the government and other social governance entities must shake out the misunderstanding of tool rationality and technology leading, and return to the logical starting point of technology serving social governance.

7.2.2 More Attention Should Be Paid to the Impact of Digital Technology Innovation Supply on the Gender Divide in Short Term

With the gradual emerging of the new track of digital economy, "Metaverse" will become an important direction of the future development of digital economy. Currently, technologies related to the Metaverse have not yet met the requirements of the application effect that the Metaverse will achieve in the future. In other words, the current digital technology has not formed a satisfactory industrial application and practice in the field of the Metaverse. Therefore, in the future, the digital economy based on the development direction of Metaverse will focus more on the continuous innovation and updating and iteration of digital technology, that is, the supply of new technologies. Hence, in the foreseeable future, the digital factors that produce significant impact on the gender divide will keep affecting from the digital technology side, namely the supply side economy activities such as the research and development of digital technology and experiments, which may continue the discrimination and prejudice against women in technical posts. In the future, when bridging the gender divide in the digital age, improving women's digital skills, promoting women's employment in digital technology posts, and breaking gender discrimination in digital technology posts will still be the main direction of efforts.

7.2.3 More Attention Should Be Paid to the Impact of Multiple Digital Application Scenarios on the Gender Divide in the Future

After the industrialized application of digital technology reaches a mature stage, or digital technology is sufficient to support various application scenarios based on the Metaverse and various application scenarios can meet the spiritual and material needs of the public, the digital economic activities in the digital age will shift from technology to application scenarios. In other words, economic entities will pay more attention to the development and supply of application scenarios at that time. The new immersive experience scenarios will be greatly enriched. By that time, more personalized application scenarios based on independent creation will emerge in the Internet space and the application and scenarios of digital technology will be more gender inclusive. The impact and effect of these application scenarios on the gender divide deserve further analysis and demonstration.

7.2.4   The Influence of Enterprises in Bridging the Gender Divide Will Continue to Increase

With the rapid popularization and updating and iteration of decentralized digital technologies such as blockchain, the future digital age will show a trend of decentralized development in many fields such as social governance. The future social governance will be more characterized by the co-governance of plural subjects. Therefore, under the background of decentralization, the power of enterprises and other plural subjects will be further highlighted, and the central governance position of the government will be further weakened, in terms of bridging the gender divide. The bridging of the gender divide and other social issues in the future will rely more on the joint participation of enterprises, social organizations and other decentralized plural subjects.

Appendix

UNIDO Report *Gender*, *Digital Transformation and Artificial Intelligence*

Achieving gender equality and women empowerment is an essential part of achieving the United Nations Sustainable Development Goals (SDGs) and Inclusive and Sustainable Industrial Development (ISID). While achieving SDG 9, United Nations Industrial Development Organization (UNIDO) continues to support women through various actions and initiatives, contributing to the achievement of SDG 5.

The book *Bridging Gender Divide in the Digital Age* is an active exploration of the topic of bridging the gender divide in the digital age. Through the analysis of the divide by its connotation and performance, the book draws lessons from combining international and domestic experience, looks forward to the future from the innovative perspective in metaverse, and then proposes solution based on UNIDO's EQUIP 10 toolkit focusing on gender equality. This book is the outstanding cutting-edge research achievement of the UNIDO ITPO Shanghai Office on gender issues.

Recently, UNIDO released the *Gender*, *Digital Transformation*, *and Artificial Intelligence* report (see below for details), emphasizing once again that gender is an issue that must be taken into account in the process of digital transformation and the development of artificial intelligence. UNIDO hopes that through this report, all parties in society will pay more attention to gender issues in the context of digital transformation and propose to take action in eight key areas to jointly build a gender-equal digital age.

This book takes the report as appendix, hoping to give readers further inspiration.

Foreword by the Director General
GENDER, DIGITAL TRANSFORMATION AND ARTIFICIAL INTELLIGENCE

The digital transformation and Artificial Intelligence (AI) hold the promise for almost everything we can dream of. Yet, even today, we can see that technology development is strongly biased against women and disadvantaged groups.

We must not accept that! The gender perspective must take center stage in our thinking, planning and implementation of digital transformation and AI.

Without conscious choices, AI will not magically eliminate biases. Much of the current data that forms the basis of even the best algorithms draws a picture we want to leave behind. At UNIDO, balancing and correcting gender bias is an integral part of our project portfolio. The fast- paced developments of technologies related to the digital transformation and AI must not be taken as an excuse to skimp on the gender question. I believe the opposite is the only fitting approach— taking the necessary precautions, but also preparations, for gender equality in AI and the digital transformation.

Building that future requires our efforts in all areas of development. We need to correct the inequality wherever we can, particularly in the digital field. How can we ensure gender balance and un-biased AI or digital transformation development, when the gender digital divide is gaping between countries, societies and even families?

However, there are developments we can influence. Raising awareness is a starting point to uncover the mechanisms that reduce women's participation as users, developers and learners of digital technologies. By design, the inclusive potential of the digital transformation must be pronounced. Capacity building for AI and digital technologies should primarily target women. This way, we not only increase participation, but, even more importantly, the skills needed to have not only gender balance in algorithms, but also in their development, adoption and further implementation.

In this background paper, UNIDO proposes actions we can take, and with this starting point, I hope we can raise the issues and start eliminating them. I firmly believe that through our attention and through our efforts, we can overcome this challenge and look into a brighter, balanced future.

Gerd Müller

Director General of the United Nations

Industrial Development Organization

EXECUTIVE SUMMARY

Fast-changing technological developments across the digital, biological, and physical spheres are transforming work places, human relations, and trade networks. As the Fourth Industrial Revolution (4IR) unfolds, it is creating jobs and business opportunities but also making some roles and activities obsolete.

Gender bias and stereotypes hinder the participation of women as users, learners, and developers of digital technologies.

Digitalization has accelerated, particularly after the COVID-19 pandemic; however, not everyone is benefiting equally from the opportunities the 4IR is creating.

Women and girls are less likely to have access to digital technologies, and they are underrepresented in technology fields, as students, academic staff, and entrepreneurs—a gap that is even more pronounced in the fields of artificial intelligence.

Digital technologies have the potential to create opportunities for women to lead, participate in, and benefit from technology developments. However, without the right policy enablers, digital technologies can reinforce gender stereotypes and deepen economic and social exclusion.

Based on a review of more than 150 initiatives across five geographical regions, this report offers recommendations on the priorities and entry points to further advance gender equality and women empowerment in the digital transformation.

Closing gender gaps is a human rights issue, but it also has economic and social benefits, from expanding markets and unlocking talent to addressing increasing skills shortages, improving financial performance, increasing innovation activity, and avoiding the reinforcement of disparities in status and power in societies.

The report reviews the current state of policies and initiatives related to the promotion and strengthening of global efforts toward gender-transformative strategies and initiatives in emerging digital technologies, with an emphasis on artificial intelligence. In addition to the field of AI, the paper focuses on the following technology areas: additive manufacturing, big data, cloud computing, cyber-security, the Internet of Things (IoT), distributed ledger technology, robotics, unmanned autonomous vehicle systems, and quantum computers.

More than 150 initiatives across Africa, Asia and the Pacific, Latin America and the Caribbean, Eastern Europe, and Western Europe and other states were reviewed within the scope of this report. The review involved desk research, the submission of input from international and civil society organizations, and interviews with key stakeholders that helped to develop case studies of good practices.

The report describes key areas of action and shared approaches and features case studies of initiatives, from international organizations funding research to understand gender gaps in technology fields, and development banks supporting women-led businesses, to academic institutions and the private sector collaborating in skills development, and civil society organizations supporting the digital inclusion of marginalized groups.

Eight key areas of action are identified, as listed below, to tackle the gaps between genders in the use, knowledge, and development of digital technologies.

1. Reducing gender skills gaps beyond coding

Efforts to develop skills with a gender perspective have overwhelmingly focused on coding abilities. However, initiatives run the risk of failing to address gender gaps in other related areas where disparities are wider, such as cloud computing, or in areas where gaps are actually widening, such as data analysis and artificial intelligence. Skills-development initiatives should therefore specialize their scope based on a sound understanding of the context-specific dynamics of the labour markets and the incremental nature of skills.

2. Gender-transformative lifelong learning approaches

Women face barriers to participation in digital technology fields throughout their lives. This puts women at risk of losing opportunities related to the digital transformation when facing the increasing need for digital competence, reskilling, and upskilling across disciplines, occupations, and sectors. Digital skills-development initiatives should therefore adopt a lifelong learning approach.

3. Gender-responsive approach in technology-driven research, design, and innovation

A gender-responsive approach is not only about fairness and justice but also about producing better knowledge, products, and services for a wider audience. Among the challenges identified, there is an increasing need to tackle digital technologies' discriminatory potential — in particular, in AI systems. Technology development and deployment, including the development and deployment of AI systems, should therefore strive for diversity in technical and leadership positions, and within teams, including cross-disciplinary competencies such as insights into mechanisms for gender discrimination.

 ## 4. Fostering multi-stakeholder partnerships

Gender bias and discrimination is manifesting in old and new ways through the digital transformation, and different stakeholders have a role to play to address these. The private sector and research organizations, for example, are key to addressing gender bias in technology-driven research, design, and innovation. Meanwhile, civil society organizations have been effective in raising concerns about the negative impacts of digital technologies on marginalized groups. Actions toward closing gender gaps in digital technology fields should therefore adopt a multi-stakeholder approach.

 ## 5. Mainstreaming gender considerations into industrial and innovation strategies

Differences in the participation of women and men in the digital transformation call for gender mainstreaming in industrial and innovation strategies, that is, assessing and addressing the implications for different gender groups of a planned action. In particular, the review of initiatives revealed a gap in measures with a gender perspective in several areas, such as support for technology adoption in business and funding for technology scale-up at the later stages of the innovation cycle.

 6. Twin green and digital transitions

Digitalization can be a key enabler of the transition toward more circular and less carbon-intensive industries. Energy and infrastructure sectors, however, suffer from gender disparities similar to those observed in digital technology fields. The circular economy and climate-neutral industry sectors are equally male dominated, especially as regards technical and leadership positions. Failure to address these intertwined gender gaps risks amplifying existing inequalities.

 7. Continuing to strengthen innovation ecosystems and infrastructure

Increasing opportunities for women also means that efforts to strengthen innovation ecosystems and infrastructure need to continue, particularly in developing countries. Governments can adopt a gender-responsive approach in the development of their innovation systems and infrastructure. This involves, for example, including gender equality conditionalities in the funding of research and innovation projects, and adopting gender-responsive public procurement strategies (gender- responsive procurement strategies).

 8. Continuing to close information gaps

A lack of gender-disaggregated data in companies, and national and international statistics, is one of the main challenges that policy-makers face when addressing gender gaps in technology fields. Lessons from digital platforms, in partnership with the private sector, can be leveraged to gain a better understanding of the use of advanced digital technologies and the potential benefits. This review also revealed the need for a better understanding of gender equality initiatives within technology companies.

For full access to the report, please visit: https: //hub. unido. org/node/ 12112.